D1295289

# MARC for Library Use:
## Understanding the USMARC Formats

## by Walt Crawford

**Knowledge Industry Publications, Inc.**
**White Plains, NY and London**

*Professional Librarian Series*

MARC for Library Use: Understanding the USMARC Formats

**Library of Congress Cataloging in Publication Data**

Crawford, Walt.
    MARC for library use.

    (Professional librarian)
    Bibliography: p.
    Includes index.
    1. MARC System.   2. Libraries--United States--
Automation.   I. Title.   II. Title: M.A.R.C. for library
use.   III. Series.
Z699.4.M2C72 1984       025.3'028'54       84-23376
ISBN 0-86729-120-6
ISBN 0-86729-119-2 (pbk.)

Printed in the United States of America

10    9    8    7    6    5    4    3    2    1

# Table of Contents

# List of Figures

# Acknowledgments

Like most one-person projects, this book represents the combined efforts of many people. Errors, assertions, clumsy wording and poor organization are all mine, but the people mentioned below deserve much of the credit for what's right about this book.

My wife, Linda Driver, has tolerated my rantings about MARC ever since we've been married; she's a professional librarian, which helps. She showed me even more tolerance during this effort, and her participation in the decision to buy a desktop computer made the book possible in the first place. Her advice on various library matters is, as always, invaluable; her support for my efforts was critical to their completion.

Many people looked at various drafts, and a few put forth extraordinary effort. Glee Harrah Cady, Assistant Director for Applications Development at RLG (and my boss), was an early supporter and a tough editor; her suggestions in October 1983 kept the first manuscript from foundering, and her editing and advice have helped the book in ways too numerous to mention. Henriette Avram and others at the Library of Congress provided detailed, careful comments on the manuscript, putting their considerable skills and substantial time into their review. John Attig at Pennsylvania State University offered detailed, insightful suggestions in his review of the manuscript. Kathleen Bales at RLG provided her insights from teaching library school courses, checked my examples for cataloging accuracy, and helped to develop the final organization of the book.

John Wescoat, Alan Tucker and Ed Glazier of RLG all provided important early reviews; Charles Stewart and Joan Aliprand of RLG also gave me helpful review comments, as did Richard Greene of OCLC and Gwen Miles Culp of Washington Library Network. Richard Greene and Gwen Miles Culp, as well as Gary McCone of the Library of Congress and Jack Cain at UTLAS, also helped by providing current figures for their institutions. Karen Smith Yoshimura of RLG located the example of vernacular cataloging used in Chapter 8.

Three agencies, Morrow Designs, MicroPro and Pearlsoft, also deserve credit. This book was prepared on my Morrow MicroDecision MD2, a well-designed desktop computer which has served me well over the past year. The speed, silence and thoughtful design of the Morrow continue to impress me; WordStar, from MicroPro, made it feasible to go through a half dozen major revisions without giving up or going completely crazy. The glossary and bibliography were prepared using Personal Pearl, a relational database manager from Pearlsoft, which also came with the Morrow. Using a database for the bibliography and glossary gave me a tremendous sense of freedom: I could, and did, add and revise entries up to submission date without worrying about re-alphabetizing or retyping.

Finally, a belated thanks to Jim Bourne, formerly of RLG, who put together the RLG Publications character set used for the figures in this book—and thanks to my employers for their explicit support, allowing me to produce drafts on RLG's system for a book which was not done for RLG or on work time.

Comments and corrections, and suggestions for revision in the event of a second edition, are welcome and should be sent to me at the Research Libraries Group, Jordan Quadrangle, Stanford, CA 94305.

Walt Crawford
Menlo Park
July 1983-May 1984

# Foreword

The MARC Distribution Service enjoyed its fifteenth birthday this year. There are some of us who have lived these 15 years "under the influence" of MARC and these individuals discovered that there was a beginning, an involvement that was difficult to escape and, thus, no apparent end. Walt Crawford joined those ranks 11 years ago.

His position as Manager of the Product Batch Group at the Research Libraries Group (RLG) provided the expertise which led to his participation as the RLG representative to MARBI, the principal organization in the United States concerned with reviewing and advising the Library of Congress (LC) on matters concerning the USMARC formats. Since MARBI works in cooperation with LC, the bibliographic utilities, other national libraries and representatives of other library associations, Walt has gained a very broad perspective on the many facets of MARC. All of this experience, a dedicated interest in the subject and his in-depth understanding of the MARC format make him highly qualified to undertake the writing of this book.

The operational MARC Distribution Service began with the development of the "MARC II" format for books, based on the experience gained in the MARC Pilot Project and the distribution, to selected participants, of LC machine-readable records for its current cataloging of books in English.

Today, the MARC formats cover not only all forms of material but also component parts, archival, location and holding information, and authority data. LC's distribution service covers all materials in all languages cataloged for its classified collections as well as names, series and subject authority records. In addition, authority and bibliographic records are contributed to the LC database by the University of Chicago, Harvard University and other Name Authority Co-op (NACO) members. Through the Linked Systems Project (LSP), a common online authority file will soon become a reality for LC, RLG and the Washington Library Network (WLN). Internationally, the UNIMARC format developed by the International Federation of Library Associations and Institutions (IFLA) provides the mechanism for exchanging records among the national bibliographic agencies, bypassing the inherent difficulties created by multiple national MARC formats.

The character of automation in the library community has changed dramatically over these 15 years—from a few individual libraries using local computer systems to today's three major bibliographic utilities, regional and special materials networks, a number of major stand-alone systems and a trend toward distributed processing for local or regional requirements. MARC records are no longer created only by LC but also by many other institutions, and are available through the bibliographic utilities and from commercial services. Union catalogs, union lists of serials and interlibrary loan systems are widespread, all based on the availability of MARC records.

From the principal activity—the production of catalog cards from machine-readable records—the library community has moved to online catalogs and computer to computer communications, all using MARC-based systems and/or MARC records.

The advances in technology greatly enhanced the potential for sharing and MARC was an important component. MARC, the precise definition of the contents (identification of data, character sets, codes, parameters for using data, etc.) of machine-readable records, permits the exchange of data from one automated system to another via magnetic tape or telecommunications. Adherence to the standard for record interchange makes increasingly possible the economical automation of the operations of individual institutions and, with a standard citation linked to the location of the item, will eventually permit more efficient and timely sharing of materials.

For all this expansion in the scope and use of MARC, no comprehensive work on MARC has existed prior to this publication. In the early years, the various MARC formats were published separately *(Books: A MARC Format,* etc.), followed by composite publication, *MARC Formats for Bibliographic Data* (MFBD). The MFBD is a specification; Walt Crawford has written an exposition on the components of the MARC format, on the applicability of the format to the various forms of material, on its use for authorities, for holdings and location data, and for linking records and fields within records. It contains an extensive bibliography and, to my knowledge, the first published glossary of MARC and MARC-related terms. In addition, it is a how-to-do-it book on the application of MARC in the library environment. Walt describes in detail, in one publication, what has been described, if at all, only at various levels and in many diverse publications. Such a book is long overdue. However, this may be the best time, since as a community we now have vastly greater experience to draw on than we did in the late 1960s or the 1970s.

This publication should provide the basis of understanding for those new to MARC, as well as those who have experience with MARC. The book will be useful to librarians at all levels, technicians involved in library automation, and students and teachers in library schools. Walt Crawford is to be commended for his effort.

Henriette D. Avram
Library of Congress

# 1

# Introduction

Many librarians create and use MARC records without ever understanding the nature of MARC itself. While no such understanding is required for cataloging, librarians need to know more about MARC as their uses of computers expand. A thorough understanding of MARC will help when dealing with vendors of services, when considering online catalogs and other automated systems, and when considering possible local development of automated systems.

MARC is the single most important factor in the growth of library automation in the United States and other countries. MARC forms the basis for storing bibliographic information in a consistent form, sharing that information and manipulating that information by computer. This book is designed to show what MARC is, how it works and how it is changing. It is also designed to help in dealing with the field of library automation as it relates to MARC.

This book does not attempt to provide a complete technical knowledge of MARC or rules for cataloging using the MARC formats. MARC content designation is thoroughly documented in the *MARC Formats for Bibliographic Data (MFBD)*,[1] in *Authorities: A MARC Format*,[2] and in field guides issued by bibliographic services such as OCLC, RLIN, WLN and UTLAS.[3] Cataloging information is available from many sources, including *AACR2*[4] and a variety of manuals and guides interpreting the rules.

## WHAT ARE MARC AND USMARC?

MARC is an acronym derived from MAchine-Readable Cataloging. Within the United States, the terms MARC, LC MARC and USMARC are interchangeable. The terms do have slightly different meanings:

1. MARC is a generic term applied to the universe of MARC formats, including UKMARC, CANMARC, InterMARC, and so on;

2. LC MARC refers to the set of options and content designation called "MARC II";

3. USMARC is a new name for LC MARC, introduced in the *Underlying Principles* document[5] in 1983. There is no sharp distinction in content between LC MARC and USMARC. The terms USMARC or MARC are also applied to MARC extensions, formats such as OCLC MARC and RLIN MARC that include data in addition to USMARC data elements.

Informally, MARC and USMARC also identify a range of standards and services:

1. The MARC Editorial Office of the Library of Congress (LC) and the MARC Distribution Services, provided by LC's Cataloging Distribution Service to distribute machine-readable copies of LC's original cataloging;

2. The *MARC Formats for Bibliographic Data* and *Authorities: A MARC Format*—standard sets of names for the elements (fields and subfields) of MARC records, used at LC, by users of the major bibliographic services (OCLC, RLIN, UTLAS and WLN) and by MARC subscribers;

3. The structure that supports USMARC and other MARC formats and provides a standard method of organizing data for communication and storage;[6]

4. Tens of millions of bibliographic records for books, films, maps, serials, sound recordings, scores and other materials, and several million authority records, created by LC and thousands of other libraries.

MARC is a set of standards for identifying, storing and communicating cataloging information. MARC tags are standard ways to identify elements of a bibliographic record such as title, edition and subject so that those elements can be manipulated by computers and used by others. MARC structure is a standard way to communicate bibliographic information between users and between computers. By establishing a common vocabulary and representation, MARC makes shared cataloging easier, more powerful and more flexible.

## WHAT GOOD IS MARC?

In original cataloging, assignment of MARC tags and subfield codes is an added cost; assignment of coded values can be a significant added cost. Why bother?

Tags and subfield codes provide a context for cataloging. They provide a consistent shorthand notation, telling a computer how to deal with the cataloging and making it easier for others to use it. Additionally, tags and subfields make possible computer-based systems that provide more access and flexibility than card catalogs.

MARC records communicate bibliographic information with more precision and flexibility than printed catalog cards. The Library of Congress uses MARC to communicate its prepublication and final cataloging to thousands of other libraries; other libraries use MARC to share original cataloging. The bibliographic services have permanently changed the course of library cataloging. Without MARC, these services could not have developed and flourished as they have, nor could users deal consistently with records from the services.

MARC also provides the flexibility needed for individual libraries. Libraries can add information to MARC records, define fields for local use and rearrange existing information, without retyping catalog cards and risking transcription error. MARC provides the vocabulary and structure to produce catalog cards and online catalog access from a single set of information. MARC increases choices for access and display while retaining the economies of shared cataloging.

## CHANGING NATURE OF THE FORMATS

The MARC formats are more than 15 years old, and they are continually evolving. MARC and MARC II have long been known as LC MARC; the Library of Congress (LC) publishes the MARC formats and takes primary responsibility for their development and maintenance. LC MARC was originally developed so that LC could distribute its cataloging in machine-readable form. Thus, it had a number of areas suited only to LC's needs.

The times have changed. The Library of Congress is the largest single creator of cataloging in the United States, but it is no longer the only major source of cataloging data in the United States. A deliberate effort, supported by the Library of Congress, has diminished the LC bias of MARC and moved to formats that are now known as USMARC.

The formats are evolving to support new forms of material and new forms of control. The formats have been separated from the cataloging code; USMARC supports *AACR2* cataloging but does not restrict cataloging to one set of rules. USMARC now provides for control of archival materials, and a national format for holdings information is in preparation. USMARC has expanded to provide for cataloging of machine-readable files and is expanding to provide better support for graphic materials such as prints and photographs.

Last, but certainly not least, a single USMARC bibliographic format is being explored; in such a format, fields would be used as appropriate for a given item, not based on their validity for a given material format.

## CHANGING USES OF THE FORMATS

At first, LC MARC was a vehicle for distribution of records from a single source. MARC has since become a vehicle for communication between systems, for storage and manipulation within national bibliographic services, and for communication to the Library of Congress from other libraries and agencies.

The use of MARC for communications is fundamental to any professionally designed library automation system, but MARC became more than a communications format shortly after it began. Libraries have used MARC formats in batch processing for over a decade. In such use, MARC has proven to be efficient, flexible and highly maintainable. Computers are getting less expensive and more powerful, and their uses in libraries are growing and changing. There will be more use of MARC as a processing format within commercial systems and within local systems. Local extensions to commercial systems seem likely to arise in the years to come, and such extensions are likely to use MARC as a processing format.

## DEFINITIONS

While most special terms in this book are defined as they appear, a few terms are so basic that they need to be defined now.

*Content designation:* The codes and conventions that identify data elements and support their manipulation. For MARC, these are tags, indicators and subfield codes.

*Fields:* Groups of one or more data elements defined and manipulated as a unit, such as the 245 (title) and 001 (record number). Each field is identified by a tag.

*Indicators:* Two characters at the beginning of each field except for control fields. Indicators provide additional information about the field.

*Subfields:* Data elements within fields. Each subfield is identified by a *subfield code* which is composed of a delimiter, shown as "‡" in this book, and a single character.

*Tags:* Labels for fields. For example, "245" is the tag for the title field.

*Bibliographic services:* Used in this book to refer to Online Computer Library Center (OCLC), the Research Libraries Information Network (RLIN), University of Toronto Library Automation Systems (UTLAS) and the Washington Library Network (WLN). These four agencies are sometimes called "bibliographic utilties" or "online networks."

*MARBI:* An ALA interdivisional committee: the American Library Association Resources & Technical Services Division / Library & Information Technology Association / Reference and Adult Services Division Committee on Representation in Machine Readable Form of Bibliographic Information.

*USMARC advisory group:* A group composed of MARBI, liaisons from LC, the National Library of Medicine, the National Agricultural Library, the National Library of Canada, the bibliographic services and other interested parties. The USMARC advisory group advises the Library of Congress on additions and changes to the USMARC formats.

*MFBD: MARC Formats for Bibliographic Data,* published by the Library of Congress. This looseleaf publication is the standard reference for content designation.

## EXAMPLES AND FIGURES

Several USMARC records are shown in this book to illustrate use of the USMARC formats. With certain exceptions, these records were all derived from actual cataloging records available on RLIN. Records used reflect a variety of cataloging sources and practices; some are pre-*AACR2* and several are non-LC cataloging. The records illustrate actual use of USMARC, and are not intended to show correct or desirable cataloging practice, an area outside the scope of this book.

Two forms of record display are commonly used in figures: a traditional formatted display similar to that used for catalog cards, and a tagged and labeled display showing each USMARC tag, subfield, indicator and coded element. The formatted display is loosely derived from the "long" display available on RLIN. The tagged display is similar in nature to displays used for input and editing by OCLC, RLIN and other bibliographic services but is not intentionally based on any of those displays.

Each bibliographic service has its own method of displaying coded elements; OCLC's "Festschr" is RLIN's "FSI." This book's tagged display is not directly based on any known system; mnemonics used are normally shortened versions of the element names, and the figures are narrower than typical online displays. Four special characters are used in some cases for clarity:

"ƀ" is an explicit blank or space;
"‡" is the subfield delimiter;[7]
"◇" is the field terminator;
"||" is the record terminator.

The subfield delimiter "‡" is used consistently throughout figures and text, usually followed by a code, as in ‡a ("subfield a"). The explicit blank "ƀ" is only used where presence or absence of a blank is ambiguous; the terminators "◇" and "||" are rarely shown except here and in Chapter 3. The subfield delimiter, field terminator and record terminator are fully explained in Chapter 3.

## FROM CATALOG CARD TO USMARC

The traditional means of storing bibliographic information is a catalog card; Figure 1.1 is a replica of a catalog card. The library catalog card is a remarkable medium, providing a large amount of information in a small amount of space. As designers of online catalogs have found, it is difficult to replace all the functions of a card catalog. Two strengths of catalog cards are their standard structure and the flexibility of that structure. For example, the tracings paragraph has a known meaning for librarians and sophisticated users, but one book may have no tracings at all, while another may have dozens.

A computer-based cataloging record should carry at least as much information as a catalog card; otherwise, it is a step backward. MARC II was designed to provide the extreme flexibility required for cataloging, without losing reasonable computer efficiency. A

**Figure 1.1 Catalog Card Replica**

```
Blixrud, Julia C., 1954-
   A manual of AACR2 examples tagged and
coded using the MARC format / by Julia C.
Blixrud and Edward Swanson. -- Lake
Crystal, Minn. : Soldier Creek Press,
1982.
   iii, 116 p. ; 28 cm.

"An adjunct to the series of manuals
illustrating cataloging using the Anglo-
American cataloging rules, second edition,
prepared by the Minnesota AACR2 Trainers."
   ISBN 0-936996-13-7

   1. Cataloging. I. Swanson, Edward, 1941-
II. Minnesota AACR2 Trainers. III. Title.
```

MARC record contains all the information on a catalog card, and some additional information as well. Figure 1.2 is a tagged display for the MARC record used to produce Figure 1.1.

Tagged displays show the content designation of USMARC and include some of the structural elements of USMARC (indicators, subfields and fields). Other structural elements of USMARC are invisible in online usage, but vital to communication and some

**Figure 1.2 Bibliographic Record, Tagged Display**

```
Rec Status:n  Legend:am℔℔   Encoding:℔   Descript:a    Link:℔
File Date:821119           DType:s       Date 1:1982   Date 2:℔℔℔℔
Country:mnu   Illus:℔℔℔℔    Intell:℔      Repro:℔       Contents:℔℔℔℔
Govt:℔        Confer:0      Fest:0        Index:0       ME/Body:1
Fiction:0     Biography:℔   Language:eng  Mod:℔         Cat Src:d
Record ID:CRLG82-B33509                   Transac:19821119-081042.0
020 ℔℔ ‡a0936996137
040 ℔℔ ‡aCU‡cCU
100 10 ‡aBlixrud, Julia C.,‡d1954-
245 12 ‡aA manual of AACR2 examples tagged and coded using the MARC
        format /‡cby Julia C. Blixrud and Edward Swanson.
260 0℔ ‡aLake Crystal, Minn. :‡bSoldier Creek Press,‡c1982.
300 ℔℔ ‡aiii, 116 p. ;‡c28 cm.
500 ℔℔ ‡a"An adjunct to the series of manuals illustrating cataloging
        using the Anglo-American cataloging rules, second edition,
        prepared by the Minnesota AACR2 Trainers."
650 ℔0 ‡aCataloging.
700 10 ‡aSwanson, Edward,‡d1941-
710 20 ‡aMinnesota AACR2 Trainers.
```

forms of processing. These elements include the leader and the directory, discussed in Chapter 3. You may never see a leader or a directory online, but those elements make USMARC processing efficient and flexible.

## USMARC BIBLIOGRAPHIC EXAMPLE, ELEMENT BY ELEMENT

The discussion that follows takes each element of the record as it appears in the tagged display of Figure 1.2, except for the leader elements in the first line (which are discussed in Chapter 3). In those cases where the mnemonic of Figure 1.2 is not a clear truncation of the data element name as given in the *MARC Formats for Bibliographic Data,* the mnemonic appears in parentheses following the name. All quoted passages below are from the *MARC Formats for Bibliographic Data.*

### Field 008: Fixed Length Data Elements

The second, third, fourth and fifth lines of Figure 1.2 show elements from Field 008, starting with File Date and ending with Cat Src. Field 008 has different meanings depending on the contents of the legend. For monographs, Field 008 contains nineteen different codes. These are described below in the order in which they appear in the field and Figure 1.2.

Date Entered On File (File Date): "821119"
This date does not usually change as the record changes.

Type of Publication Date Code (DType): "s"
Date 1, which follows, is a single known or probable date; Date 2 is not used and is left blank.

Date 1: "1982"
The book was published in 1982.

Date 2: "ƀƀƀƀ"
Not used when Type of Publication Date Code = "s".

Country of Publication or Production Code: "mnu"
This book was published in Minnesota.

Illustration Code (Illus): "ƀƀƀƀ"
There are no illustrations.

Intellectual Level Code (Intell): "ƀ"
This code describes the intellectual level of the intended audience; currently, the only values available for books are "j" for juvenile and "ƀ," used here, for "unknown or not applicable."

Form of Reproduction Code (Repro): "ƀ"
Not a reproduction.

Nature of Contents Code (Contents): "ƀƀƀƀ"
Single-character codes can be used to specify certain types of materials used frequently for reference purposes, such as book reviews ("o"), bibliographies ("b") or yearbooks ("y"). None of these codes were applicable.

Government Publication Code (Govt): "ƀ"
Not a government publication.

Conference Publication Indicator (Confer): "0"
Not a conference publication.

Festschrift Indicator (Fest): "0"
Not a festschrift.

Index Indicator: "0"
No index.

Main Entry in Body of Entry Indicator (ME/Body): "1"
The main entry also appears in the body of the entry.

Fiction Indicator: "0"
This work is nonfiction.

Biography Code: "ƀ"
No biographical material.

Language Code: "eng"
The predominant language of the book is English.

Modified Record Code (Mod): "ƀ"
The record is not modified; that is, the MARC record contains the same information
which would be found in manual cataloging copy.

Cataloging Source Code (Cat Src): "d"
Non-LC cataloging.

The sixth line of Figure 1.2 shows two other control fields: field 001, labeled "Record
ID," and field 005, labeled "Transac."

## Field 001: Control Number (Record ID)

Field 001 is mandatory in all MARC records and must be unique within the system
that originates the record. Field 001 does not have a fixed length or fixed pattern.[8]

## Field 005: Date and Time of Latest Transaction (Transac)

This field records the date and time of the "latest transaction." The contents state
that the last transaction took place on November 19, 1982 (19821119) at 8:10 a.m. (and 42
seconds) (081042.0). The contents follow ANSI standards: X3.38-1971 for calendar date,
X3.43-1977 for local time.

Eventually, all communicated MARC records should include Field 005. It allows a
receiving agency to do two things unambiguously:

1. Determine whether a received record is, in fact, a more current version than the
record already in place;

2. If a tape or transmitted file contains more than one copy of a record, determine which copy is the latest.

The former capability is critical for authorities work and useful for bibliographic work. The latter is important for those receiving transaction tapes from some bibliographic services. When the 005 was approved, it was assumed that the information would be provided by the computer system that generates the MARC record for transmission, rather than by keyboard data entry. To date, all known implementations of Field 005 do provide for automatic generation of the field.

**Field 020: International Standard Book Number (ISBN)**

The two indicators for field 020 are always blank. The field can contain three subfields: ‡a, International Standard Book Number (and binding information), ‡c, Terms of availability, and ‡z, Cancelled or invalid ISBN. An obsolete subfield ‡b contained binding information, now included as parenthetical information within subfield ‡a (or subfield ‡c, if price is given without an ISBN). For this record, the ISBN was transcribed without a price. ISBNs are stored without hyphens; for most (but not all) ISBNs, hyphens can be supplied on printed products by computer algorithm. In this case, the data would appear on a catalog card as "ISBN 0-936996-13-7."

**Field 040: Cataloging Source**

As with field 020, the two indicators for field 040 are not defined and are always blank. Field 040 can contain four subfields: ‡a, "Original cataloging agency other than LC," ‡b, "Code for language of cataloging," ‡c, "Transcribing agency code," and ‡d, "Modifying agency code." In this case, the record was cataloged and transcribed by the agency with NUC code "CU."

**Field 100: Main Entry—Personal Name**

Field 100 begins the main portion of the bibliographic description. Indicator 1 is "1": the name includes a single surname. This information is useful in sorting entries or in preparing index entries. Indicator 2 is "0": Main entry/subject relationship is irrelevant. A system would not be expected to generate a subject entry from the contents of field 100. Subfield ‡a is the Name; subfield ‡d the Dates (of birth, death or flourishing).

**Field 245: Title Statement**

Indicator 1 is "1": a title added entry should be generated from this field. Indicator 2 is "2": there are two nonfiling characters at the beginning of the first subfield: "Aƀ." For filing purposes, the title begins "MANUAL OF *AACR2* EXAMPLES". Subfield ‡a is the short title or title proper; subfield ‡c is the statement of responsibility. Because of the first indicator, this field generates the tracing shown as "III. Title" in Figure 1.1, and would also generate an added entry under the title (in cases where added entries are generated).

**Field 260: Imprint Statement**

Indicator 1 is "0": the name of the publisher, distributor, etc., is present in the imprint. Currently, indicator 2 is not defined in Books, and it is blank. Subfield ‡a gives the Place of publication, distribution, etc.: "Lake Crystal, Minn." Subfield ‡b gives the Name of publisher, distributor, etc.: "Soldier Creek Press." Subfield ‡c gives the Date of publication, distribution, etc.: "1982."

**Field 300: Physical Description**

Neither indicator is defined. Subfield ‡a gives Extent: "iii, 116 p." Subfield ‡c gives Dimensions: "28 cm." Since this book is not illustrated, there is no subfield ‡b (Other physical details).

**Field 500: General Note**

"This field contains general unformatted notes for information that is not specifically tagged elsewhere in the format but which would provide additional data about the work." The indicators are not defined, and subfield ‡a contains the general note. The double quotes around the note indicate that it was taken directly from the book.

**Field 650: Subject Added Entry—Topical Heading**

Indicator 1 specifies the level of the subject heading. No information on level was provided in this case. Indicator 2 specifies the source of the subject heading. In this case, "0" identifies a Library of Congress subject heading (LCSH). Subfield ‡a contains the Topical heading/place element, "Cataloging." Other subfields are used to record general subject subdivisions (‡x), chronological subject subdivisions (‡y), and geographic subject subdivisions (‡z). Field 650 appears in the Figure 1.1 tracings paragraph as "1. Cataloging." The field might also generate an added entry under the heading "CATALOGING."

**Field 700: Added Entry—Personal Name**

Field 700 has the same first indicator meaning and subfield structure as field 100; in this record, the same first indicator and subfields appear. The second indicator of field 700 has a different meaning from that for 100. Currently, for Books the second indicator is "Type of added entry"; "0" is "Alternative entry." The added entry is for the coauthor of the book; this field generates the tracing "I. Swanson, Edward, 1941–."

**Field 710: Added Entry—Corporate Name**

Indicator 1 shows the Type of corporate name: "2" identifies a name as "Name (direct order)." Indicator 2 indentifies the Type of added entry (Alternative, secondary, or analytical): "0" identifies an alternative entry. Subfield ‡a gives the Name: "Minnesota *AACR2* Trainers." This field generates the Figure 1.1 tracing "II. Minnesota *AACR2* Trainers."

## FORMATTED DISPLAYS FROM USMARC RECORDS

Figure 1.1 shows the most common form of formatted display, a main entry catalog card. When bibliographic data are stored in USMARC form, displays can be varied to meet different needs. Three examples of possible formatted displays are shown in Figure 1.3.

**Figure 1.3 Bibliographic Record, Selective Formatted Displays**

```
Blixrud, Julia C. A MANUAL OF AACR2 EXAMPLES TAGGED AND CODED USING
    THE MARC FORMAT. 1982.

[Compact bibliographic display]
```

```
Blixrud, Julia C., 1954-
  A manual of AACR2 examples tagged and coded using the MARC format
/ by Julia C. Blixrud and Edward Swanson. -- Lake Crystal, Minn. :
Soldier Creek Press, 1982.
  iii, 116 p. ; 28 cm.

ID: CRLG82-B33509

["Partial" bibliographic display]
```

```
 AUTHOR:  Blixrud, Julia C., 1954-
  TITLE:  A manual of AACR2 examples tagged and coded using the MARC
          format.
    PUB:  Soldier Creek Press, 1982.
SUBJECT:  Cataloging.
   ISBN:  0-936996-13-7

["Labelled" bibliographic display]
```

## NOTES AND REFERENCES

1. Library of Congress. Automated Systems Office. *MARC Formats for Bibliographic Data.* Washington, DC: Library of Congress; 1980. Looseleaf (updated quarterly).

2. Library of Congress. Automation Planning and Liaison Office. *Authorities: A MARC Format.* Washington, DC: Library of Congress; 1981. [160] p. Updated in June 1983.

3. "Bibliographic service" is also an imprecise term; the Library of Congress is (among other things) a bibliographic service, as are a number of other agencies and commercial firms. No suitable collective term describes the four nonprofit organizations that operate large online shared cataloging systems (OCLC, RLG/RLIN, WLN and UTLAS). In each case, the organization has its own special characteristics and functions. The term "bibliographic utilities," while popular, is considered objectionable by some of the four agencies mentioned above.

4. *Anglo-American Cataloguing Rules.* 2nd ed. Chicago: American Library Association; 1978. 620 p.

5. "The USMARC Formats: Underlying Principles." *LC Information Bulletin.* 1983 May 9.

6. The formal record structure underlying MARC is technically not MARC; it is established as ANSI Z39.2-1979. For the purposes of this book, the choices made for MARC within ANSI Z39.2-1979 are called the MARC structure.

7. Subfield delimiters are sometimes shown as slashed equal signs or dollar signs "$."

8. A longstanding misconception has held that Field 001 is fixed at 12 characters and has a predetermined format. This has never been true. LC MARC records as created by the Library of Congress are a minimum of 12 characters long, but are frequently longer (when revision dates are included). Other systems may use shorter or longer record numbers and may structure the record number in any manner. The record number shown, which in no way resembles an LC Card Number, is perfectly legitimate.

# 2

# MARC Formats for Bibliographic Data

The designers of MARC II had in mind a single format for all bibliographic material.[1] The work required to build such a comprehensive set of content designation, however, would have delayed the appearance of the format considerably. As has often been the case, pragmatism prevailed over elegance. When MARC was first developed, it appeared as a format for books.[2] Later, a somewhat similar format was developed for serials. Other formats were added, until by 1976 (with publication of the MARC Music format) there were six MARC formats for bibliographic information. In 1980, the separate format publications were replaced by the *MARC Formats for Bibliographic Data*,[3] called *MFBD* in this book. *MFBD* documents a family of formats: the bibliographic family.

## THE COMMON CORE OF BIBLIOGRAPHIC FIELDS

A bibliographic record has common characteristics, no matter what item the record describes.

1. There will always be a title or identifying name. An entry for an author is the same sort of entry no matter what the material. Some items don't have any author entries, and some have many. Sometimes it is reasonable to call one of the author entries a main entry, and sometimes it isn't.

2. Most nonfiction items have subjects; they are about someone or something. Subjects can be people, corporations, conferences or topics; they can also be titles or geographic names. Some items aren't "about" anything, and some are "about" quite a number of things.

3. Catalogers may need to make notes about any sort of item being cataloged. Any item might have restrictions on use, might require a citation or summary, or might simply need some general notes.

4. Most items are published, produced or released at a specific location and time by a specific person or agency.

5. Finally, all bibliographic items need to be described physically.

These attributes are common to everything that can be cataloged, and they form the basic descriptive language of cataloging and of USMARC. They are the core bibliographic data elements, common to all bibliographic formats.

Figure 2.1 lists the commonly defined fields subject to authority control. These fields are all suitable for use as access points and make up the bulk of fields specifically intended as access points.

The common 0XX fields shown in Figure 2.2 provide coded information, most of it not available on a catalog card. Some 0XX fields identify a record or the item it describes. 001 and 005 specifically identify one version of a single USMARC record. Other 0XX

**Figure 2.1 Bibliographic Fields Subject to Authority Control**

| | |
|---|---|
| 100 | Main entry - personal name |
| 110 | Main entry - corporate name |
| 111 | Main entry - conference or meeting |
| 130 | Main entry - uniform title heading |
| 400* | Series statement - personal name/title (traced) |
| 410* | Series statement - corporate name/title (traced) |
| 411* | Series statement - conference or meeting/title (traced) |
| 600 | Subject added entry - personal name |
| 610 | Subject added entry - corporate name |
| 611 | Subject added entry - conference or meeting |
| 630 | Subject added entry - uniform title heading |
| 650 | Subject added entry - topical heading |
| 651 | Subject added entry - geographic name |
| 700 | Added entry - personal name |
| 710 | Added entry - corporate name |
| 711 | Added entry - conference or meeting |
| 730 | Added entry - uniform title heading |
| 800 | Series added entry - personal name/title |
| 810 | Series added entry - corporate name/title |
| 811 | Series added entry - conference or meeting/title |
| 830 | Series added entry - uniform title heading |
| * Fields 400-411 are not defined in Films or in Archival and Manuscripts Control. | |

**Figure 2.2 Common Bibliographic Fields: 0XX**

```
001       Control number
005       Date and time of latest transaction
008       Fixed length data elements
   008/00-05  Date entered on file
   008/15-17  Place of publication or production code
   008/35-37  Language code
   008/38     Modified record code
   008/39     Cataloging source code

010       LC control number (LCCN)
011       Linking LCCN
035       Local system control number
037       Stock number
039       Level of bibliographic control and coding detail
040       Cataloging source
041       Language code
045       Chronological code or date/time

052       Geographic classification code
055       Call numbers/class numbers assigned in Canada
066       Character set present
072       Subject category code
```

fields contain call numbers, show who has cataloged the item and transcribed that cataloging into USMARC, and provide codes that can serve as special access points or that qualify other access points. As an example of qualified access, a person might wish to locate works by Shakespeare published in Norwegian; the language code (088/35-37) could qualify a search on Main entry—personal name.

Figure 2.3 shows the commonly defined bibliographic fields that are not normally considered subject to authority control. These fields include several of the most commonly used: title, imprint, physical description, untraced series and general note.

Figures 2.1, 2.2 and 2.3 show the most commonly used fields, those which are defined for all formats. There are also quite a few fields defined for more than one format, but not defined for all of them. These fields, as they appeared in mid-1984, are listed in Figures 2.4 and 2.5, using standard *MFBD* two-letter codes:[4]

BK   Books Format
FI   Films Format
MS   Manuscripts Format
MP   Maps Format
MU   Music Format
SE   Serials Format
DF   Machine Readable Data Files Format

**Figure 2.3 Common Bibliographic Fields: 2XX-8XX**

| | |
|---|---|
| 240 | Uniform title |
| 242 | Translation of title by cataloging agency |
| 245 | Title statement |
| 260 | Publication, distribution, etc. (Imprint) |
| 265 | Source for acquisition / subscription address |
| 300 | Physical description |
| 440 | Series statement - title (traced) |
| 490 | Series untraced or traced differently |
| 500 | General note |
| 506 | Restrictions on Access |
| 520 | Summary, abstract, annotation, scope, etc. note |
| 580 | Linking entry complexity note |
| 773 | Host item entry |
| 880 | Alternate graphic representation |

## SUBFIELDS IN THE MARC FORMATS

Subfields serve to define individual elements within a field. Many USMARC fields, including most notes, use only a nonrepeatable subfield ‡a, having the same name as the field itself. Where multiple subfields are used, they frequently follow patterns. Figure 2.6 shows the subfield patterns that are used more than once in 0XX fields, as well as samples of each pattern, including some fields with additional subfields. The most common 0XX subfield pattern contains a number in subfield ‡a and a cancelled or invalid number in subfield ‡z. Field 022 (ISSN) splits incorrect and cancelled ISSNs into two subfields, ‡y, and ‡z, respectively; field 020 (ISBN) adds subfield ‡c (terms of availability).

Fields subject to authority control have relatively consistent subfields, matched by those in authority records. Figure 2.7 gives the full set of subfields for field 100, then shows the additional subfields in each related personal name field (400, 600, 700 and 800).

Most of the subfields in field 100 also appear in fields 110 and 111, but a few subfields are differently defined in each of those fields. Once a pattern is set, it is followed: 410, 610, 710 and 810 relate to field 110 in exactly the same way as 400, 600, 700 and 800 relate to 100: the additional subfields are identical. The same is true for 111, 411, 611, 711 and 811; these relationships are shown in Figure 2.8.

Figure 2.8 also gives the subfields for the remaining authority-controlled fields; few new subfields appear. Fields 650 and 651 are simply defined, using mostly the three standard subject subdivisions (‡x: General subject subdivision, ‡y: Chronological subdivision,

**Figure 2.4 Fields Defined in More than One Format: 0XX**

| | | |
|---|---|---|
| 007 | Physical description fixed field | BK FI MS MP MU SE |
| 008/06 | Type of date code | BK FI MS MP MU DF |
| 008/07-10 | Date 1 | BK FI MS MP MU DF |
| 008/11-14 | Date 2 | BK FI MS MP MU DF |
| 008/18 | Frequency code | SE DF |
| 008/19 | Regularity code | SE DF |
| 008/22 | Intellectual level code | BK FI MU |
| 008/23 | Form of reproduction code | BK MS MU SE |
| 008/28 | Government publication code | BK FI MP SE DF |
| 008/29 | Conference publication indicator | BK SE |
| 008/31 | Index indicator | BK MP |
| 008/32 | Main entry in body of entry ind. | BK FI MU |
| 015 | National bibliography number | BK MP SE |
| 017 | Copyright registration number | BK FI MP MU DF |
| 018 | Copyright article fee code | BK SE |
| 020 | ISBN | BK FI MP MU DF |
| 025 | Overseas acquisition number | BK FI MP SE |
| 033 | Capture date and place | FI MU |
| 034 | Coded mathematical data | BK MP SE |
| 042 | Authentication agency code | BK MP SE |
| 043 | Geographic area code | BK FI MS MU SE |
| 044 | Country of producer code | FI MU |
| 050 | LC call number | BK FI MP MU SE DF |
| 051 | Copy, issue, offprint | BK MU SE |
| 060 | NLM call number | BK FI MS MP MU SE |
| 070 | NAL call number | BK FI MS MP MU SE |
| 071 | NAL copy statement | BK SE |
| 074 | GPO item number | BK FI MP MU SE |
| 082 | Dewey Decimal classification number | BK FI MU SE DF |
| 086 | Government Document class. number | BK FI MP MU SE |

‡z: Geographic subdivision). Figure 2.9 shows a few field examples taken from *MARC Formats for Bibliographic Data*.

Chapter 8 includes the subfields for field 773, Host Item Entry; the other linking entry fields in the range 760 to 788 have similar subfields, consistently defined across the range of fields. Figure 2.10 shows five other major fields and their subfields, and Figure 2.11 gives some examples of these fields.

## INDICATORS IN THE MARC BIBLIOGRAPHIC FORMATS

Indicators, like subfields, follow patterns. As of mid-1984, indicators have six frequent uses in the bibliographic fields and a handful of miscellaneous uses. Figure 2.12 includes all indicators defined for USMARC bibliographic fields as of mid-1984. The numbers "1:" and "2:" preceding lists of fields show which indicator is defined for that use, the first or second.

**Figure 2.5 Fields Defined in More than One Format: 2XX-8XX**

| | | |
|---|---|---|
| 214 | Augmented title | BK DF |
| 241 | Romanized title (OBSOLETE) | BK FI MS MP MU DF |
| 243 | Uniform title, collective | BK FI MS MU |
| 250 | Edition statement | BK FI MP MU SE DF |
| 255 | Mathematical data area | BK MP SE |
| 263 | Projected publication date | BK MU SE |
| 302 | Item count / page count | BK MS |
| 315 | Frequency | MP DF |
| 350 | Price / value | BK FI MS MU SE |
| 362 | Dates of publication / volumes | MP SE DF |
| 501 | "With" note | BK FI MP MU |
| 502 | Dissertation note | BK FI MS MP MU DF |
| 503 | Bibliographic history note | BK MU DF |
| 504 | Bibliography / discography note | BK MP MU SE |
| 505 | Contents note (formatted) | BK FI MP MU DF |
| 510 | Citation note (brief form) | BK FI MS MP MU SE |
| 511 | Participant / performer note | FI MU |
| 518 | Data on capture session note | FI MU |
| 521 | Users/intended audience note | SE DF |
| 533 | (Photo)reproduction note | BK FI MS MP MU SE |
| 534 | Original version note | BK FI MS MP MU SE |
| 536 | Funding information note | BK DF |
| 541 | Provenance note | MS MU |
| 555 | Cumulative index / finding aids | MS SE |
| 652 | Subject entry - reversed geographic | BK MP SE |
| 653 | Subject entry - uncontrolled term | BK DF |
| 655 | Genre heading | BK MP MU SE |
| 740 | Added entry-title traced differently | BK FI MS MP MU DF |
| 765 | Original language entry | BK SE |
| 767 | Translation entry | BK SE |
| 770 | Supplement / special issue entry | BK SE |
| 772 | Parent record entry | BK SE |
| 775 | Other edition available entry | BK SE |
| 776 | Additional physical form available | BK SE |
| 780 | Preceding entry | BK SE |
| 785 | Succeeding entry | BK SE |
| 787 | Nonspecific relationship entry | BK SE |
| 840 | Series added entry - title | BK FI MS MP MU SE |
| 850 | Holdings | BK MP SE DF |

**Figure 2.6 Common 0XX Subfield Patterns and Sample Fields**

```
‡a  [number]
‡z  Cancelled/invalid [number]
Other subfields may also be defined
Fields: 010  020  022  024  027  030  035  086
```

```
‡a  [number]
‡b  Source
Other subfields may also be defined
Fields: 017  028  032  036  037
```

```
‡a  Classification number
‡b  Item number
Other subfields may also be defined
Fields: 050  051  060  061  070  071
```

```
010 ♭♭ ‡a♭♭♭81691938♭‡z♭♭♭82692384♭
020 ♭♭ ‡a0877790019 (black leather)‡z0877780116 :‡c$14.00
035 ♭♭ ‡a(OCoLC)814782‡z(OCoLC)7374506
```

```
017 ♭♭ ‡aA68778‡bU.S. Copyright Office
028 31 ‡a256A090‡bDeutsche Grammaphon Gesellschaft
028 01 ‡aSTMA8007‡bTamla Motown
036 ♭♭ ‡aCPS 495441‡bCenter for Political Studies, University of
       Michigan, Ann Arbor.
037 ♭♭ ‡aFSWEC-77/0420‡bNational Technical Information Service,
       Springfield, Va. 22161‡fMagnetic tape‡c$175.00
```

```
050 00 ‡aG107.9‡b.F57 1976
```

## Nonfiling Characters

In each field where defined, the nonfiling characters indicator is a number from 0 to 9 showing how many characters of the first subfield should be ignored in sorting. Figure 2.11 shows typical uses of the nonfiling characters indicator in field 245. Nonfiling characters indicators are an example of the limited sorting support provided in USMARC. No such indication is available for the title subfield of author/title fields such as 700.

## Notes and Added Entries Control

These indicators can be used to suppress unwanted notes and to generate needed added entries. Title added entry indicators (as in 2XX fields) usually use "0" for "no title added entry" and "1" for "added entry." Note indicators in the linking entry fields 760 to 787 use "0" for "display a note" and "1" for "do not display a note." Some fields use a wider range of values: field 028 (publisher number for music) uses a single indicator to specify both note and added entry, with four possible combinations represented by four values. *(Text continues on page 22)*

**Figure 2.7 Subfields for Personal Name Fields**

```
100 Main entry - personal name

    ‡a Name (surnames and forenames)
    ‡b Numeration
    ‡c Titles and other words associated with the name
    ‡d Dates (of birth, death, or flourishing)
    ‡e Relator
    ‡f Date (of a work)
    ‡k Form subheading
    ‡l Language
    ‡n Number of part/section
    ‡p Name of part/section
    ‡q Qualification of name (fuller form)
    ‡t Title (of a work)
    ‡u Affiliation
    ‡4 Relator code
```

```
400 Series statement - personal name/title (traced)
    Additional subfields:
    ‡v Volume or number
    ‡x ISSN
```

```
600 Subject added entry - personal name
    Additional subfields:
    ‡g Miscellaneous information
    ‡h Medium
    ‡m Medium of performance (for music)
    ‡o Arranged statement (for music)
    ‡r Key (for music)
    ‡s Version
    ‡x General subject subdivision
    ‡y Chronological subdivision
    ‡z Geographic subdivision
    ‡2 Source of heading or term
```

```
700 Added entry - personal name
    Additional subfields defined as for 600: ‡g  ‡h  ‡m  ‡o  ‡r  ‡s
    Other additional subfields:
    ‡x ISSN
    ‡5 Institution to which copy-specific added entry applies
```

```
800 Series added entry - personal name/title
    Additional subfields defined as for 600, 700: ‡h  ‡m  ‡o  ‡r  ‡s
    Other additional subfield:
    ‡v Volume
```

**Figure 2.8 Subfield Variations for X10, X11, X30, 650, 651**

```
110 Main entry - corporate name
    Subfields defined as in 100: ǂa ǂe ǂf ǂk ǂl ǂn ǂp ǂt ǂu ǂ4
    Other subfields:
    ǂb Each subordinate unit in hierarchy
    ǂc Place
    ǂd Date (of conference or meeting)
```
```
410, 610, 710, 810:
    Same additional subfields as 400, 600, 700, 800
```
```
111 Main entry - conference or meeting
    Subfields defined as in 100: ǂa ǂf ǂk ǂl ǂn ǂp ǂt ǂu ǂ4
    Other subfields:
    ǂb Number (of conference or meeting) (OBSOLETE)
    ǂc Place
    ǂd Date (of conference or meeting)
    ǂe Subordinate unit in name
    ǂg Miscellaneous information
    ǂq Name of meeting following place element
```
```
411, 611, 711, 811:
    Same additional subfields as 400, 600, 700, 800
```
```
130 Main entry - uniform title heading
    Subfields defined as in 100: ǂf ǂk ǂl ǂn ǂp ǂt
    Subfields defined as in 600: ǂg ǂh ǂm ǂo ǂr ǂs
    Other subfields:
    ǂa Uniform title heading
    ǂd Date (of treaty signing)
```
```
630:
    Additional subfields ǂx, ǂy, ǂz, ǂ2 as in 600
730:
    Additional subfields ǂx, ǂ5 as in 700
830:
    Additional subfield ǂv as in 800
```
```
650, 651:
    ǂa Heading or place element (650: Topical, 651: Geographic)
    ǂb Name following place entry element  (651: Geographic)
    Other subfields as in 600-630: ǂx  ǂy  ǂz  ǂ2
```

**Figure 2.9 Fields Subject to Authority Control: Examples**

```
100 00 ‡aFriedrich‡bII,‡cder Grosse, King of Prussia,‡d1712-1786.
100 01 ‡aFrancesco d'Assisi,‡cSaint.‡kLegend.‡pVita Thomae
       Celanensis.‡pTractatus secundus.‡lEnglish.

110 10 ‡aUnited States.‡tConstitution.‡n1st-10th amendments.
110 20 ‡aDemocratic Party (Tex.).‡bState Convention‡d(1857 :‡cWaco)

111 20 ‡aOlympic Games‡d(1976 :‡cMontreal, Quebec).‡eOrganizing
       Committee.‡eArts and Culture Program

130 0ხ ‡aBible.‡pN.T.‡pRomans.‡sRevised standard.
130 0ხ ‡aMonopoly.
130 00 ‡aConcertos,‡mviolin, string orchestra,‡rD major.

600 10 ‡aShakespeare, William‡d1564-1616.‡tHamlet.
600 10 ‡aBach, Johann Sebastian,‡d1685-1750.‡tSuites,‡mvioloncello,
       ‡nBWV 1009,‡rC major.
600 10 ‡aNixon, Richard M.‡q(Richard Milhous),‡d1913- ‡xPersonality.

610 10 ‡aUnited States.‡bArmy‡xHistory‡yCivil War, 1861-1865.

630 45 ‡aThe Studio magazine.‡pContemporary paintings‡xPeriodicals.
630 00 ‡aRural Japan today.‡h[Filmstrip]

650 ხ0 ‡aAmish.
650 ‡2 ‡aKidney‡xtransplantation.
650 17 ‡aCareer Exploration.‡2ericd

700 11 ‡aIrvine, Thomas Francis,‡eed.
700 11 ‡aHarrison, Tinley Randolph,‡d1900-‡tPrinciples of internal
       medicine.‡s9th ed.

800 1ხ ‡aPoe, Edgar Allan,‡d1809-1849.‡tWorks.‡lGerman.‡f1922.
       ‡sRosl ;‡v1. Bd.

830 ხ0 ‡aStoria della Cina.‡lEnglish ;‡vv. 2
```

*(Text continued from page 19)*
## Display Constant Control

"Display constants" are text strings used to precede fields or subfields when they are displayed or printed, but not stored as part of the fields or subfields. "ISSN ," "Issued with: ," and "Continued by: " are some of the many suggested display constants defined for USMARC. Indicators are frequently associated with suggested display constants. Several of the "further qualification" indicators serve to control display constants, and some of the "source of information/authority file" indicators are used in some systems to modify display mechanisms. USMARC defines display constants for a number of fields; in some cases, the fields may be more functional without the display constant.

The "display constant control" indicators allow for explicit suppression of field-level display constants (always using value "8"), or, in some cases, for a range of alternative display constants using other values. In most cases, display constant control indicators are defined for fields that have existing cases of blank indicators. The blank, as usual, means "no information supplied"—which, in this case, means that the field-level display constant is proper.

### Source of Information or Authority File

These indicators are used in the fields that were originally only used by national libraries. For call number fields, the indicator shows whether the call number was assigned by the national library or by some other agency. For subject fields, the indicator can show a specific subject authority file or list, refer to a code in subfield ‡2 as the source, or show that the source is not specified.

**Figure 2.10 Subfields for Fields 240, 245, 250, 260, 300**

```
240 Uniform title
    The subfields for field 240 are identical to those for field 130
```

```
245 Title statement
    ‡a Short title / title proper
    ‡b Remainder of title
    ‡c Remainder of title page transcription / statement of
       responsibility
    ‡h Medium
    ‡n Number of part/section
    ‡p Name of part/section (of a work)
```

```
250 Edition statement
    ‡a Edition statement
    ‡b Remainder of edition statement
```

```
260 Publication, distribution, etc. (Imprint)
    ‡a Place of publication, distribution, etc.
    ‡b Name of publisher, distributor, etc.
    ‡c Date of publication, distribution, etc.
    ‡d Plate or publisher number (OBSOLETE)
    ‡e Place of manufacture
    ‡f Manufacturer
    ‡g Date of manufacture
```

```
300 Physical description
    ‡a Extent
    ‡b Other physical details
    ‡c Dimensions
    ‡e Accompanying material
```

## Main Entry / Subject Relationship

All 1XX fields have the same second indicator in Books, Music, and Serials; "0" for "main entry/subject relationship irrelevant," "1" for "Main entry is subject." If the value "1" appears, a system may be able to generate a subject tracing (and subject added entry for a split catalog) directly from the main entry. The Library of Congress no longer assigns value "1," and the subject fields have additional subfielding available, but some systems still use this method to conserve energy and file space (since value "1" eliminates double keying and double storage of the entry).

## Further Qualification of Field Contents

Many indicators say more about the contents of the field, serving to qualify the tag. The first indicator in fields 100, 400, 600, 700 and 800 specifies whether a personal name appears as a forename only ("0"), includes a single surname ("1"), includes multiple surnames ("2") or appears as a name of family only ("3"). This information is useful in sorting and retrieval, as are similar indicators in conference and corporate name fields. Some further qualifications affect display constants, such as the eight possible values for field 780 (Preceding Entry) and nine possible values for field 785 (Succeeding Entry).

**Figure 2.11 Fields 240, 245, 250, 260, 300: Examples**

```
100 10 ‡aEdwards, Jonathan,‡d1703-1758.
240 10 ‡aWorks.‡f1957.
245 14 ‡aThe works of Jonathan Edwards /‡cPerry Miller, general
        editor.
```

```
245 00 ‡aOn the Little Big Horn;‡bor, Custer's last stand.‡h[Motion
        picture]
245 02 ‡aA Population story‡h[motion picture] :‡bcollision with the
        future /‡cEncyclopaedia Brittanica Educational Corporation.
245 10 ‡aMusique.‡pGuitare =‡bMusic. Guitar.
```

```
250 ‡‡ ‡aEnglish edition.
250 ‡‡ ‡a2d ed., rev. and enl. /‡bby W. H. Chaloner.
```

```
260 0‡ ‡aBruxelles :‡bLibrairie Vanderlinder,‡c1964, dep. 1973.
260 0‡ ‡aParis :‡bGauthier-Villars ;‡aChicago :‡bUniversity of
        Chicago Press,‡c1955.
260 0‡ ‡aLondon :‡bArts Council of Great Britain,‡c1976‡e(Twickenham
        :‡fCTD Printers,‡g1974)
```

```
300 ‡‡ ‡a271 p. :‡bill. ;‡c21 cm. +‡e1 answer book.
300 ‡‡ ‡a1 videoreel (Ampex 7003) (15 min.) :‡bsd., b&w ;‡c1/2 in.
300 ‡‡ ‡a40 slides :‡bcol. +‡e1 sound disc (30 min. : 33 1/3 rpm,
        mono. ; 12 in.)
```

**Figure 2.12 Indicator Usage in the MARC Formats for Bibliographic Data**

| | |
|---|---|
| Nonfiling characters | 1: 130, 630, 730, 740<br>2: 211, 214, 222, 240-245,<br>440, 830, 840 |
| Notes and added entries control | 1: 210, 211, 212, 214, 222,<br>240-247, 760-787<br>2: 028, 247 |
| Display constant control | 1: 036, 516, 520, 521, 522,<br>523, 524, 537, 556, 565,<br>567, 581 |
| Source of information/authority file | 2: 050, 060, 072, 082, 600,<br>610, 611, 630, 650, 651,<br>655 |
| Main entry / subject relationship | 2: 100, 110, 111, 130 |

Further qualification of field contents:

| | |
|---|---|
| Type of number | 1: 024, 028 |
| Type of date or date/time | 1: 033, 045 |
| Type of scale | 1: 034 |
| Type of edition | 1: 082 |
| Type of personal name | 1: 100, 400, 600, 700, 800 |
| Type of corporate name | 1: 110, 410, 610, 710, 810 |
| Type of conference/meeting name | 1: 111, 411, 611, 711, 811 |
| Type of title | 2: 246 |
| Format of date | 1: 362 |
| Type of contents note | 1: 505 |
| Type of participant or performer | 1: 511 |
| Additional information on repository | 1: 535 |
| Type of added entry | 2: 700, 710, 711, 730, 740 |
| Type of relationship | 2: 780, 785 |

Miscellaneous

| | |
|---|---|
| Level of international interest | 1: 022 |
| Specifications .. field applies | 1: 039 |
| Work is or includes translation | 1: 041 |
| Existence in national library | 1: 050, 060, 070 |
| Presence of publisher in imprint | 1: 260 |
| Relationship: publisher/added entry | 2: 260 |
| Existence of pronoun for main entry | 2: 400, 410, 411 |
| Nature of the source | 1: 510 |
| Fiction or nonfiction | 1: 517 |
| Presence of series statement/original | 1: 534 |
| Repetitious/nonrepetitious note | 1: 550 |
| Level of subject term | 1: 650, 653 |

## USMARC AND *MFBD*

The *MARC Formats for Bibliographic Data (MFBD)* combines many varieties of information into a single publication, making up the primary reference for content designation in USMARC bibliographic formats. Most of the information in this and the following chapters is derived from *MFBD,* but represents only a tiny portion of the information available there.

### Coded Values

Nearly one-fourth of the main text of *MFBD* concerns fields 007, 008 and 009. Each coded value is explained in detail: values defined for the code, how each value is used, and frequently instructions on assigning values, together with notes on LC practice. This portion of *MFBD* grew considerably in the early 1980s as LC and others worked through each code to make its values distinct, explicit and assignable. A relatively simple example of *MFBD* explanation for a coded value follows below, taken from the material for field 007, position 11, for sound recordings: "Kind of Cutting" (code values "h": Hill-and-dale cutting; "1": Lateral or combined cutting; "n": Not applicable, "u": Unknown):

A one-character alphabetic code specifies the kind of cutting. The primary use of this byte is to identify discs which contain only hill-and-dale information. Most contemporary discs (i.e., all quadraphonic discs and nearly all stereophonic discs) contain both vertical and lateral information and are coded "1." Monophonic discs are normally lateral only.

Hill-and-dale cutting—A vertical cutting, with no lateral information intended for reproduction. All cylinders and some early discs have this cutting.

Lateral or combined cutting—A cutting containing lateral information intended for reproduction; such discs may also have vertical components intended for reproduction.

Some descriptions are shorter; many are much longer. The intent is to make coded values useful and clear enough so that nonspecialists can assign values correctly.[5]

### Descriptions and LC Practice Notes

Most of the text of *MFBD* is descriptions of fields, LC practice notes, and examples. Descriptions give uses for fields, relate fields to other fields, cite *AACR2* practice where appropriate, and sometimes include historical notes. LC practice appears in many cases. Besides serving as the master reference for USMARC bibliographic formats, *MFBD* is the data dictionary for LC MARC distribution services.

### Appendices

Several appendices enhance the value of *MFBD*. Appendix I.A, the table of tags, indicators, and subfields, gives the full set of content designators in a reasonably compact form (running just over 100 pages), but without description. Despite the name, Appendix I.A also includes coded values. Appendix I.B provides a keyword index to names of fields and subfields. Appendix II includes various lists of codes, including geographic area codes, language codes, and country codes; as new coded values are defined, new sections are added. Appendix III gives tape format and character specifications for LC MARC, and Appendix IV gives the history of each field in the USMARC bibliographic formats.

# NOTES AND REFERENCES

1. Avram, Henriette D. *MARC, Its History and Implications.* Washington, DC: Library of Congress; 1975: 7.

2. Library of Congress. Automated Systems Office. *Books: A MARC Format.* Washington, DC: Library of Congress; 1970.

3. Library of Congress. Automated Systems Office. *MARC Formats for Bibliographic Data.* Washington, DC: Library of Congress; 1980.

4. These tables are up to date as of mid-1984. Addition of Archival and Manuscripts Control and Visual Materials will make these tables incorrect; information on Machine Readable Data Files is tentative.

5. In the example of 007/11, librarians working in music archives would need almost none of the explanation. The original definition for "1" (Lateral), however, would confuse knowledgeable librarians working with modern recordings, for the reasons noted in the description. As often happens, this code was originally created to serve a special group, primarily those working with early recordings. Nearly all phonodiscs made since 1965 have both lateral and vertical information intended for reproduction; with the redefinition and clarification noted above, the code can be assigned by a wider group of users. It was not necessary to distinguish between combined and lateral cutting, because another code (007/04: Kind of sound) makes the necessary distinctions.

# 3

# The Structure of USMARC

When you build a MARC record, you label the data using tags, indicators and sub-field codes. When a bibliographic service writes a record to tape, it adds several other structural elements to provide the fundamental structure of a USMARC record. The fundamental structure of MARC is established in national and international standards; USMARC is a specific implementation of these standards, taking specific choices from a range of possibilities.

## ANSI Z39.2-1979: WHAT IT SAYS, WHAT IT MEANS

The American National Standards Institute (ANSI) is the parent body for standards organizations in the United States. All ANSI standards are voluntary. ANSI committees are formed in various interest areas where there are enough organizations interested in standards to keep a committee going. The National Information Standards Organization (Z39) was formerly ANSI committee Z39, dealing with Standardization in the Field of Library Work, Documentation, and Related Publishing Practices. It is the "library standards" organization in the United States.

ANSI Z39.2-1979 is the *American National Standard for Bibliographic Information Interchange on Magnetic Tape.*[1] Standard Z39.2 was first promulgated in 1971, and has always been the basis for the structure of MARC records. It "specifies the requirements for a generalized interchange format which will accommodate describing all forms of material susceptible of bibliographic description, as well as related data such as authority records." The standard "does not specify the content of the bibliographic description and does not, in general, assign meaning to tags, indicators, or data-element identifiers." Z39.2-1979 specifies an overall schema for a record.

Each MARC record must begin with a leader 24 characters long, as shown in Figure 3.1. All numeric elements (record length, indicator count, indentifier length, base address

**Figure 3.1 MARC Leader as Defined by ANSI Z39.2-1979**

| RECORD LENGTH | STATUS | TYPE OF RECORD | BIBLIOGRAPHIC LEVEL | RESERVED FOR FUTURE USE |
|---|---|---|---|---|
| 0-4 | 5 | 6 | 7 | 8-9 |

| INDICATOR COUNT | IDENTIFIER LENGTH | BASE ADDRESS | IMPLEMENTATION DEFINED POSITIONS | ENTRY MAP |
|---|---|---|---|---|
| 10 | 11 | 12-16 | 17-19 | 20-23 |

and entry map) must be character numerics (characters "0"-"9"). The entry map, which describes the structure of directory entries, has four single-digit positions:

Position 20: Length of length-of-field;
Position 21: Length of starting character position;
Position 22: Length of implementation-defined portion;
Position 23: Reserved.

The directory contains "at least one entry" for each variable field and begins at position 24, immediately following the entry map. The first portion of a directory entry is always a three-character tag, which is not specified in the entry map. Each directory entry consists of up to four portions, all but the tag being defined by the entry map. The directory identifies each field in the record by a three character tag and shows where the field begins and how long it is. The structure of a directory entry is shown in Figure 3.2.

**Figure 3.2 MARC Directory Structure as Defined by ANSI Z39.2-1979**

| TAG | LENGTH OF FIELD | STARTING CHARACTER POSITION | IMPLEMENTATION DEFINED PORTION |
|---|---|---|---|

The standard allows a wide range of implementations. A format need not have any indicators or subfields to be a Z39.2 format. A format could also have eight indicators per field, and subfield codes that were six characters long, and still be a Z39.2 format. An implementation could even have different directory structures for different records, since the leader in each record defines that record's directory.

ANSI Z39.2-1979 does provide a basic structure for records.[2] A properly designed computer program can check that the first five characters of a record are all numeric and that positions 10–16 and 20–23 are all numeric. Given that, and the assumption that the record is a Z39.2-1979 record, the program can read the directory and locate fields within the record. The program can even locate and identify subfields. This can all be done without knowing anything about the producer of the record, the conventions followed, or even what sort of MARC format is being processed. The leader provides enough information to allow a program to break a record and its fields into component parts.

## USMARC: AN IMPLEMENTATION OF ANSI Z39.2-1979

USMARC is a specific implementation of ANSI Z39.2-1979, making specific choices from the options provided in the standard. The descriptions below include choices made for USMARC within ANSI Z39.2-1979.

### The Leader

USMARC defines all three of the Implementation Defined Positions, positions 17–19, and has fixed values for five of the positions. Figure 3.3 shows the structure of the USMARC leader, including fixed values.

**Figure 3.3 USMARC Leader**

| Logical Record Length | Record Status | - - - Legend - - - - | | | Indicator Count "2" |
| | | Type of Record | Bibliographic Level | Unde-fined | |
| 00-04 | 05 | 06 | 07 | 08-09 | 10 |

| Subfield Code Count "2" | Base Address of Data | Encoding Level | Descriptive Cataloging Form | Linked-Record Code |
| --- | --- | --- | --- | --- |
| 11 | 12-16 | 17 | 18 | 19 |

| - - - - - - - - - Entry Map - - - - - - - - - - - - - - - - - | | | |
| Length of the length-of-field portion "4" | Length of the starting-character-position portion "5" | Length of the Implementation-defined portion "0" | Unde-fined pos. "0" |
| 20 | 21 | 22 | 23 |

Figure 3.4 is the same MARC record used in Figures 1.1 and 1.2 in Chapter 1, in a format showing all of the MARC record structure. This format is called a "formatted dump," and is typical of listings used by programmer/analysts working on MARC records. This record is used to give examples for each element of the leader, as described below.

**Figure 3.4 Bibliographic Record Formatted Dump**

```
Leader:00745nam♭♭2200181♭a♭4500
Direct:001001400000 005001700014 008004100031 020001500072
       040001100087 100003000098 245011400128 260005500241
       300002600296 500016700322 650001600489 700002800505
       7100030005330
Tag  I  Text
001     CRLG82-B335090
005     19821119081042.00
008     821119s1982♭♭♭♭mnu♭♭♭♭♭♭♭♭♭♭♭000100eng♭d0
020  ♭♭  ‡a09369961370
040  ♭♭  ‡aCU‡cCU0
100  10  ‡aBlixrud, Julia C.,‡d1954-0
245  12  ‡aA manual of AACR2 examples tagged and coded using the MARC
        format /‡cby Julia C. Blixrud and Edward Swanson.0
260  0♭  ‡aLake Crystal, Minn. :‡bSoldier Creek Press,‡c1982.0
300  ♭♭  ‡aiii, 116 p. ;‡c28 cm.0
500  ♭♭  ‡a"An adjunct to the series of manuals illustrating cataloging
        using the Anglo-American cataloging rules, second edition,
        prepared by the Minnesota AACR2 Trainers."0
650  ♭0  ‡aCataloging.0
700  10  ‡aSwanson, Edward,‡d1941-0
710  20  ‡aMinnesota AACR2 Trainers.0‖
```

## Logical Record Length

The first five characters of any MARC record, positions 0–4, contain five numeric characters. These five characters are a right-justified and zero-filled number that gives the total length of the record.

Example: "00745"
The record has 745 characters in all.

## Record Status

The record status is stored in position 5. This single-character alphabetic code defines the status of the record. The record status is added by the agency that prepares a USMARC record for transmission, to be used by the agency that receives the record. Common values for Record Status are "n" (New), "c" (Changed) and "d" (Deleted); LC has also used "a" (Increase in encoding level) and "p" (Increase in encoding level from prepublication record). In bibliographic records, there is really only one specifically useful value for Record Status; if it is "d," the record is deleted and should be removed from any current files. Value "c" can only be used to distinguish new records for changes if the receiving agency is certain that it has all records ever created by the generating agency. In practice, most agencies treat "c" and "n" alike, adding the record if it isn't already present, replacing it if it is.

Example: "n"
This is a new record.

## Legend

The legend identifies and describes the record, implying the general content of a record and the meaning of the content designators. The legend says which USMARC format the record belongs to: a record with the legend "amɓ ɓ" is always a Books record. Four characters are reserved for the legend, but only positions 6 and 7, Type of Record and Bibliographic Level, have ever been used or defined in USMARC.

Example: "amɓ ɓ"
The record describes language material, printed or microform ("a") which is a monograph ("m").

## Type of Record

The format of a record can usually be determined from the Type of Record code. Authorities records have value "z"; the proposed Holdings Format uses values "x" and "y." All other records are bibliographic records; values include "j" (Sound recordings, musical), "a" (Language material, printed or microform), "c" (Music, printed or microform) and "e" (Maps, printed or microform).

## Bibliographic Level

"Bibliographic Level" is only defined for the bibliographic formats. The two most common values are "m" (Monograph) and "s" (Serial). With the inclusion of analytics and archival control, four more values are useful: "a" (Component part, monographic), "b" (Component part, serial), "c" (Collection) and "d" (Subunit). Collections are groups of materials treated together for cataloging and control; subunits are components of a collection.

## Indicator Count

Although ANSI Z39.2-1979 allows 0 to 9 indicators per field, USMARC has always specified two. As a result, position 10 of the Leader is always "2."

## Subfield Code Count

USMARC always uses two-character subfield codes: the delimiter "‡" and a single-character identifier. As a result, position 11 of a USMARC leader is always "2."

**Base Address of Data**

Like the Logical Record Length, the Base Address is a five-character, right-justified, zero-filled number. This number shows the offset at which the first data character is found (the first character of field 001). This address is important because starting character positions in directory entries are given as offsets from this base. The Starting Character Position for field 001 is always "00000," by definition. In order to find a specific field, a program must add the Base Address to the Starting Character Position.

The base address serves two valuable purposes. First, it is more efficient to have directory searching end at a given position (the base address minus one) than to test for the field terminator at each entry. Second, the base address allows low-overhead modification of MARC records. Suppose that you have an incoming USMARC record to which you need to add one local field. Adding the field would make the directory 12 characters longer; without the base address, all the starting positions would be different and you would need to rebuild the entire directory, even if the new field was at the end of the record. Because MARC uses a base address, all you need do is add an item to the directory, add the field at the end of the record, and increment the base address by 12: the rest of the directory is still valid.

Example: "00181"
The first character of the field 001 is the 181st character of the record. The leader is always 24 characters long, and the directory in USMARC records is always a sequence of 12-character entries, ending with a field terminator. This record has 13 directory entries (13 fields); thus, the base address is 24 + (12 * 13) + 1. The number of fields in a record is always equal to the base address, minus 25, divided by 12.

**Encoding Level**

This single character identifies the degree of completeness of the record. Blank is "full." Normally, a blank in any coded position means nothing, that is, that no information has been provided. The use of blank for "full" is a historical anomaly. Initially, the values in this position reflected preliminary stages of Library of Congress cataloging; only full records were distributed. Now, Cataloging-in-Publication records are distributed (as are other partial records); other values for less-than-full encoding levels are needed, since USMARC is used more for non-LC cataloging.

Example: "b"
Full level: the book was inspected.

**Descriptive Cataloging Form**

This single alphabetic character indicates the form of descriptive cataloging used in the record. As currently defined, it can specify either the form of descriptive cataloging or the form of punctuation. Blank means that no information is given; you cannot assume either *AACR2* or ISBD (International Standard for Bibliographic Description) form. Value "a" means "*AACR2.*" Value "i" means "full ISBD" without regard to the cataloging rules. Other values specify partial or provisional ISBD form. Descriptive Cataloging Form is not defined for Authorities or Holdings; the position is left blank in that case.

Example: "a"
The book was cataloged using *AACR2* provisions for both description and choice and form of access points.

### Linked-Record Code

Position 19 of the leader was defined in 1982 as part of the solution to coding analytics in USMARC. Two values are possible: blank, "related record not required to fully process the record," and "r," "related record required to fully process the record." All records prior to 1984, and most records since then (including most analytics), will have a blank. Most catalogers doing analytics would put a brief citation in the "In" field, field 773.

Value "r" is used where the cataloger feels that the  most up-to-date complete bibliographic record for the host item (the book or serial) is required. Therefore, the cataloger codes only a record control number to identify the host. In the latter case, no system could present a complete display or printed reference to the record at hand without fetching the related record, to provide the "In" value. The linked record code allows system designers to check for such a situation at the beginning of the record.

Example: "ƀ"
Related record not required to fully process the record.

### Entry Map

The entry map defines the structure of directory entries; all USMARC records have an entry  map of "4500," indicating that the length-of-field portion of a directory entry is 4 characters long, the starting-character-position portion is 5 characters long, and there is no implementation-defined portion. The final zero is a placeholder.

## THE DIRECTORY

The directory consists of a series of entries, one for each field in the record, showing the tag of the field, its length, and its starting position relative to the first field in the record. The leader allows a program to recognize a record and establish basic processing aspects. The directory allows a program to locate data in a record quickly and easily.

The variable control fields (fields 001–009 and 00a–00z) are always represented at the beginning of the directory, and are always in ascending order. The first directory entry is always for field 001. If the next tag is 005 (as it usually is), you can be sure that there are no 002, 003 or 004 fields.

After you get past the variable control fields, the tags are sequenced by first character; a record can have a 600 field followed by a 651 followed by a 650 followed by a 600. This allows a cataloger to define the order of fields within a range as desired. You cannot have a 710 followed by a 651, since the first characters would then be out of order.

From a programming viewpoint, first-digit sequencing provides valuable information. If you're processing subject entries and you see a tag beginning with "7," "8," or "9," you're through with subjects (6xx). However, if you're looking for personal names as subjects (600) and you see a 610, you're not necessarily through; the tag after the 610 might well be a 600.

Fields do not need to be stored in the same order as the directory. Except for control fields, any field can start anywhere in the record. This flexibility helps make maintenance practical. Suppose that you get a USMARC record and want to add hyphens to the 020 (ISBN). The easiest way to do that is to move the new 020 to the end of the record. All you need to do is change the 020 directory entry and the record length; the rest of the directory, and the rest of the record, is fine. If you insert the expanded 020 where the old one was, all fields following the 020 will have different starting character positions, and most of the directory must be rebuilt. In this case, the record contains both an old unhyphenated ISBN and a new hyphenated one; the old unhyphenated 020 isn't covered by the directory. Proper MARC handling programs always take the starting character position and length of each field from the directory; thus, the "garbage" in the record is effectively invisible. It is also legitimate, though rare, for two different fields to have precisely the same content. A system could carry the text once, and have two directory entries (with different tags) pointing to the same text.

**Uses for the Directory**

The directory does represent avoidable overhead; each tag could be stored at the beginning of its field. If you're processing an entire record, field by field, this would be roughly as efficient and save nine characters per field. But when you're processing USMARC, you aren't always looking at every field, and you aren't always looking at fields in strict sequential order. If you're preparing a quick finding list, you may only want to deal with fields 100–111, 245 and 09x. You don't care what's in any of the other fields —and you don't want to have to process them to get to the fields you need.

The processing required to find fields from the directory is simple and efficient in most computers. For applications that look at a lot of fields, it can be made even more efficient: pointers to each "range" of tags (1xx, 2xx, etc.) can reduce processing time even further. Processing an extremely long text string to find individual elements is considerably less efficient in most computers, and somewhat more difficult to design. The directory also lends stability to existing programs. If a program is looking for fields 245 and 260, it doesn't matter if three more fields between 245 and 260 have been defined since the program was implemented. Since the program isn't looking for any intermediate fields, it will run equally well using records that contain them, thanks to the directory.

## VARIABLE FIELDS

Bibliographic information, coded and textual, is divided into fields. All fields are variable length; some simply consist of a series of codes, but most are subdivided into indicators and subfields.

### Variable Control Fields

Variable control fields have tags beginning with "00." They differ from other fields in that they do not have indicators or subfields. A given control field has either a single data element or a series of data elements identified by relative character position. Control fields are sometimes called "fixed-length fields": this name is incorrect and misleading. While control fields may contain fixed-length data elements, control fields are not inherently fixed-length.

Only one control field is mandatory in USMARC: field 001, the Control Number. This field is variable length, and processing systems that have assumed a fixed length have had problems. While the LC Card Number which appears in 001 fields for MARC distribution tapes is fixed length up to the end of the number itself, suffixes and revision dates can follow that number. Other control fields generally serve either to identify a record or a version of a record, or to provide coded values that can be used to select or process records. Field 005 contains a date/time stamp. Field 008 contains a number of coded values including country of publication, language and (for serials) frequency and regularity. The contents of the 008 are defined by the contents of the legend. Fields 007 and 009 contain other coded data elements; these fields have several different versions, which are defined by the first character of the field itself.

### Variable Data Fields and Tags

Fields with tags which don't begin with "00" are variable data fields. If you use USMARC directly or indirectly, you probably use tags; they represent the most common method for identifying data for entry or maintenance. Each bibliographic service provides its own documents that list and describe the available tags, including those added to USMARC by the service. The *MARC Formats for Bibliographic Data* includes all nationally defined bibliographic tags, indicators and subfields.

Tags are the level of content designation used to define independent elements of a record. Because tags are stored in fixed-length directory elements, they can be retrieved quickly and easily in computer processing, allowing flexible processing of the contents of a record. In most cases a variable data field is independently useful within the context of the bibliographic record. The remaining two levels of content designation depend on the context of the variable field within which they are contained.

## INDICATORS

Each USMARC variable data field begins with two indicators. Indicators serve a number of functions in USMARC fields. Some indicators expand on the tag, defining the field contents more narrowly. For instance, the second indicator for Field 780 (Preceding Entry) specifies the type of preceding entry. Other indicators say something about the source of the data or specify the display constant to be used with the field. Indicators can give the length of an initial article to aid in sorting, or can control access to or display of a field's data.

## SUBFIELDS

The lowest level of content designation in USMARC is the subfield. Subfield codes always serve to identify data elements, at whatever level is thought necessary. A field with no subordinate levels will have a subfield ‡a (for instance, field 501: "With" Note). A field with a complex set of data elements may have many more; quite a few fields have 14 different defined subfields. Subfields generally help to clarify field contents and can allow those contents to be manipulated for special purposes.

The contents of a subfield can only be interpreted within the context of the field. The combination of a field and subfield gives specific significance to data, but the data may not be independently useful. Consider a 110 field "20‡aBell and Howell.‡bMicro Photo Division." The tag says that this is a Main Entry—Corporate Name; the indicators say that it is a Name (direct order) and that the relationship between the main entry and subjects is irrelevant. Within the context of a 110, subfield ‡b identifies a subordinate unit in a hierarchy—but "Micro Photo Division" is meaningless in and of itself; the subfield and its contents are dependent on the remainder of the field for context.

Subfield codes allow hierarchical indexing and authority control. Subfield codes allow selective display under certain conditions. They also serve many other purposes. Because text processing is required, subfields are generally more difficult to process than fields; however, subfields involve less overhead. They are appropriate where a data element is not independent, but does need to be identifiable.

## DELIMITERS

A delimiter is a character with a unique meaning, used to mark a location within a record. All MARC formats use delimiters to separate elements. USMARC uses three types of delimiters, known as the subfield delimiter, the field terminator and the record terminator. The subfield delimiter is part of the subfield code, and is essential in processing USMARC. It is defined as ASCII 1/15, or hexadecimal 1F. This book uses the double dagger "‡" to indicate the subfield delimiter; the subfield delimiter is sometimes shown as "$" when no double dagger is available in a character set.

The field terminator appears at the end of the directory and of each field. It is defined as ASCII 1/14, or hexadecimal 1E. The field terminator is redundant information since the length of field is given in the directory. Some processing programs use the field terminator as a convenient way of knowing that the end of field has been reached. In text processing, this is sometimes easier than using the length of field. There is no common graphic representation for the field terminator.

The record terminator is always the last character in the logical record, and is coded as ASCII 1/13, or hexadecimal 1D. One easy test of the validity of a USMARC transmission is to take the Logical Record Length and look at the character at that character position. If it is not a record terminator, something is wrong with the record. Until quite recently, LC MARC records carried the record terminator in place of the last field terminator. This saved one character, but made it more difficult for programs to use the field terminator (since any field might end with a record terminator; fields need not be stored in any particular order). Current practice adds the record terminator at the end of the record, so that the final field still ends with a field terminator. MARC processing programs designed for stability will check to see that the next-to-last character in an incoming record is a field terminator. If it is not, the programs may change the record terminator to a field terminator, since there are no significant processing uses for the record terminator. There is no common graphic representation for the record terminator.

## USMARC: Transmission Form

When a USMARC record is communicated on tape, it is written as a long string of characters. That string is difficult for a person to interpret, but easy for a computer to process. Figure 3.5 shows the record which appeared in Figure 3.4, in a simulation of the actual transmission form. The long character string is broken down into 50-character pieces for convenience. The offset is given for each line: "offset," here and elsewhere, means "distance from the first character." The first character is at Offset 0. You should never have to read a record in the format of Figure 3.5; it wasn't designed for people. This format allows a computer to deal with the flexibility of USMARC without losing efficiency.

### Figure 3.5 USMARC Record in Transmission Format

```
Offset        Text
     0        00745nam♭♭2200181♭a♭4500001001400000000500170001400
    50        80041000310200015000720400011000871000030000982450
   100        11300128260005500241300002600296500001670032265000 1
   150        60048970000280050571000300053◊CRLG82-B33509◊19821
   200        119081042.0◊821119s1982♭♭♭♭mnu♭♭♭♭♭♭♭♭♭♭000010♭eng
   250        ♭d◊♭♭‡a0936996137◊♭♭‡aCU‡cCU◊10‡aBlixrud, Julia C.
   300        ,‡d1954-◊12‡aA manual of AACR2 examples tagged and
   350         coded using the MARC format /‡cby Julia C. Blixru
   400        d and Edward Swanson.◊0♭‡aLake Crystal, Minn. :‡bS
   450        oldier Creek Press,‡c1982.◊♭♭‡aiii, 116 p. ;‡c28 c
   500        m.◊♭♭‡a"An adjunct to the series of manuals illust
   550        rating cataloging using the Anglo-American catalog
   600        ing rules, second edition, prepared by the Minneso
   650        ta AACR2 Trainers."◊♭0‡aCataloging.◊10‡aSwanson, E
   700        dward,‡d1941-◊20‡aMinnesota AACR2 Trainers.◊‖
```

# NOTES AND REFERENCES

1. American National Standards Institute. *American National Standard Format for Bibliographic Information Interchange on Magnetic Tape.* New York: ANSI; 1979. (ANSI Z39.2-1979). All citations in this chapter are from ANSI Z39.2-1979 or the *MARC Formats for Bibliographic Data.* Some material is reproduced with permission from American National Standard Z39.2-1979, copyright 1979 by the American National Standards Institute. Copies of this standard may be purchased from the American National Standards Institute at 1430 Broadway, New York, NY 10018.

2. ANSI Z39.2-1979 does contain some additional specifications. Tags are always three characters long, and are partially defined: tags beginning with "00" specify variable control fields, and tags "001," "002" and "003" are defined or reserved. Tags 004–009 and 00a–00z are open to definition, and all other tags, specifying variable data fields, are open to definition. The standard also specifies the placement and order of control fields. These fields must be in ascending order and the fields must follow the directory. Other fields need not be in any given sequence. Field 001 must consist of basic characters and a record must contain exactly one 001. Z39.2 does not restrict the number, length or content of variable data fields. Little is said about variable fields; the standard specifies that indicators come before subfield codes and data and that the same number of indicator positions must appear in each variable data field. Further, each "data element identifier" (subfield code) must come before the data it identifies.

# 4

# Books and Serials

The oldest and most widely used USMARC formats are used to describe printed language materials: books and serials.

## THE BOOKS FORMAT

A library is, at heart and by etymology, a place of books. Libraries began with books or their equivalent, and libraries are still thought of primarily as places to find books. The first MARC bibliographic format was a format for books. The Books format is the best established and possibly the most stable format. Use of the Books format outweighs use of all other formats combined by a wide margin.

With the exception of three coded data elements in field 008 and three fields defined for technical reports, all of the fields in the Books format are either common to all USMARC bibliographic formats or are defined in more than one format. By and large, the Books format is the core USMARC format.

Three coded positions are unique to books:

008/30     Festschrift indicator
008/33     Fiction indicator
008/34     Biography code

Figures 4.1 and 4.2 show a USMARC Books record. The Books coded elements were all named in Chapter 1; this example shows some different values and some additional fields. Descriptive cataloging form "i" is used for items cataloged under the provisions of *AACR1,* revised chapter 6, which was based on ISBD(M): the record is in full ISBD form. This book was published in Illinois ("Country:ilu"), and has illustrations ("Illus:a ƀ ƀ ƀ").

It includes bibliographies ("Contents: b b̆ b̆ b̆") and is a conference publication ("Confer:1"). There is an index ("Index:1"), the main entry does appear in the body of the entry ("ME/Body:1"),[1] the book is in English ("Language:eng") and the cataloging source was not the Library of Congress ("Cat Src:d").

The main entry is a conference or meeting name (Field 111). The indicators show, respectively, that the name appears in direct order ("2") and that the main entry/subject relationship is irrelevant ("0"). Subfields ‡a, ‡b, ‡c and ‡d identify the name, number, place and date of the conference, respectively. The title is an added entry and has no initial article; subfields ‡a, ‡b and ‡c identify the short title, remainder of title and statement of responsibility. The imprint explicitly includes the full name of the publisher. The field contains place of publication, name of publisher and date of publication. The physical description is complete, with subfields ‡a, ‡b and ‡c for extent, other physical details, and dimensions.

The series note 490 is for a series traced differently (first indicator "1"), rather than a series not traced; field 811 is the different tracing. The single note is a Bibliography/Discography note, field 504. Three topical subject added entries appear (field 650); each second indicator is "0," identifying a Library of Congress Subject Heading (LCSH). Each field includes a topical heading followed by one or more general subject subdivisions in subfield ‡x. One personal name added entry follows (field 700); indicators state that the name has a single surname and is an alternative entry. Field 740 gives a different title tracing, a secondary entry (second indicator "1"). The final field is the traced equivalent to

**Figure 4.1 Books Format Record, Formatted Display**

```
Clinic on Library Applications of Data Processing, 8th, University
   of Illinois, 1970.
   MARC uses and users : papers presented at the 1970 Clinic on
Library Applications of Data Processing conducted by the University
of Illinois Graduate School of Library Science, April 26-29, 1970 /
edited by Kathryn Luther Henderson. -- Urbana, Ill. : University of
Illinois, Graduate School of Library Science, c1971.
   ix, 113 p. ; ill. : 24 cm. -- (Proceedings of the 1970 Clinic on
Library Applications of Data Processing)

   Includes bibliographical references and index.
   ISBN 087845019X

   1. Libraries--Automation--Congresses. 2. MARC System--Congresses.
3. Machine readable bibliographic data--Congresses. I. Henderson,
Kathryn Luther. II. Title. III. Title: Library applications of
data processing, 1970. IV. Series: Clinic on Library Applications of
Data Processing. Proceedings ; 1970.
```

the 490 series note; like the main entry, it is a conference name in direct order. Subfields ‡a, ‡t and ‡v identify the name of the meeting, title of the work and volume or number, respectively.

The Books format was recently enriched to support cataloging of technical reports. Subfields were added to many fields, and three new fields were defined. These fields, shown in Figure 4.3, are unique to Technical Reports; they are not used for other monographs.

The record illustrated in Figures 4.4 and 4.5 is for a technical report, though, like many such records, it does not use any special fields or subfields. It has relatively simple subfielding, but does show some interesting use of MARC fields, a case of a repeating set of subfields (260 ‡a,‡b), and a case of a "bibliographic" field that does not display or print in typical bibliographic displays (265). This report is assigned a beginning and ending date of publication ("Dtype:m"); the beginning date is 1979 and the ending date is not yet known ("Date 2:9999"). The report is illustrated and is a federal publication ("Govt:f").

**Figure 4.2 Books Format Record, Tagged Display**

```
Rec Status:n   Legend:am      Encoding:b     Descript:i     Link:b
File Date:800828              Dtype:s        Date 1:1971    Date 2:bbbb
Country:ilu    Illus:abbb     Intell:b       Repro:b        Contents:bbbb
Govt:b         Confer:1       Fest:0         Index:1        ME/Body:1
Fiction:0      Biography:b    Language:eng   Mod:b          Cat Src:d
Record ID:CRLG18054889-B                    Transac:19801021-051510.0
020 bb ‡a087845019X
040 bb ‡aNjR‡cNjR
111 20 ‡aClinic on Library Applications of Data Processing,‡b8th,
       ‡cUniversity of Illinois,‡d1970.
245 10 ‡aMARC uses and users :‡bpapers presented at the 1970 Clinic
       on Library Applications of Data Processing conducted by the
       University of Illinois Graduate School of Library Science, April
       26-29, 1970 /‡cedited by Kathryn Luther Henderson.
260 0b ‡aUrbana, Ill. :‡bUniversity of Illinois, Graduate School of
       Library Science,‡c1971.
300 bb ‡aix, 113 p. ;‡bill. :‡c24 cm.
490 1b ‡aProceedings of the 1970 Clinic on Library Applications of
       Data Processing
504 bb ‡aIncludes bibliographical references and index.
650 b0 ‡aLibraries‡xAutomation‡xCongresses.
650 b0 ‡aMARC System‡xCongresses.
650 b0 ‡aMachine readable bibliographic data‡xCongresses.
700 10 ‡aHenderson, Kathryn Luther.
740 01 ‡aLibrary applications of data processing, 1970.
811 2b ‡aClinic on Library Applications of Data Processing.
       ‡tProceedings ;‡v1970.
```

**Figure 4.3 Technical Reports: Unique Fields**

```
027      Standard Technical Report Number (STRN)
088      Report number
513      Type of report and period covered note
```

**Figure 4.4 Technical Report, Formatted Display**

```
Crawford, Richard.
  Computer automation of continuous-flow analyzers for trace
constituents in water / R. W. Crawford. -- Livermore, Calif. : Dept.
of Energy, Lawrence Livermore Laboratory ; [Springfield, Va. : for
sale by the National Technical Information Service], 1979-
  v. : ill. ; 28 cm. -- (UCRL ; 52532 Vol.4, pt.1)

  Work performed by the UCLLL under contract no.  W-7405-ENG-48.
  Jan. 18, 1979.
  Contents: v. 4. Description of program segments. pt. 1. TAAIN.
  Supt. of Docs. no.: E 1.28:UCRL-52532/v.
  (pbk.)

  1. Trace elements in water. 2. Automatic data collection  systems.
3. Computer programs. I. Lawrence Livermore Laboratory.  II. Title.
```

Field 020‡a (International Standard Book Number) was modified in 1980 to include binding information as a qualifier. As interpreted here, the "qualifier" exists without qualifying anything, as there is no ISBN. Field 035 contains the local system number (the local system, in this case, being DGPO, the Government Printing Office). Field 040 shows that the record was cataloged and transcribed by GPO, subfield ‡d indicates that it was modified by RLIN (CStRLIN) during the course of loading. Field 074 is the GPO item number. Field 086, a Government document classification number, contains a numeric subfield, ‡2: Source (i.e., government document classification scheme). The value of the subfield, "sudocs," is used to create the display value "Supt. of Docs. no.:."

The imprint includes two ‡a-‡b combinations, the first representing the publisher, the second the distributor; the date is also entered. Field 265, Source for acquisition/subscription address, is not normally displayed in formatted displays. The 490 field in this case is for an untraced series (the first indicator is "0"). Two 500 fields give general notes, and a 505 field (Formatted contents note) gives the complete contents (first indicator "0").

# THE SERIALS FORMAT

If books are at the heart of the traditional library, serials are the dominant format in most scientific fields, and are an area of great concern to many librarians. The MARC serials format has been in use for many years, and is the basis for one of the library field's most successful cooperative programs, CONSER. At least one university library is estimated to hold more than 250,000 different serial titles, and the RLIN database includes more than 1.25 million serial records.

### Figure 4.5 Technical Report, Tagged Display

```
Rec Status:n  Legend:am    Encoding:ƀ    Descript:i    Link:ƀ
File Date:800521           DType:m       Date 1:1979   Date 2:9999
Country:cau   Illus:aƀƀƀ   Intell:ƀ      Repro:ƀ       Contents:ƀƀƀƀ
Govt:f        Confer:0     Fest:0        Index:0       ME/Body:1
Fiction:0     Biography:ƀ  Language:eng  Mod:ƀ         Cat Src:d
Record ID:DCDG6342511-B                  Transac:19800521-120000.0
020 ƀƀ ‡a(pbk).
035 ƀƀ ‡a(DGPO)8016620
040 ƀƀ ‡aDGPO‡cDGPO‡dCStRLIN
074 ƀƀ ‡a429-T-4 (microfiche)
086 ƀƀ ‡aE 1.28:UCRL-52532/v.‡2sudocs
100 10 ‡aCrawford, Richard.
245 10 ‡aComputer automation of continuous-flow analyzers for trace
       constituents in water /‡cR. W. Crawford.
260 0ƀ ‡aLivermore, Calif. :‡bDept. of Energy, Lawrence Livermore
       Laboratory ;‡a[Springfield, Va. :‡bfor sale by the National
       Technical Information Service],‡c1979-
265 ƀƀ ‡a5285 Port Royal Road, 22161
300 ƀƀ ‡av. :‡bill. ; ‡c28 cm.
490 0ƀ ‡aUCRL ; 52532 Vol.4, pt.1
500 ƀƀ ‡aWork performed by the UCLLL under contract no.
       W-7405-ENG-48.
500 ƀƀ ‡aJan. 18, 1979.
505 0ƀ ‡av. 4. Description of program segments. pt. 1. TAAIN.
650 ƀ0 ‡aTrace elements in water.
650 ƀ0 ‡aAutomatic data collection systems.
650 ƀ0 ‡aComputer programs.
710 20 ‡aLawrence Livermore Laboratory.
```

The serials format has a large set of unique content designators, as shown in Figure 4.6. Full serials cataloging requires elements relating to frequency, previous title and other aspects which are irrelevant for non-serial publications. Serials cataloging must follow a publication through time, dealing with publication patterns, changes in title, supplements and special issues, numbering peculiarities and other issues related to ongoing publications.

**Figure 4.6 Serials Format: Unique Fields**

| | |
|---|---|
| 008/06 | Publication status code |
| 008/07-10 | Beginning date of publication |
| 008/11-14 | Ending date of publication |
| 008/20 | ISDS center code |
| 008/21 | Type of serial code |
| 008/22 | Physical medium code |
| 008/24 | Nature of entire work code |
| 008/25-27 | Nature of contents code |
| 008/30 | Title page availability code |
| 008/31 | Index availability code |
| 008/32 | Cumulative index availability code |
| 008/33 | Original alphabet of title code |
| 008/34 | Successive / latest entry indicator |
| 022 | International Standard Serial Number (ISSN) |
| 030 | CODEN designation |
| 032 | Postal registration number |
| 061 | National Library of Medicine (NLM) copy statement |
| 210 | Abbreviated title |
| 212 | Variant access title |
| 222 | Key title |
| 246 | Varying form of title |
| 247 | Former title or title variations |
| 310 | Current frequency |
| 320 | Current frequency control information |
| 321 | Former frequency |
| 330 | Publication pattern |
| 331 | Former publication pattern |
| 512 | Earlier or later volumes separately cataloged note |
| 515 | Numbering peculiarities note |
| 525 | Supplement note |
| 530 | Additional physical form available note |
| 546 | Language note |
| 547 | Former title complexity note |
| 550 | Issuing body note |
| 570 | Editor note |
| 760 | Main series entry |
| 762 | Subseries entry |
| 777 | Issued with entry |

''Seriality'' distinguishes the Serials format from the Books format. Both cover printed-language materials; items are cataloged as Serials because they are issued in successive parts bearing numerical or chronological designations and are intended to be continued indefinitely. Maps also appear serially, as do other materials that contain images other than printed language; the problems of seriality for other formats are being considered by the USMARC advisory group as an aspect of format integration.

Figures 4.7 and 4.8 show the record of one of the more unusual disputes in recent library literature. This record is for *LJ, Library journal*. This title appeared when *Library Journal* began carrying its well-known initialism in prominent letters on the cover and in the masthead and running title. The National Serials Data Program determined that this was a new title, and assigned a new ISSN. *Library Journal* maintained that the title had not changed, and continued to carry the low ISSN originally assigned. This phase of the dispute lasted for two years, the life span of *LJ, Library journal*.

The first five mnemonics shown in Figure 4.8 are from the leader and show a corrected or changed record ("Rec Status:c") for language material, printed or microform, serial ("Legend:as"), in non-ISBD form (pre-*AACR1* rev.) ("Descript:ƀ"). Some of the coded values from field 008 are different for serials; the codes and their values for this serial are as follows:

Date entered on file (File date): "760512"
May 12, 1976

Publication status code (PubStat): "d"
Dead.

Beginning date of publication (BegDate): "1974"

Ending date of publication (EndDate): "1976"

Country of publication (Country): "nyu"
New York.

Frequency code: "s"
Semimonthly (twice a month).

## Figure 4.7 Serials Record, Formatted Display

```
LJ, Library journal.
   v. 99, no. 12-v. 101, no. 8; June 15, 1974-Apr. 15, 1976.
   [New York, Bowker]
   2 v. ill. 29 cm.

   Semimonthly (monthly, July-Aug.)
   Continues: Library journal (1876) ISSN 0000-0027
   Continued by: Library journal (1976) ISSN 0363-0277
   ISSN 0360-3113 = LJ, Library journal

   1. Library science--Periodicals. 2. Libraries--United States.

LCCN: 75648584//r76
035: (OCoLC)2171727
L.C. CALL NO: Z671.L7
```

**Figure 4.8 Serials Record, Tagged Display**

```
Rec Status:c  Legend:as    Encoding:ƀ    Descript:ƀ   Link:ƀ
File Date:760512          PubStat:d     BegDate:i974  EndDate:1976
Country:nyu   Frequency:s  Regular:n     ISDS:1       SerType:p
Medium:ƀ      Repro:ƀ      Nature:ƀ      Contents:ƀƀƀ Govt:ƀ
Confer:0      Titlepg:u    Index:u       Cum Indx:u   Alpha:ƀ
Suc/Lat:0     Language:eng Mod:ƀ         Cat Src:ƀ
Record  ID:DCLC75648584-S               Transac:19760512-120000.0
010 ƀƀ ‡a75648584//r76
022 ƀƀ ‡a0360-3113‡y0000-0027
035 ƀƀ ‡a(OCoLC)2171727
040 ƀƀ ‡dNSDP‡dOCL‡dNSDP‡dRCS‡dCStRLIN
042 ƀƀ ‡alc‡ansdp
043 ƀƀ ‡an-us---
050 0ƀ ‡aZ671‡b.L7
060 ƀƀ ‡aZ 671 L6963
082 ƀƀ ‡a020/.5
210 0ƀ ‡aLJ, Libr. j.
222 00 ‡aLJ, Library journal
245 00 ‡aLJ, Library journal.
246 10 ‡aLibrary journal.
260 00 ‡a[New York,‡bBowker]
265 ƀƀ ‡a(Subscription Dept.) Box 67, Whitinsville, Mass.
300 ƀƀ ‡aƀ2 v.‡bill.‡c29 cm.
310 ƀƀ ‡aSemimonthly (monthly, July-Aug.)
350 ƀƀ ‡a$16.20
362 0ƀ ‡av. 99, no. 12-v. 101, no. 8; June 15, 1974-Apr. 15, 1976.
650 ƀ0 ‡aLibrary science‡xPeriodicals.
650 ƀ0 ‡aLibraries‡zUnited States
780 00 ‡tLibrary journal‡c(1876)‡x0000-0027
785 00 ‡tLibrary journal‡c(1976)‡x0363-0277
```

Regularity code (Regular): "n"
Normalized irregular (irregular in a predictable manner).

ISDS center code (ISDS): "1"
United States.

Type of serial code (SerType): "p"
Periodical.

Physical medium code (Medium): "ƀ"
Not a special medium (e.g., microfilm, Braille).

Form of reproduction code (Repro): "ƀ"
Not a reproduction.

Nature of entire work code (Nature): "ƀ"
No specified nature (e.g., book reviews, abstracts).

Nature of contents code (Contents): "ƀƀƀ"
No specified nature of contents.

Government publication code (Govt): "ƀ"
Not a government publication.

Conference publication indicator (Confer): "0"
Not a conference publication.

Title page availability code (Titlepg): "u"
Unknown (whether separate title page is available).

Index availability code (Index): "u"
Unknown (whether volume indexes are available).

Cumulative index availability code (Cum Indx): "u"
Unknown (whether cumulative indexes are available).

Original alphabet of title code (Alpha): "ƀ"
No alphabet given.

Successive/Latest entry indicator (Suc/Lat): "0"
Successive entry (*AACR*) cataloging.

Language code (Language): "eng"
Publication is predominantly in English.

Modified record code (Mod): "ƀ"
Record is not modified.

Cataloging source code (Cat Src): "ƀ"
Library of Congress cataloging.

The record contains an 010 (LC card number) longer than 12 characters, because of a revision date; field 022 (International Standard Serial Number—ISSN) includes subfields ‡a (ISSN) and ‡z (Cancelled or invalid ISSN), where the ‡z is the ISSN actually carried on *Library Journal* during part of the dispute. Field 042 (Authentication agency code) says that both LC and the National Serials Data Program have authenticated the record. Field 043 (Geographic area code) indicates that the work relates to the United States. Field 050 (LC call number) has a first indicator "0," showing that the serial is in LC; the call number includes subfields ‡a and ‡b, giving classification number and item number, respectively. Field 060 (NLM call number) places the entire call number in subfield ‡a (and has a slightly different Cutter number). Field 082 contains a Dewey Decimal Classification number.

The record contains a wealth of title information. Field 210 (Abbreviated title) contains the abbreviated title assigned by the International Serials Data System (ISDS). Since the first indicator is "0," no title added entry should be made for this field. Field 222 (Key title) has both indicators set to "0," meaning that the 245 field is not required for the ISDS variant title, and that 222 is not required for an added entry; the second indicator says that there are no nonfiling characters. Field 245 is the title, and no title added entry is needed (in this case, because the title is the main entry). The fourth title field, 246 (Varying form of title) does take an added entry (first indicator is "1"). Field 260 (Imprint) has two "0"'s for indicators. The first says that the publisher's name is present in the imprint. The second indicates that the publisher is not the same as the issuing body (if any) transcribed in an added entry. The place (‡a) and name (‡b) are recorded. Field 265 gives a subscription address.

Field 300 is defined identically in all formats; field 310 gives the current frequency, while field 350 contains the list price. Field 362 (Dates of publication and volume designation) has a first indicator "0," meaning that the date is in formatted style. The second 650 (Topical subject entry) field includes subfield ‡z, a geographic subdivision. The last two fields are linking fields; both fields have a wide range of available subfields to identify a related record, and both use the second indicator to define a display constant. The first indicator is set to "0" to display a note in both cases. Field 780 (Preceding entry) has a second indicator of "0," meaning "Continues"; subfields ‡t, ‡c and ‡x contain the title, qualifying information and ISSN of the related work, respectively. Field 785 (Succeeding entry) also has a second indicator of "0," meaning "Continued by"; the same subfields appear, carrying the same categories of information.

The record in Figures 4.7 and 4.8 is relatively simple for a serials record. In 1976, *Library Journal* removed the troublesome "LJ," and a new, even simpler record was created: to LJ's disappointment, a third ISSN was assigned, which the serial did carry in place of the original. As a result of the dispute, the original record for *Library Journal* was relegated to the secondary role of describing a "dead" serial, *Library Journal* from 1876 to 1974. Figures 4.9 and 4.10 show that record.

The record in Figure 4.10 has nearly the same coded values as that in Figure 4.8, except that the older record has "Contents:o," indicating presence of book reviews, and "Cum indx:1," indicating availability of a cumulative index. Naturally, the dates differ also. The 210 and 222 both contain subfield ‡b (Qualifying information). The 222 has a first indicator of "1," indicating that the 245 is required for the ISDS variant title and that the 222 is required for an added entry. The 246 (Varying title) has a first indicator of "1," calling for a title added entry, and a second indicator of "6," identifying the varying title as a "Caption title." Field 310 (Frequency) is qualified by a ‡b subfield (Dates of current frequency), as is field 321 (Former frequency).

In addition to the 500 (General note), this record includes six 510 fields (Citation note, brief form), each with first indicator "0" (coverage for item is unknown), and several including subfield ‡x (ISSN). Field 520 (Summary, abstract, annotation, scope, etc. note) carries a field-level display constant, adding "Summary:" when the note is displayed. Field 555 identifies the cumulative index and carries a display constant "Indexes:." Field 570 (Editor note) does not carry a field-level display constant.

Each 700 field (Added entry—personal name) has a first indicator "1" (Single surname) and second indicator "1" (Secondary entry); most have subfields ‡a, ‡d and ‡e, containing name, dates and relator, respectively; in each case, the relator is "ed." Both

**Figure 4.9 Serials Record, Formatted Display**

```
Library journal.
   v. 1-99, no. 11; Sept. 30, 1876-June 1, 1974.
   [New York, R. R. Bowker Co., etc.]
   99 v. ill., ports., maps. 24-29 cm.

   Monthly, Sept. 1876-Dec. 1919
   Semimonthly (monthly, July-Aug.) Jan. 1, 1920-
   Caption title: American library journal 1876/77
   Official organ of the Library Associations of America and the
Kingdom, Nov. 1877-June 1882; of the American Library Association,
July 1882-Aug. 1907.
   Indexed by: Biography index ISSN 0006-3053
   Indexed by: Library literature ISSN 0024-2373
   Indexed by: Poole's index to periodical literature
   Indexed by: Public affairs information service
   Indexed by: Readers' guide to periodical literature ISSN 0034-0464
   Indexed by: Library and information science abstracts ISSN
0034-0464
   Summary: Includes, beginning Sept. 15, 1954 (and on the 15th of
each month, Sept.-May) a special section: School library journal,
ISSN 0000-0035, (called Junior libraries, 1954-May 1961). Issued also
separately.
   Indexes: Vols. 1-22, Sept. 1876-Dec. 1897. 1 v.
   Editors: 1876-79, M. Dewey, R. R. Bowker; 1880, F. Leypoldt, M.
Dewey; 1881-93, C. A. Cutter and others; 1894-Nov. 15, 1933, R. R.
Bowker; Dec. 1, 1933-Feb. 15, 1943, B. E. Weston; Mar. 1, 1943-May
15, 1951, K. Brown; June 1, 1951-June 1, 1974, H. E. Wessells.
   Issued with: Junior libraries
   Issued with: School library journal ISSN 0000-0035
   Continued by: LJ, Library journal ISSN 0360-3113
   ISSN 0000-0027 = Library journal (1876)

   1. Library science--Periodicals. 2. Libraries--United States--
Periodicals. I. Dewey, Melvil, 1851-1931, ed. II. Bowker, Richard
Rogers, 1848-1933, ed. III. Leypoldt, Frederick, 1835-1884, ed. IV.
Cutter, Charles Ammi, 1837-1903, ed. V. Weston, Bertine Emma, 1898-
ed. VI. Brown, Karl, 1896- ed. VII. Wessels, Helen E., ed. VIII.
American Library Association. IX. Library Association. X. Junior
libraries. XI. School library journal.

   LCCN: 0412654//r54
   035: (OCoLC)1755854
   L.C. CALL NO: Z671.L7
   ID: DCLC0412654-S
```

**Figure 4.10 Serials Record, Tagged Display**

```
Rec Status:c  Legend:as     Encoding:ƀ    Descript:ƀ    Link:ƀ
File Date:751101             PubStat:d     BegDate:1876  EndDate:1974
Country:nyu  Frequency:s     Regular:n     ISDS:1        SerType:p
Medium:ƀ     Repro:ƀ         Nature:ƀ      Contents:oƀƀ  Govt:ƀ
Confer:0     Titlepg:u       Index:u       Cum Indx:1    Alpha:ƀ
Suc/Lat:0    Language:eng    Mod:ƀ         Cat Src:ƀ
Record  ID:DCLC0412654-S                   Transac:19751101-120000.0
010 ƀƀ ‡a0412654//r54
022 0ƀ ‡a0000-0027
035 ƀƀ ‡a(OCoLC)1755854
040 ƀƀ ‡cMUL‡dCtY‡dOCoLC‡dMH‡dDLC‡dNSDP‡dm.c.‡dNSDP‡dRCS
042 ƀƀ ‡alc‡ansdp
043 ƀƀ ‡an-us---
050 0ƀ ‡aZ671‡b.L7
060 ƀƀ ‡aZ 671 L6963
082 ƀƀ ‡a020.5
210 0ƀ ‡aLibr. j.‡b(1876)
222 10 ‡aLibrary journal‡b(1876)
245 00 ‡aLibrary journal.
246 16 ‡aAmerican library journal‡f1876/77
260 00 ‡a[New York,‡bR. R. Bowker Co., etc.]
300 ƀƀ ‡a99 v.‡bill., ports., maps.‡c24-29 cm.
310 ƀƀ ‡aSemimonthly (monthly, July-Aug.)‡bJan. 1, 1920-June 1, 1974.
321 ƀƀ ‡aMonthly,‡bSept. 1876-Dec. 1919
362 0ƀ ‡av. 1-99, no. 11; Sept. 30, 1876-June 1, 1974.
500 ƀƀ ‡aOfficial organ of the Library Associations of America and
       the United Kingtom, Nov. 1877-June 1882; of the American Library
       Association, June 1882-Aug. 1907.
510 0ƀ ‡aBiography index‡x0006-3053
510 0ƀ ‡aLibrary literature‡x0024-2373
510 0ƀ ‡aPoole's index to periodical literature
510 0ƀ ‡aPublic affairs information service
510 0ƀ ‡aReaders' guide to periodical literature‡x0034-0464
510 0ƀ ‡aLibrary and information science abstracts‡x0024-2179
520 ƀƀ ‡aIncludes, beginning Sept. 15, 1974 (and on the 15th of each
       month, Sept.-May) a special section: School library journal, ISSN
       0000-0035, (called Junior libraries, 1954-May 1961). Issued also
       separately.
555 ƀƀ ‡aVols. 1-22, Sept. 1876-Dec. 1897. 1 v.
570 ƀƀ ‡aEditors: 1876-79, M. Dewey, R. R. Bowker; 1880, F. Leypoldt,
       M. Dewey; 1881-93, C. A. Cutter and others; 1894-Nov. 15, 1933,
       R. R. Bowker; Dec. 1, 1933-Feb. 15, 1943, B. E. Weston; Mar. 1,
       1943-May 15, 1951, K. Brown; June 1, 1951-    H. E. Wessells.
650 ƀ0 ‡aLibrary science‡xPeriodicals.
650 ƀ0 ‡aLibraries‡zUnited States‡xPeriodicals.
700 11 ‡aDewey, Melvil,‡d1851-1931,‡eed.
700 11 ‡aBowker, Richard Rogers,‡d1848-1933,‡eed.
```

**Figure 4.10 Serials Record, Tagged Display (Cont'd)**

```
700 11  ‡aLeypoldt, Frederick,‡d1835-1884,‡eed.
700 11  ‡aCutter, Charles Ammi,‡d1837-1903,‡eed.
700 11  ‡aWeston, Bertine Emma,‡d1898-‡eed.
700 11  ‡aBrown, Karl,‡d1896-‡eed.
700 11  ‡aWessels, Helen E.,‡eed.
710 21  ‡aAmerican Library Association.
710 21  ‡aLibrary Association.
730 b2  ‡aJunior libraries.
730 b2  ‡aSchool library journal.
777 1b  ‡tJunior libraries
777 1b  ‡tSchool library journal‡x0000-0035
785 00  ‡tLJ. Library journal‡x0360-3113
```

710 fields (Added entry—corporate name) have first indicator "2," showing a name in direct order, and second indicator "1" for secondary entry. The two 730 fields (Added entry—uniform title heading) have second indicator "2," showing analytical entries. Finally, the two 777 fields are also linking entry fields giving "Issued with" entries. In both cases, the first indicator set to "1" means that a note should not be displayed. (This indicator is ignored for the formatted display, which simulates a fuller online display rather than a more selective catalog card entry.)

The original record for *Library Journal* carries quite a bit of information, and shows some of the features available in the Serials format. The power of USMARC is partly its flexibility for display; where space is at a premium, the record in Figure 4.10 could generate a display as compact as Figure 4.11, while retaining the wealth of information for future needs.

**Figure 4.11 Serials Record, Compact Display**

```
LIBRARY JOURNAL. v. 1-99, no. 11; Sept. 30, 1876-June 1, 1974. ([New
   York, R. R. Bowker Co., etc.])
```

## NOTES AND REFERENCES

1. The "main entry in body of entry" indicator has potential use in systems that display the access point at the head of an entry (catalog cards and other printed products typically do this). If the main entry also appears in the body of the entry, the display need not provide the main entry following the access point, but can follow the access point with the title; while the display would not follow traditional unit record rules, it would be fully intelligible.

# 5

# Formats for Other Materials

The Books and Serials formats are both specifically oriented to text on paper or microform. Three other MARC formats were developed in the 1970s for other forms of material: maps, music and "films," which subsumed everything not covered elsewhere. The other format developed during the 1970s was for manuscripts. As with the Serials format, it distinguishes items on the basis of publication aspects rather than material aspects. During the 1980s, another format was developed to describe machine-readable data files, and substantial changes were made to the Films format to accommodate paintings, photographs, and other two-dimensional graphics. Further changes to the Films format (now called the Visual Materials format), in order to support three-dimensional materials, are expected. The Manuscripts format is discussed in Chapter 6. The other material formats are discussed below, in alphabetical order.

## THE FILMS FORMAT

This format has always been somewhat misnamed. In effect, it has been the "everything else format": graphics, sculpture, instructional materials, kits and realia are all cataloged using this format. So are films and video in various forms. The Films format is much less complex than Serials and somewhat more complicated than Books. Cataloging issues may well be more complex in Films, but those complexities are reflected in content more than in designation. The Films format has repeatable 300 (physical description) and 007 (coded physical description) fields since it includes kits, which can include sound recordings, microfiche and other materials.

Figure 5.1 lists the USMARC fields uniquely defined for Films. Several fields that are specifically useful for films are defined for films and music. Such fields include 033 (Capture date and place), 044 (Country of producer code), 511 (Participant/performer note) and 518 (Data on capture session note). Figures 5.2 and 5.3 show a reasonably typical Films record, for a videocassette release of a film classic.

**Figure 5.1 Films Format: Unique Fields**

```
008/18-20    Length (running time)
008/21       In LC collection (obsolete)
008/23-27    Accompanying matter code
008/33       Type of material code
008/34       Technique code

023          Standard Film Number
261          Imprint statement for films (pre-AACR1 Rev) (obs.)
301          Physical description for films (pre-AACR2) (obs.)
308          Physical description for films (Archival)
359          Rental price
508          Credits note
517          Categories of films note (Archival)
527          Censorship note (Archival)
```

**Figure 5.2 Films Record, Formatted Display**

```
Citizen Kane [videorecording] / RKO Radio Pictures, a Mercury
  production ; producer/director, Orson Welles ; screenplay, Herman
  J. Mankiewicz, Orson Welles. -- Los Angeles, CA : Nostalgia
  Merchant, 1978.
  1 videocassette (120 min.) : sd., b&w ; 1/2 in.

  Cast: Orson Welles, Joseph Cotton, Dorothy Comingore, Agnes
Moorehead, Everett Sloane.
  Credits: Photographer, Gregg Toland ; editors, Robert Wise, Mark
Robson ; music, Bernard Herrman.
  Issued in 1941 as a motion picture.
  Summary: A story of the rise and fall of a great man as the result
of his accumulation of wealth and subsequent isolation from the
world.

  1. Feature films. I. Welles, Orson, 1915- II. RKO Radio Pictures,
inc.
```

**Coded Elements**

The first five elements are from the leader. The record has been revised or corrected ("Rec Status:c") and represents an item in the principal audiovisual media, monographic ("Legend:gm"). The "principal audiovisual media" include motion pictures, filmstrips, slides, transparencies and videorecordings. The record is complete ("Encoding:b"),

**Figure 5.3 Films Record, Tagged Display**

```
Rec Status:c   Legend:gm    Encoding:ƀ    Descript:a    Link:ƀ
GMD:v          SMD:f        Orig/Rep:|    Color:b        Present:n
SoundSep:a     MedSound:h   Width:o
File Date:830303            DType:s       Date 1:1978    Date 2:ƀƀƀƀ
Country:usƀ    Length:120   In LC:u       Intell:g       Accomp:ƀƀƀƀƀ
Govt:ƀ         ME/Body:0    Type:v        Technique:1    Language:eng
Mod:ƀ          Cat Src:d
Record ID:CRLG83-F11                      Transac:19830304-132756.0
040 ƀƀ ‡aCSjCiC‡cCSjCiC‡dCStRLIN
245 00 ‡a Citizen Kane‡h[videorecording] /‡cRKO Radio Pictures, a
       Mercury production ; producer/director, Orson Welles ;
       screenplay, Herman J. Mankiewicz, Orson Welles.
260 ƀƀ ‡aLos Angeles, CA :‡bNostalgia Merchant,‡c1978.
300 ƀƀ ‡a1 videocassette (120 min.) :‡bsd., b&w ;‡c1/2 in.
511 1ƀ ‡aOrson Welles, Joseph Cotton, Dorothy Comingore, Agnes
       Moorehead, Everett Sloane.
508 ƀƀ ‡aPhotographer, Gregg Toland ; editors, Robert Wise, Mark
       Robson ; music, Bernard Herrman.
500 ƀƀ ‡aIssued in 1941 as a motion picture.
520 ƀƀ ‡aA story of the rise and fall of a great man as the result of
       his accumulation of wealth and subsequent isolation from the
       world.
650 ƀ0 ‡aFeature films.
700 11 ‡aWells, Orson,‡d1915-
710 21 ‡aRKO Radio Pictures, inc.
```

*AACR2* ("Descript:a"), and self-contained ("Link:ƀ"). The second and third lines in Figure 5.3 represent elements of one version of field 007, which has different versions depending on the first character of the field. This version is eight characters long; the individual elements are as follows:

General Material Designation (GMD): "v"
Videorecording.

Specific Material Designation (SMD): "f"
Videocassette.

Original vs. Reproduction Aspect (Orig/Rep): "|"
The usefulness of this position, and the possibility of assigning it in a meaningful way, are currently questioned; at the moment, the fill character ("no attempt to code") is the only recommended value.

Color: "b"
Black-and-white.

Presentation format (Present): "n"
This code identifies a motion picture as anamorphic, 3D, standard sound, or other formats. The code is only useful for motion pictures, not for videorecordings; "n" (Not applicable) is always coded for videorecordings.

Sound on medium or separate (SoundSep): "a"
The sound track is on the medium (typical for videorecordings).

Medium for sound (MedSound): "h"
This code can identify a sound track as optical, magnetic, or, if separate from the medium, as to the medium of the sound track (disc, tape reel, etc.). In this case, the sound track is carried with the visual information on videotape: "h" indicates "videotape."

Width or dimensions (Width): "o"
1/2 inch (width of the videotape itself).

The remaining coded values (except for Record ID and Transac, which represent fields 001 and 005) are from Field 008. Several are common and should be familiar by now: File Date, Country, Govt, ME/Body, Language, Mod, and Cat Src. New codes, and old codes with new values, follow:

Length: "120"
The running time of the videocassette is 120 minutes. This code will be renamed "Running time for motion pictures and videorecordings" as part of the Visual Materials changes.

In LC collection (In LC): "u"
Unknown. This code will be made obsolete as part of the Visual Materials changes.

Intellectual level code (Intell): "g"
General (the film is intended for general audiences). This code has a wider range of values in Films than in other formats: preschool, primary, adult, specialized and others. The values provided do not allow direct coding of MPAA ratings ("G," "PG," "R," "X").

Accompanying matter code (Accomp): "ḃḃḃḃḃ"
This field is used primarily in archival cataloging, and allows recording of up to five categories of matter such as stills, posters, lobby cards and script material.

Type of material code (Type): "v"
Videorecording.

Technique code (Technique): "1"
Live action.

Most variable data fields in this record have already been encountered. Field 245 contains an additional subfield, ‡h (Media qualifier); fields 260 and 300 describe the videocassette actually being cataloged, not the original film. Field 511 is a participant or performer note; the first indicator identifies the type of participant or performer and establishes a display constant. "1" indicates "Cast," giving a display constant of "Cast:." Field 508 (Credits note) carries a field-level display constant "Credits:," as shown in Figure 5.2. The second indicator in fields 700 and 710 has a different meaning in Films than in other formats; "1" in this case means "Added entry used on printed card."

## VISUAL MATERIALS FORMAT: CHANGES FROM FILMS

Proposal 82-21, "Additions/Changes to the Films format so as to accommodate two-dimensional material," was prepared by the Library of Congress in 1982 and first submitted to the USMARC advisory group at meetings in October 1982. The changes were discussed in June and September 1983, and approved during the American Library Association's Midwinter Conference in 1984. The proposal changes the name of the format to "Visual Materials," makes four existing fields obsolete, and adds a large number of fields, subfields and indicators to the format. Changes also include editorial revision of *MFBD* for consistency and to reflect the needs of agencies that catalog graphic materials. Changes provide full support for Chapter 8 of *AACR2* and for the extended rules in LC's publication *Graphic Materials: Rules for Describing Original Items and Historical Collections.*[1]

When this proposal was originally presented, the USMARC advisory group was busily reviewing the Archival and Manuscripts Control format. Many of the elements desired for original and historical graphics are needed for archival materials; the review group suggested that the newer proposal be modified to take advantage of Archival and Manuscripts Control (AMC) fields. With the expert guidance and editorial work of Phyllis Bruns, Library of Congress, the proposal was revised in such a way that it draws the formats closer together and makes them more consistent.

Three varieties of proposed changes clarify Films and support graphic materials. Some fields and codes are labeled obsolete; some fields, subfields and coded values are added; and some elements are renamed, redefined or defined more sharply to meet additional needs. Figure 5.4 shows fields in the Films format which will be obsolete in the Visual Materials format.

Figure 5.5 shows fields in the Visual Materials format which were not in the Films format prior to 1984. Those fields new to USMARC are marked with a star "*"; fields ex-

**Figure 5.4 Visual Materials: Obsolete Films Fields**

| Field | Name | Note |
|-------|------|------|
| 008/21 | In LC Collection | 1 |
| 301 | Physical description for films (Pre-AACR2) | 2 |
| 350 | Price/Value | 3 |
| 359 | Rental Price | 3 |

Notes on obsolete fields:
1. This position will be left blank; presence of a film in LC's collection is not part of the universal bibliographic description
2. Field 300 will be used for physical description in all cases.
3. Terms of availability can be carried in field 020 (ISBN), even if there is no ISBN.

**Figure 5.5 Visual Materials: New Fields**

| | |
|---|---|
| +351 | Organization and arrangement |
| +400 | Series statement - personal name/title (traced) |
| +410 | Series statement - corporate name/title (traced) |
| +411 | Series statement - conference or meeting/title |
| +507 | Scale note |
| +521 | Users/Intended Audience note |
| +524 | Preferred citation of described materials |
| +530 | Additional physical form available note |
| +540 | Terms governing use and reproduction |
| +541 | Immediate source of acquisition |
| +545 | Biographical or historical note |
| +555 | Cumulative index/finding aids note |
| +561 | Provenance |
| +581 | Publications note |
| +583 | Actions |

*585     Exhibitions note

Example:
```
 585 ᵇᵇ ‡aExhibited: "Visions of City & Country: Prints and
     Photographs of Nineteenth-Century France," organized by
     Worchester Art Museum and the American Federation of
     Arts, 1982.
```

| | |
|---|---|
| +655 | Genre/Form Heading |

*755     Physical characteristics access

Example:
```
 755 ᵇᵇ ‡aLithograph‡zGermany.‡2[Thesaurus code]
```

*781     Subsequent publication of material entry

Example, including related note.
```
 580 ᵇᵇ ‡aPublished as cover of Vanity Fair, July 1930.
 781 1ᵇ ‡tVanity Fair‡gJuly 1930
 (First indicator = 1: Do not print a note)
```

tended to Visual Materials from other formats are marked with a plus " +." In addition to new fields, Visual Materials will add new subfields to existing Films fields and new coded values in the leader, 007 and 008; a new version of the 007 will be added specifically supporting graphic materials. No new control fields or fields in the main entry or title paragraph will be added, though some subfields will migrate from other formats into Films. One new Physical Description field is suitable for Visual Materials; fields 400, 410 and 411 will be added to the format (mostly for the sake of consistency). Eleven "notes" fields will be added to Films; one of these is new to USMARC. Subfields and indicator values will be added in some other 5XX fields. Subfields will be added to a number of other existing fields: ‡3 (Materials specified) in all 6XX fields and ‡4 (Relator code) in the 600, 610, 611, 700, 710, 711, 800, 810 and 811 fields. Three new added entry fields are proposed.

A large proportion of the proposed changes serve the special needs of those cataloging original and historical graphic materials, including museum curators. Most of those changes will have no effect on those currently using the Films format for motion pictures and videorecordings, but added 007 codes will allow explicit coding of the prevalent video formats (Beta, VHS, Laser disc, CED disc, and a few others).

## THE MAPS FORMAT

Map catalogers deal with more than "maps"; they deal with the whole range of cartographic materials, including globes and other special devices. Map cataloging has a special vocabulary which extends that of books and serials cataloging. As shown in Figure 5.6, the Maps format has relatively few unique elements, and only one unique variable data field; most map cataloging uses elements common to several formats. This is partly because atlases can be cataloged in the Books format and some cartographic materials are cataloged using Serials; as a result, fields 034 (Coded mathematical data) and 255 (Mathematical data area), which contain scale data in coded and textual form, are defined in all three formats.

Figures 5.7 and 5.8 show a Maps record cataloged by the Library of Congress. The record is new ("Rec Status:n"), for a map, printed or microform, monographic ("Legend:em"); the record is complete ("Encoding:ƀ"), and in *AACR2* form ("Descript:a"). There are four new codes in field 008; other codes indicate publication in California ("Country:cau"), presence of an index ("Index:1"), and that LC is the source of cataloging ("Cat Src:ƀ"). The four new codes are as follows:

Relief code (Relief): "ƀƀƀƀ"
The map does not show relief. Four positions allow up to four types of relief (contours, shading, hachures, bathymetry, color, etc.) to be recorded.

Base map elements code (Base): "ƀƀƀ"
The projection used is not specified on the map. This element is divided into two parts: map projections and prime meridian data. Two-character codes identify projections (Mercator, Dimaxion, Orthographic, and many others); one-character codes identify prime meridians (Greenwich, Paris, Ferro, Philadelphia, Washington, DC, or Other).

Record group code (Rec Gp): "a"
This is a single map (rather than a series, serial or globe).

Special format characteristics code (Format): "ƀƀ"
This map had no special format characteristics. The codes allow for one or two special characteristics, identifying wall maps, maps on calendars, playing cards, etc.

**Figure 5.6 Maps Format: Unique Fields**

| | |
|---|---|
| 008/18-21 | Relief code |
| 008/22-24 | Base map elements code |
| 008/25 | Record group code |
| 008/33-34 | Special format characteristics code |
| 315 | Frequency |
| 507 | Scale note |

**Figure 5.7 Maps Record, Formatted Display**

```
Compass Maps (Firm)
  Map of Modesto, California. -- 1981 ed. -- Scale [ca. 1:26,000]. --
Modesto, CA : Modesto Chamber of Commerce, [1981]
  1 map : col. ; 57 x 55 cm., folded to 23 x 10 cm.

  Panel title: City map of Modesto with Stanislaus County and its
communities.
  Indexed.
  Indexed maps of Stanislaus County and "Map of Turlock and
vicinity", "Map of Oakdale and vicinity", "Map of Riverbank and
vicinity", 15 local maps, ill., and advertisements on verso.

  1. Modesto (Calif.)--Maps. 2 Stanislaus County (Calif.)--Maps.  3.
Turlock (Calif.)--Maps. I. Modesto Chamber of Commerce.

  LCCN: 82692187/MAPS
  L.C. CALL NO: G4364.M6 1981.C6
  ID: DCLC82692187-M
```

Field 020 (ISBN) is used to store the price (in the ‡c subfield). Field 034 carries coded mathematical data. The first indicator specifies the type of scale; "1" indicates "single scale." Subfield ‡b contains the constant ratio linear horizontal scale, "26000." Other subfields could contain a variety of coded information on scale, coordinates, declination, and right ascension, providing a key access point for cartographic materials. This field has a textual equivalent in field 255; in this case, the statement of scale (subfield ‡a) gives a textual equivalent: "Scale [ca. 1:26,000]." Field 052 provides another form of access: geographic classification codes. Subfield ‡a contains a geographic classification area code, each ‡b a sub-area code. Between the two occurrences of 052, sub-area codes identify Modesto ("‡a4364‡bM6"), Turlock (". . .‡bT9"), and Stanislaus County ("‡a4364‡bS8"); as is typical for field 052, there are matching 651 fields for each access point.

**Figure 5.8 Maps Record, Tagged Display**

```
Rec Status:n  Legend:em    Encoding:ƀ    Descript:a    Link:ƀ
File Date:820330            DType:s       Date 1:1981   Date 2:ƀƀƀƀ
Country:cau   Relief:ƀƀƀƀ   Base:ƀƀƀ     Rec Gp:a      Govt:ƀ
Index:1       Format:ƀƀ     Language:eng  Mod:ƀ         Cat Src:ƀ
Record ID:DCLC82692187-M                 Transac:19820330-120000.0
010 ƀƀ ‡a82692187/MAPS
020 ƀƀ ‡c$0.50
034 1ƀ ‡b26000
050 0ƀ ‡aG4364.M6 1981‡b.C6
052 ƀƀ ‡a4364‡bM6‡bT9
052 ƀƀ ‡a4364‡bS8
110 2ƀ ‡aCompass Maps (Firm)
245 00 ‡aMap of Modesto, California.
250 ƀƀ ‡a1981 ed.
255 ƀƀ ‡aScale [ca. 1:26,000].
260 0ƀ ‡aModesto, CA :‡bModesto Chamber of Commerce,‡c[1981]
265 ƀƀ ‡aModesto Chamber of Commerce, 1401 F. St., P.O. Box 844,
       Modesto, CA 95353
300 ƀƀ ‡a1 map :‡bcol. ;‡c57 x 55 cm., folded to 23 x 10 cm.
500 ƀƀ ‡aPanel title: City map of Modesto with Stanislaus County and
       its communities.
500 ƀƀ ‡aIndexed.
500 ƀƀ ‡aIndexed maps of Stanislaus County and "Map of Turlock and
       vicinity", "Map of Oakdale and vicinity", "Map of Riverbank and
       vicinity", 15 local maps, ill., and advertisements on verso.
651 ƀ0 ‡aModesto (Calif.)‡xMaps.
651 ƀ0 ‡aStanislaus County (Calif.)‡xMaps.
651 ƀ0 ‡aTurlock (Calif.)‡xMaps.
710 20 ‡aModesto Chamber of Commerce.
```

## MRDF: THE MACHINE-READABLE FILES FORMAT

During 1980 and 1981, a working group of U.S. and Canadian librarians prepared a MARC format for Machine-Readable Data Files (MRDF). MARBI and the rest of the USMARC advisory group discussed the proposed format during those two years, finally approving the new format in October 1981. Lenore Maruyama of LC's Network Development Office compiled the format document, while Sue Dodd of the University of North Carolina, Chapel Hill prepared a cataloging manual.[2] Because 1981, 1982 and 1983 were exceptionally busy years for USMARC development, the format was not scheduled for integration into *MFBD* unitl Update 9 in 1984. MRDF did receive testing prior to approval, as UTLAS developed a test system which helped to refine the proposed format. After approval of the format, OCLC began early analysis, resulting in a number of proposed changes to the format prior to publication in *MFBD*.

As defined in *AACR2,*

A machine-readable data file is defined as a body of information coded by methods that require the use of a machine (typically a computer) for processing. Examples are files stored on magnetic tape, punched cards (with or without a magnetic tape strip), aperture cards, punched paper tapes, disk packs, mark sensed cards, and optical character recognition font documents. The term *machine-readable data file* embraces both the data stored in machine-readable form and the programs used to process that data.[3]

The format was developed with primary attention to data files as used on large computers. When cataloging data files, the nature of the data is important, while the physical format is changeable and relatively minor. As a result, *AACR2* and the MRDF format both concentrate on content with little attention to physical form.

The advent of mass-produced microcomputer software requires more attention to physical form; physical and technical details are important for microcomputer software, and they are constant for a given edition of such software. A patron who wants to check out a LOGO interpreter needs to know what form the interpreter is in and what computers it will run on; if the patron has an IBM PCjr with disk drive, an Atari 1200XL cartridge will be of little use. Microcomputer software requires different rules and elements, and involves a much larger group of users. Some libraries have already begun cataloging microcomputer software on the major bibliographic services, using the Films format.

Most 008 positions for MRDF are derived from other material formats. Field 036, Original study number, can carry an identification number given when the file was created. Field 036 is specifically designed for files that result from studies. Field 211 adds yet

**Figure 5.9 Machine-Readable Data Files: New Fields**

| | |
|---|---|
| 008/26 | Type of file |
| 008/27 | Type of machine |
| 036 | Original study number |
| 211 | Acronym or shortened title |
| 351 | File structure / sort sequence |
| 516 | Kind of file or data |
| 521 | Users or intended audience |
| 522 | Geographic coverage |
| 523 | Chronological coverage of data/dates of collection |
| 537 | Source of data |
| 538 | Technical details |
| 556 | Information about documentation |
| 565 | Number of cases / variables |
| 567 | Methodology |
| 581 | Primary publications |

another variant title possibility, one which is quite common for databases and other machine-readable data files. Field 351 contains information about the file structure and sort sequence. The ten new notes fields make up the bulk of the new fields needed for MRDF, which also uses the core bibliographic fields. Figure 5.9 shows the new MRDF fields. Figure 5.10 shows examples for most of them.

**Figure 5.10 Machine-Readable Data Files: Examples for New Fields**

| |
|---|
| 351 ᵇᵇ ‡aFixed-length, nonhierarchical‡bMonth by carrier code and flight number<br>351 ᵇᵇ ‡aRectangular‡bEnumeration district and block group tract within county within state<br>351 ᵇᵇ ‡aSPSS system file |
| 516 ᵇᵇ ‡aComputer programs (Subroutines/modules)<br>516 ᵇᵇ ‡aText (Law reports and digests) |
| 521 ᵇᵇ ‡aLawrence Livermore Laboratory, G-Division, Physics Dept.<br>521 ᵇᵇ ‡aClinical students, postgraduate house officers. |
| 522 ᵇᵇ ‡aCounty-level data from four Northwestern states (Idaho, Montana, Oregon, Washington). |
| 523 ᵇᵇ ‡aBritish speeches from 1870-1914 and German speeches from 1871-1912. |
| 537 ᵇᵇ ‡aSurvey of Consumer Finances, conducted annually from 1946-1971 by the Economic Behavior Program, Survey Research Center, University of Michigan.<br>537 ᵇᵇ ‡aDefense Mapping Agency digitized 1:250,000 maps. |
| 538 ᵇᵇ ‡aWritten in FORTRAN H with 1.5K source program statements.<br>538 ᵇᵇ ‡aTechnical details: Operates on IBM 360 and 370 under OS SVS and OSMVS with 9K bytes internal memory; requires IBM 2740 terminal with special narrow platen and form feeding features. |
| 556 ᵇᵇ ‡aDocumentation also available as FSWEC-77/0387-1. |
| 565 ᵇᵇ ‡a300 variables. |
| 567 ᵇᵇ ‡aTotal civilian noninstitutional population of the United States.<br>567 ᵇᵇ ‡aThe model employs the integration of a set of coupled nonlinear ordinary differential equations by simple Euler differentiating. |
| 581 ᵇᵇ ‡aCampbell, Angus. "Interpreting the Presidential Victory," Milton C. Cummings (ed.) The National Election of 1964. Washington: Brookings, 1965. |

## THE MUSIC FORMAT

The USMARC Music format covers two different material formats: sound recordings and printed and manuscript music. "Music" is really not an adequate name for the format. All sound recordings are cataloged in the "music" format, including plays, humor, and other nonmusic presentations. Scores (printed and manuscript music) sometimes appear to have more in common with books than with sound recordings. However, both sound recordings and scores require uniform titles much more commonly than other materials, as both tend to have nondistinctive titles.

### Musical Scores

The Music format has a moderate number of unique elements and fields, listed in Figure 5.11. OCLC and RLG both decided independently to treat Music as two formats. Figures 5.12 and 5.13 show a record for a printed score; Figures 5.14 and 5.15 show a record for a sound recording.

Most coded values have already been encountered; the legend ("cm") identifies the material as music, printed or microform, monograph, commonly known as a score. Five new codes appear; they are as follows:

Form of composition code (Compos): "zz"
A two-character code indicates the form of composition, such as suites, toccatas, waltzes, rock music, ricercars, bluegrass and mazurkas. Code "zz" indicates some form not found in the list of codes.

Format of music manuscript or printed music (Score): "b"
Full score, miniature or study size.

Existence of parts (Parts): "ƀ"
No parts exist.

Accompanying matter code (Accomp): "ehiƀƀƀ"
The score is accompanied by a biography of the composer or author ("e"), technical information on the music ("h"), and historical information ("i").

Literary text code for sound recordings (Text): "nƀ"
Not applicable: not a sound recording.

Field 028 (Publisher number for music) is a control number and retrieval item that can also generate notes and added entries. The field has two defined indicators; the first indicator specifies the type of publisher number (issue, matrix, plate or other); the second specifies printing of a note or an added entry (or both). Subfield ‡a contains the number, subfield ‡b the source. The first 028 in Figure 5.13 is an "other publisher number" (first indicator "3"); the second is a plate number (first indicator "2"); both have second indicator "2," calling for a note but no added entry.

Field 041 (Language code) uses the first indicator to state whether the item is or includes a translation; "0" says that it is not and does not. Several subfields allow storage of

**Figure 5.11 Music Format: Unique Fields**

| 008/18-19 | Form of composition code |
| 008/20 | Format of music manuscript or printed music |
| 008/21 | Existence of parts |
| 008/24-29 | Accompanying matter code |
| 008/30-31 | Literary text code for sound recordings |

| 024 | Standard Recording Number (SRN) |
| 028 | Publisher number for music |
| 047 | Form of composition code |
| 048 | Number of instruments or voices code |
| 254 | Musical presentation area |
| 262 | Imprint statement for sound recordings (pre-AACR2) |
| 305 | Physical description for sound recordings (pre-AACR2) |

**Figure 5.12 Scores Record, Formatted Display**

```
Satie, Erik, 1866-1925.
  [Gymnop'edies; arr.]
  Gymnop'edies / Erik Satie ; two orchestrated by Claude Debussy ;
edited by Peter Dickinson. -- London ; New York : Eulenburg, c1980.
  1 miniature score (xi, 19 p.) ; 19 cm.

  Originally for piano.
  Pref. in English, French, and German.
  Publisher's no.: 1376.
  Pl. no.: EE 6695.

  1. Orchestral music, Arranged--Scores. I. Debussy, Claude,
1862-1918. II. Dickinson, Peter. III. Title.
```

language codes for different aspects of a work; subfield ‡g contains language codes of accompanying material other than summaries or librettos (e.g., program notes); as stated in the second 500 note, this printed music includes a preface in English, French and German, recorded in 041 ‡g as "gerengfre." Field 045 (Chronological code or date/time) uses the first indicator to show "type of date/time"; "0" indicates "Single date/time." Subfield ‡b contains chronological date/time; the "d" indicates "A.D.," the next four characters give the year: thus, the work is associated with A.D. 1896.

Field 048 (Number of instruments or voices code) provides coded access to number and type of instruments or voices. Subfield ‡a gives performer or ensemble codes, subfield ‡b contains soloist codes. Each subfield consists of a two-letter code for an instrument, ensemble or voice, and a two-digit code (optional) for the number of parts. Figure 5.12 includes a simple 048: "‡aoa," "Larger ensemble—full orchestra."

**Figure 5.13 Scores Record, Tagged Display**

```
Rec Status:c  Legend:cm    Encoding:ᵬ   Descript:a   Link:ᵬ
File Date:830311           DType:s      Date 1:1980  Date 2:ᵬᵬᵬᵬ
Country:enk   Compos:zz     Score:b      Parts:ᵬ      Intell:ᵬ
Repro:ᵬ       Accomp:ehiᵬᵬ  Text:nᵬ      ME/Body:1    Language:ᵬᵬᵬ
Mod:ᵬ         Cat Src:d
Record ID:CRLG36910-C                    Transac:19830830-052714.0
028 32  ‡a1376‡bEulenburg
028 22  ‡aEE 6695‡bEulenburg
040 ᵬᵬ  ‡cNN‡dNN‡dCtY-Mus
041 0ᵬ  ‡ggerengfre
045 0ᵬ  ‡bd1896
048 ᵬᵬ  ‡aoa
100 10  ‡aSatie, Erik,‡d1866-1925.
240 10  ‡aGymnop´edies;‡oarr.
245 10  ‡aGymnop´edies /‡cErik Satie ; two orchestrated by Claude
        Debussy ; edited by Peter Dickinson.
260 0ᵬ  ‡aLondon ;‡aNew York :‡bEulenburg,‡cc1980.
300 ᵬᵬ  ‡a1 miniature score (xi, 19 p.) ;‡c19 cm.
500 ᵬᵬ  ‡aOriginally for piano.
500 ᵬᵬ  ‡aPref. in English, French, and German.
650 ᵬ0  ‡aOrchestral music, Arranged‡xScores.
700 10  ‡aDebussy, Claude,‡d1862-1918.
700 11  ‡aDickinson, Peter.
```

## Sound Recording Example

Figures 5.14 and 5.15 show a MARC record providing extensive coded access, none of which would be available through normal card catalogs. This record also includes 13 new coded elements in the form of an 007 field. Apart from the 007 elements (the second, third and fourth lines of Figure 5.15), codes are similar to those in the previous example. Legend "jm" is for Sound recordings, musical, monograph; country "dcu" is the District of Columbia; form of composition "cg" is "Concerti grossi," and accompanying material codes "ghi" denote "technical and/or historical information on instruments (g)" as well as technical information on music and historical information. The elements from field 007 follow:

General Material Designation (GMD): "s"
Sound recording.

Specific Material Designation (SMD): "d"
Sound disc.

Original versus Reproduction aspect (Orig/Rep): "|"
No attempt made to assign.

Speed: "b"
33 1/3 rpm (disc).

**Figure 5.14 Sound Recording Record, Formatted Display**

```
Bach, Johann Sebastian, 1685-1750.
  [Brandenburgische Konzerte]
  The Brandenburg concerti [sound recording] / Johann  Sebastian
Bach. -- Washington, D. C. : Smithsonian Institution, c1978 (New York
: Columbia Special Products).
  3 sound discs (97 min.) : 33 1/3 rpm ; 12 in. -- (Smithsonian
collection of recordings)

  Title on container: The six Brandenburg concerti.
  Performers from the Aston Magna Foundation for Music ; Albert
Fuller, artistic director.
  "Performed and recorded on original instruments for the first time
in America."
  Recorded during the Aston Magna Summer Festival, Great Barrington,
Mass., June-July, 1977.
  The concerti "occupy five sides of the three discs in this set...
The sixth side ... is blank, save for a spiral groove designed to
protect your turntable."
  Manual sequence.
  Program notes by Albert Fuller ([12] p. : ill. ; 30 cm.) and notes
on the recordings by James Morris ([1] p. ; 26 cm.) laid in
container.
  Contents: Concerto I in F, BWV 1046 (20 min.) -- Concerto II in F,
BWV 1047 (11 min., 44 sec.) -- Concerto III in G, BWV 1048 (11 min.,
28 sec.) -- Concerto IV in G, BWV 1049 (15 min., 30 sec.) -- Concerto
V in D, BWV 1050 (21 min., 5 sec.)  -- Concerto VI in B-flat, BWV
1051 (17 min., 10 sec.).
  Smithsonian : P3 14834.

  1. Concerti grossi. I. Fuller, Albert. prf II. Aston Magna
Foundation for Music. prf III. Title. IV. Title: The six  Brandenburg
concerti. V. Series.
```

   Kind of sound (Sound): ''s''
Stereophonic (electric).

   Groove width/Groove pitch (Groove): ''m''
Microgroove/fine.

   Dimensions (sound recording) (Dimens): ''e''
12 in.

   Tape width (Width): ''n''
Not applicable (not a tape).

   Tape configuration (Config): ''n''
Not applicable (not a tape). This code would designate full track, half track, quarter track
and other tape track configurations.

**Figure 5.15 Sound Recording Record, Tagged Display**

```
Rec Status:n   Legend:jm   Encoding:ƀ   Descript:a   Link:ƀ
GMD:s          SMD:d       Orig/Rep:|   Speed:b      Sound:s
Groove:m       Dimens:e    Width:n      Config:n     Kind:m
Material:p     Cutting:l   RepChar:n
File Date:840302           DType:s      Date 1:1978  Date 2:ƀƀƀƀ
Country:dcu    Compos:cg   Score:ƀ      Parts:ƀ      Intell:ƀ
Repro:ƀ        Accomp:ghiƀƀ Text:ƀ      ME/Body:1    Language:ƀƀƀ
Mod:ƀ          Cat Src:d
Record ID:CRLG84-R428                   Transac:19840302-164557.0
028 02 ‡aP3 14834‡bSmithsonian
028 00 ‡aP 14835‡bSmithsonian
028 00 ‡aP 14836‡bSmithsonian
028 00 ‡aP 14837‡bSmithsonian
033 2ƀ #a197706--‡a197707--‡b3764‡cG7
040 ƀƀ #aRPB‡cRPB‡dWaBeW
045 0ƀ #bd1721
048 ƀƀ #aba02‡awb03‡awd01‡asa02‡asb01‡asc01‡asz02‡akc01
048 ƀƀ #abb01‡awh01‡awb01‡asa03‡asb01‡asc01‡asz01‡akc01
048 ƀƀ #asa03‡asb03‡asc03‡asz01‡akc01
048 ƀƀ #awh02‡asa03‡asb01‡asc01‡asz01‡akc01
048 ƀƀ #awa01‡asa02‡asb01‡asc01‡asz01‡akc01
048 ƀƀ #asb02‡asg02‡asc01‡asz01‡akc01
100 10 #aBach, Johann Sebastian,‡d1685-1750.
240 10 #aBrandenburgische Konzerte
245 14 #aThe Brandenburg concerti‡h[sound recording] / ‡cJohann
       Sebastian Bach.
260 0ƀ #aWashington, D. C. :‡bSmithsonian Institution,‡cc1978‡e(New
       York :‡fColumbia Special Products).
300 ƀƀ #a3 sound discs (97 min.) :‡b33 1/3 rpm ; ‡c12 in.
306 ƀƀ #a002000‡a001144‡a001128‡a001530‡a002105‡a001710
440 ƀ0 #aSmithsonian collection of recordings
500 ƀƀ #aTitle on container: The six Brandenburg concerti.
511 0ƀ #aPerformers from the Aston Magna Foundation for Music ;
       Albert Fuller, artistic director.
500 ƀƀ #a"Performed and recorded on original instruments for the
       first time in America."
518 ƀƀ #aRecorded during the Aston Magna Summer Festival, Great
       Barrington, Mass., June-July, 1977.
500 ƀƀ #aThe concerti "occupy five sides of the three discs in this
       set...The sixth side ... is blank, save for a spiral groove
       designed to protect your turntable."
500 ƀƀ #aManual sequence.
500 ƀƀ #aProgram notes by Albert Fuller ([12] p. : ill. ; 30 cm.) and
       notes on the recordings by James Morris ([1] p. ; 26 cm.) laid
       in container.
505 0ƀ #aConcerto I in F, BWV 1046 (20 min.) -- Concerto II in F, BWV
       1047 (11 min., 44 sec.) -- Concerto III in G, BWV 1048 (11 min.,
       28 sec.) -- Concerto IV in G, BWV 1049 (15 min., 30 sec.) --
```

**Figure 5.15 Sound Recording Record, Tagged Display (Cont'd)**

```
        Concerto V in D, BWV 1050 (21 min., 5 sec.) -- Concerto VI in
        B-flat, BWV 1051 (17 min., 10 sec.).
  650 ƀ0 ‡aConcerti grossi.
  700 11 ‡aFuller, Albert.‡4prf
  710 21 ‡aAston Magna Foundation for Music.‡4prf
  740 40 ‡aThe six Brandenburg concerti.
```

Kind of disc, cylinder or tape (Kind): "m"
Mass-produced (most commercial discs).

Kind of material (Material): "p"
Plastic.

Kind of cutting (Cutting): "1"
Lateral or combined cutting (that is, not hill-and-dale).

Special reproduction characteristics (RepChar): "n"
Not applicable: no special reproduction characteristics. This code identifies Dolby-B encoded tapes, dbx encoded tapes and discs, CX encoded discs and other cases where special reproduction characteristics are required. If this recording is typical of 1978 classical recordings, Dolby-A was used during the recording process, but the resulting disc does not require Dolby processing (no commercial discs require Dolby processing for reproduction). The characteristics coded are reproduction characteristics rather than recording characteristics.

Field 033 (Capture date and place) provides coded access to the date and place of recording (or filming). The first indicator gives the type of date; "2" indicates a range of dates. Subfield ‡a gives capture date; in this case, from June 1976 to July 1976 ("‡a197706—‡a197707—"). Subfield ‡b contains a geographic classification area code, subfield ‡c a geographic classification sub-area code; together, they note that the recording was made in Great Barrington, Mass. ("‡b3764‡cG7").

Field 048 is used to the fullest plausible extent for this record. Each concerto has a separate 048 giving its instrumentation. The first 048 indicates that the first concerto has two parts for horns, three for oboes, one for bassoon, two for violin, one for viola, one for violoncello, two for other bowed strings and one for harpsichord (taking the subfields as they appear). The second concerto uses one trumpet, one recorder, one oboe, three violins, one viola, one violoncello, one other string and one harpsichord. The third uses three violins, three violas, three violoncelli, one other string and a harpsichord. The fourth uses two recorders, three violins, one viola, one violoncello, one other string and a harpsichord. The fifth uses one flute, two violins, one viola, one violoncello, one other string and a harpsichord. The sixth uses two violas, two viola da gambas, one violoncello, one other string and a harpsichord.

Field 260 differentiates the publisher from the manufacturer; subfields ‡a and ‡b give the place of publication and publisher (Washington, DC: Smithsonian Institution), while subfields ‡e and ‡f give the place of manufacturer and manufacturer (New York : Columbia Special Products). Field 306 (Duration of sound recordings) gives each concerto as a separate subfield ‡a, recording each in minutes and seconds: the time is actually transcribed in hours, minutes and seconds as "hhmmss"; thus, "‡a001144" is 11 minutes, 44 seconds. Field 511 represents a different use of the Participant/Performer note than the Films example; in this case, the first indicator is "0," denoting "General (i.e., no print constant generated)." Field 518 (Data on capture session note) contains information on the recording session, giving the textual equivalent to field 033 and adding the name of the festival.

**Music Format and Shared Cataloging**

Music cataloging on the national bibliographic services is a prime example of widespread cooperation. As of late 1983, RLIN had over 160,000 music records, and OCLC had many more—and none of those records were distributed by the Library of Congress in a MARC distribution service. While music catalogers will certainly appreciate direct availability of LC records in machine-readable form, anticipated in 1984, lack of such records has not prevented the format from getting substantial use.

## NOTES AND REFERENCES

1. Betz, Elizabeth W. *Graphic Materials: Rules for Describing Original Items and Historical Collections.* Washington,DC: Library of Congress; 1982. 155 p.

2. Dodd, Sue A. *Cataloging Machine-Readable Data Files: An Interpretive Manual.* Chicago: American Library Association; 1982. xix, 247 p.

3. *Anglo-American Cataloguing Rules.* 2nd ed. Chicago: American Library Association; 1978: 202-203. 620 p.

# 6

# Archival and Manuscripts Control

The MARC Manuscripts format was first published in 1973. Some 40,000 records have been entered in that format on OCLC, but it has never been a widely used format. Figure 6.1 shows fields uniquely defined for the old Manuscripts format. Some of them have become part of the new Archival and Manuscripts Control format.

The MARC Manuscripts format was designed to meet the known needs of manuscript catalogers, but was perceived by archivists as inadequate for their needs; in fact, the LC manuscripts division itself never used the format. Archivists are primarily interested in controlling material. Material is handled in a variety of ways, producing various levels of intellectual and physical control—and that control, rather than complete description, is the primary reason to build records. The Manuscripts format, couched in the language and needs of library catalogers, appeared to require too much and to provide too little to be suitable for archivists.[1]

**Figure 6.1 Manuscripts Format: Unique Fields**

| | |
|---|---|
| 008/18-19 | Illustration code |
| 008/30 | Case file indicator |
| 008/32 | Processing status code |
| 008/33 | Collection status code |
| 008/34 | Level of collection control code |
| 303 | Unit count |
| 304 | Linear footage |
| 535 | Repository note |
| 540 | Literary rights note |
| 543 | Solicitation information note |
| 545 | Biographical tracings note |

Archival and manuscript materials are, almost by definition, unique. As a result, MARC has less use as a tool for shared cataloging within the community of archivists. Also, most archivists work outside normal library contexts and have not adopted a standard code of descriptive practice. As we know, USMARC has many virtues besides providing a basis for shared cataloging; the formats serve to organize information, store complex bibliographic data, allow online retrieval on well-established national systems, communicate information in a consistent manner, and manipulate data for a variety of uses. For archivists to be able to gain these advantages, the format needed to be revised to provide for the descriptive and control requirements of archives. Steven L. Hensen of the Library of Congress described the situation in *Archives, Personal Papers, and Manuscripts: A Cataloging Manual for Archival Repositories, Historical Societies, and Manuscript Libraries:*

The emphasis is on cataloging of groups of personal papers, and corporate, governmental and family archives, which can include record groups, series, sub-groups, sub-series, etc. This approach is used and encouraged for two reasons: First, the size of most modern manuscript and archival collections has led archivists and manuscript curators to prefer limited cataloging control over all of their holdings rather than detailed control over only some of their holdings, thus, collective description is the only practical response to the overwhelming cataloging burdens that would be presented by item level description. Second, it is the approach most likely to observe the principle of archival unity which recognizes that, in organically-generated collections at least, it is the collective whole as the sum of the interrelationships of its components that has significance and that the individual item or sub-series within a collection usually derives its importance from its context. In most manuscript cataloging, the analog to the book is not the individual manuscript, but the collection of which the item may be a part.[2]

Several groups began working on related projects in 1981: a revised MARC format, a descriptive cataloging manual, and an implementation for archival processing. David Bearman headed the National Information Systems Task Force (NISTF) of the Society of American Archivists, working toward a format which would serve the needs of librarians and archivists; Steven L. Hensen of the Library of Congress prepared a cataloging manual; and Alan Tucker and Barbara Brown coordinated a Research Libraries Group Special Formats Task Force, working toward implementation. The Library of Congress was represented on both task forces; the Rare Books and Manuscripts Section of ALA's Association of College and Research Libraries (ALA ACRL RBMS) was also involved in working toward a new format.

After extensive review by the USMARC advisory group, MARBI approved the revisions to the Manuscripts format in January 1983, transforming it into the Archival and Manuscripts Control format. In October 1982, the Society of American Archivists (SAA) also approved the format, and will publish an interpretive version of the format. LC and SAA share responsibility for maintenance of the format.

## GENERAL PRINCIPLES FOR ARCHIVES

The introduction of LC's preliminary distribution of Archival and Manuscripts Control content designators states the general principles for the format:

The USMARC archival and manuscripts control content designators allow an archival-control approach rather than the "form" or "medium" approach provided by the other USMARC formats. However, some content designators from other USMARC formats (e.g., field 260—Imprint Statement) have been included, making the revised format capable of accommodating both collections of materials (published or unpublished, in any medium or form) and single items. An institution has an option of using either this format or another USMARC format appropriate to the form of the material in hand when creating a MARC record for a single item (e.g., a codex manuscript).

Two general principles were followed in developing the USMARC archival and manuscripts control content designators:

1. No content designator in the existing *MFBD* manuscripts format was made obsolete unless its use was considered confusing or illogical (e.g., the 4xx and 8xx series fields).

2. No content designator was defined or extended from other USMARC formats unless there was specific need for it (e.g., field 050—LC Call Number was not extended; field 505—Contents Note (Formatted) was extended).[3]

The Archival and Manuscripts Control format (abbreviated as AMC for the remainder of this chapter) is concerned with control, more so in some ways than with bibliographic description. Archival materials go through many stages of processing over long periods of time. These materials may have access restrictions, and are usually not described down to the individual item level.

## AMC CHANGES FROM MANUSCRIPTS

Three varieties of changes combine to transform MARC Manuscripts into the AMC format. Some content designators (fields, subfields, indicator values and coded data) are labeled obsolete (that is, not appropriate for use in AMC). Some content designators are added. Finally, some elements are renamed or redefined to meet archival control needs. Figure 6.2 shows fields defined for Manuscripts which are not considered valid for AMC.

### Newly Defined Fields, Subfields and Codes

New fields, subfields and codes fall into two groups. Some are new to USMARC. Most of these are newly defined for AMC but may be extended to material formats either explicitly or through format integration. Others have been defined for other formats and are extended to AMC. Those fields that are new to USMARC are starred (*) in Figure 6.3. Those that existed in other formats are marked with a plus (+). In addition to new fields, many subfields will be added to existing Manuscripts fields, in some cases completely transforming the existing definition. Some fields will be renamed, and new values are defined for some existing codes.

In addition to new fields, AMC adds a number of content designators at lower levels. In the legend, bibliographic level "d" adds an intermediate level between item and collection. Encoding level "n" is added, because the concept of encoding level may not apply to the record at hand. A new subfield ‡e in field 040 is a free-text area to allow specification of description conventions beyond the codes available in the leader's Descriptive Cataloging Form. This subfield will be extended across formats; it can be used to note an addi-

**Figure 6.2 Obsolete Manuscripts Fields**

| | |
|---|---|
| 008/18-19 | Illustration code |
| 008/30 | Case file indicator |
| 008/32 | Processing status code |
| 008/33 | Collection status code |
| 008/34 | Level of collection control |
| 037 | Stock number |
| 055 | Call number/class numbers assigned in Canada |
| 060 | National Library of Medicine call number |
| 070 | National Agricultural Library call number |
| 080 | Universal Decimal Classification |
| 302 | Item count / page count |
| 303 | Unit count |
| 304 | Linear footage |
| 350 | Price / value |
| 400 | Series statement - personal name/title |
| 410 | Series statement - corporate name/title |
| 411 | Series statement - conference / title |
| 440 | Series statement - title |
| 490 | Series untraced or traced differently |
| 534 | Original version note |
| 543 | Solicitation information note |
| 800 | Series added entry - personal name |
| 810 | Series added entry - corporate name |
| 811 | Series added entry - conference |
| 830 | Series added entry - uniform title |
| 840 | Series added entry - title |

tional set of conventions or an alternative set of conventions. Subfield ‡3 (Materials specified) is added to many fields, serving as an informal intra-record link to bring together various pieces of information about some portion of the material; the subfield is discussed further in Chapter 8.

Two new fields are in the physical description area. Field 340 (Medium) is a textual replacement for the coded physical descriptions of other formats (field 007); as designed, the field is a clear candidate for entry into other formats, particularly Machine-Readable Data Files. Field 351 was created for Machine-Readable Data Files as "File structure / sort sequence"; the scope of the field was expanded and its name was changed as it was extended to AMC.

Extensive and complex notes fields are the heart of the Archival and Manuscripts

**Figure 6.3 Archival and Manuscripts Control: New Fields**

| | |
|---|---|
| *340 | Medium |
| +351 | Organization and arrangement |
| +505 | Contents note (formatted) |
| +521 | Users / Intended Audience note |
| *524 | Preferred citation of described materials |
| +530 | Additional physical form available |
| *544 | Location of associated materials |
| +546 | Language note |
| *561 | Provenance |
| *562 | Copy and version identification |
| +565 | Case file characteristics note |
| +581 | Publications note |
| *583 | Actions |
| *584 | Accumulation and frequency of use |
| *656 | Index term - occupation |
| *657 | Index term - function |
| +752 | Place of publication/printing access |
| *851 | Location |

Control format. Field 583 is specifically a control field, used to record past and future actions regarding part or all of a collection; other "note" fields also have control aspects. Some of the "old" fields extended to AMC came from the Machine-Readable Data Files format. Similarly, some of the AMC definitions will eventually be extended to other formats. Certain AMC "note" fields make up a category of information not traditionally part of a bibliographic record. For practical purposes, these new fields constitute a processing control segment.

Most archivists do not distinguish between name as subject and name as creator. As shown in fields 656 and 657, "index term" is the common archival term equivalent to both "added entry" and "subject added entry." The original proposals for AMC disallowed 600-611 and 700-711, substituting a series of "Index term" fields. The format as approved allows use of either form of added entry; cataloging and practice manuals will specify the preferred form for given situations. Archival users of the AMC format may never create a 7XX field, while Rare Books and Special Collections catalogers may continue to maintain the distinction between subjects and other added entries.

Finally, one important field for Archival and Manuscripts Control does not appear in Figure 6.3 because it is defined for all formats: field 773, Host Item Entry. This field, discussed in Chapter 8, supports analytic cataloging; for archives, it supports the multiple levels of description and control which may be needed in an archival collection.

## ARCHIVAL AND MANUSCRIPTS CONTROL EXAMPLE

Archival and Manuscripts Control records tend to be large and complex. A single record may well have 10 or 20 source and action notes (fields 541 and 583); records can quite easily have several dozen added entries. Added entries for some records will be limited by the maximum record size possible in any given system; one real record used for testing the RLG implementation had over 170 added entry fields.

Figures 6.4 and 6.5 show most of an Archival and Manuscripts Control record, excluding fields 541 and 583. In many cases, fields 541 and 583 would not display with the

**Figure 6.4 Archival and Manuscripts Control Record, Formatted Display**

```
Anderson, Luther, 1880-1940.
  Luther Anderson papers, 1899-1940 (inclusive)
  2.75 linear ft. (7 boxes)

  Scrapbooks also available on microfilm (402 frames on 1 reel,
  35mm.) from Manuscripts and Archives, Yale University Library, at
  cost.  Order no. HM128.
  Taught school in Kansas and became principal of the Lindsborg,
  Kansas, high school, 1901-1903; 1907-1911 taught European history at
  the Imperial University in Peking; returned in 1911 as special
  correspondent for the Chicago Daily News, and travelled through China
  and the Philippines until 1915; 1915-1920, taught at High School of
  Commerce in Springfield, Mass.; taught part-time at Northeastern
  University, 1920-1928; 1928 began teaching at American International
  College in Springfield.
  Summary: Teacher and journalist.  Correspondence, writings,
  scrapbooks and photographs relating to his career as a journalist in
  Peking (1911-1914) and his post as teacher of English and aesthetics
  at the American International College in Springfield, Mass.
  (1928-1940).
  Gift of Helen Carlson Anderson, 1967.
  Indexes: Unpublished finding aid in repository.
  Luther Anderson Papers.  Manuscripts and Archives, Yale University
  Library.
  Location: Manuscripts and Archives, Yale University Library, Box
  1603A Yale Station, New Haven, CT 06520.

  1. Phelps, William Lyon, 1865-1943. 2. Sandz'en, Birger, 1871-1954.
  3. Anderson, Luther, 1880-1940. 4. Chinese letters. 5. Journalism.
  6. Scandinavian literature. 7. China--History--Revolution, 1911-1912.
  8. Philippine Islands--Politics and government--1898-1935. 9. United
  States--Travelers. 10. China--Description and travel. 11. Asia. 12.
  Scrapbooks. 13. Photoprints. 14. Journalists. lcsh 15. Educators.
  lcsh
```

remainder of the record, since these fields may contain confidential or sensitive information. Examples of 541 and 583 fields appear in Chapter 8, in the discussion of intra-record links.

    This record has been corrected or revised ("Rec Status:c"). The legend specifies language material, manuscript ("b"), collection ("c"). Descriptive cataloging form is unstated. The Archival and Manuscripts Control field 008 has no unique elements (and few elements in all). However, the new format will bring changes (across formats) in the names of some existing elements, which are shown here: "Country" becomes "Place" (of publication, production or execution); "GMD" (007 position 0) becomes "Category" (of material). Of the 008 codes shown, only one is new: "DType:i" shows inclusive dates (1899-1940). This record includes an 007 field, for the microform version of the scrapbooks; the field appears in the second and third lines of Figure 6.5, and is explained as follows:

    Category of material (Category): "h"
Microform.

    Specific material designation (SMD): "d"
Microfilm reel.

    Original versus reproduction aspect (Orig/Rep): "|"

    Polarity: "a"
Positive: dark characters against a light background.

    Dimensions (microform) (Dimen): "f"
35 mm (microfilm).

    Reduction ratio (Ratio): "u|||"
Unknown. This code has two parts: a one-character general ratio, and an optional three-digit specific reduction ratio. Thus, a typical computer output microfiche would be coded "c048" for "high reduction, 48x."

    Color: "b"
Monochrome (e.g., black-and-white).

    Emulsion on film (microforms) (Emulsion): "a"
Silver halide.

    Generation: "c"
Service copy (Intended for use rather than for production).

    Base of film (microforms) (Base): "a"
Safety base.

    Field 040 includes a subfield ‡e; "appm" is the agreed coding for *Archives, Personal Papers, and Manuscripts*.[3] Field 300 includes another new subfield, ‡f (Packaging unit). Field 530 (Additional physical form available) uses most available subfields: ‡3, ‡a, ‡b, ‡c and ‡d show, respectively, materials specified, note, source, conditions and order number. Field 520 (Summary, abstract, annotation, scope) also shows an added subfield: ‡b (expan-

**Figure 6.5 Archival and Manuscripts Control Record, Tagged Display**

```
Rec Status:c   Legend:bc     Encoding:ƀ    Descript:ƀ     Link:ƀ
Category:h     SMD:d         Orig/Rep:|    Polarity:a     Dimen:f
Ratio:u---     Color:b       Emulsion:a    Generation:c   Base:a
File Date:840208             DType:i       Date 1:1899    Date 2:1940
Place:ctu      Language:eng  Mod:ƀ         Cat Src:d
Record ID:CRLG84-A67                       Transac:19840209124502.0
040 ƀƀ ‡aCtY‡cCtY‡eappm
100 1ƀ ‡aAnderson, Luther,‡d1880-1940.
245 00 ‡aLuther Anderson papers,‡f1899-1940 (inclusive)
300 ƀƀ ‡a2.75 linear ft.‡f(7 boxes).
530 ƀƀ ‡3Scrapbooks‡aalso available on microfilm (402 frames on 1
    reel, 35mm.)‡bfrom Manuscripts and Archives, Yale University
    Library,‡cat cost.‡dOrder no. HM128.
545 ƀƀ ‡aTaught school in Kansas and became principal of the
    Lindsborg, Kansas, high school, 1901-1903; 1907-1911 taught
    European history at the Imperial University Peking; returned in
    1911 as special correspondent for the Chicago Daily News, and
    travelled through China and the Philippines until 1915;
    1915-1920, taught at High School of Commerce in Springfield,
    Mass.; taught part-time at Northeastern University, 1920-1928;
    1928 began teaching at American International College in
    Springfield.
520 ƀƀ ‡aTeacher and journalist. Correspondence, writings, scrapbooks
    and photographs relating to his career as a journalist in Peking
    (1911-1914) and his post as teacher of English and aesthetics at
    the American International College in Springfield, Mass.
    (1928-1940).‡bHe also lectured on Scandinavian culture and on
    Chinese politics. Manuscripts and advertising brochures document
    this aspect of his life. Although his correspondence is mostly
    routine, there are a number of letters of interest from William
    Lyon Phelps and Sven Birger Sandzen, head of the art school at
    Bethany College (Kansas) where Anderson had studied.
561 ƀƀ ‡aGift of Helen Carlson Anderson, 1967.
555 ƀƀ ‡aUnpublished finding aid‡bin repository.
524 ƀƀ ‡aLuther Anderson Papers. Manuscripts and Archives, Yale
    University Library.
600 10 ‡aPhelps, William Lyon,‡d1865-1943.
600 10 ‡aSandz'en, Birger,‡d1871-1954.
600 10 ‡aAnderson, Luther,‡d1880-1940.
650 ƀ0 ‡aChinese letters.
650 ƀ0 ‡aJournalism.
650 ƀ0 ‡aScandinavian literature.
651 ƀ0 ‡aChina‡xHistory‡xRevolution, 1911-1912.
651 ƀ0 ‡aPhilippine Islands‡xPolitics and government‡y1898-1935.
651 ƀ0 ‡aUnited Statex‡xTravelers.
651 ƀ0 ‡aChina‡xDescription and travel.
651 ƀ0 ‡aAsia.
```

**Figure 6.5 Archival and Manuscripts Control Record, Tagged Display (Cont'd)**

```
655 ƀƀ ‡aScrapbooks.
655 ƀƀ ‡aPhotoprints.
656 ƀ7 ‡aJournalists.‡2lcsh
656 ƀ7 ‡aEducators.‡2lcsh
851 ƀƀ ‡aManuscripts and Archives,‡bYale University Library,‡cBox
        1603A Yale Station, New Haven, CT 06520.
```

**Figure 6.6 Archival and Manuscripts Control Record: Added Entries**

```
PHILIPPINE ISLANDS--POLITICS AND GOVERNMENT--1898-1935
Anderson, Luther, 1880-1940.
  Luther Anderson papers, 1899-1940 (inclusive)
  2.75 linear ft. (7 boxes).
[ID: CRLG84-A76]
```

```
CHINA--HISTORY--REVOLUTION, 1911-1912.
Anderson, Luther, 1880-1940.
  Luther Anderson papers, 1899-1940 (inclusive)
  2.75 linear ft. (7 boxes).
[ID: CRLG84-A76]
```

sion of summary note). (Note that subfield ‡b does not appear on the formatted display of Figure 6.4.) Finally, field 851 (location) includes subfields ‡a, ‡b and ‡c: the custodian, institutional division and street address; other possible subfields include country of repository (‡d), location of packaging units (‡e), item number (‡f) and materials specified (‡3). Figure 6.6 shows a few of the additional entries that could be generated in a printed guide for the collection (or in online searching).

## NOTES AND REFERENCES

1. Even with the implementation of the Archival and Manuscripts Control format, MARC records built by archivists will usually serve as a pointer to more detailed non-machine-readable finding aids in the repository.

2. Hensen, Steven L. *Archives, Personal Papers, and Manuscripts: A Cataloging Manual for Archival Repositories, Historical Societies, and Manuscript Libraries.* Washington, DC: Library of Congress; 1983. 51 p. Material quoted is on pages 1–2.

3. Library of Congress. MARC Standards Office. *USMARC Archival and Manuscripts Control Content Designators (January 1983).* 1983 June: first page. Unpaged. Distributed informally prior to inclusion in the USMARC formats.

# 7

# Authorities and Holdings

The USMARC formats described so far make up a family of formats, the bibliographic family. Two other types of USMARC formats have been defined, each making up a "family" with a single member: Authorities and Holdings.

## AUTHORITIES

Authorities provide information about headings: names, subjects, uniform titles. Some authority records show the form of an established heading, that is, the form of a name to be used in building bibliographic records. A record for an established heading may also show other forms of the name as See From tracings and other established headings as See Also From tracings. The record may also give explanatory notes, may note how the established form was chosen, or might even note reference works which did not serve to establish a form of name. Other authority records do not contain established headings, but provide explanatory references for nonestablished headings.

Authority files have been maintained manually for decades, so that libraries could assure consistent entry of names and avoid repetitive decision-making on form of name. The Library of Congress has one of the largest bodies of authority information on names and subjects; most other libraries follow LC policy where possible, to avoid duplicate effort and to allow best use of LC cataloging information.

### Authority Format: Preliminary Edition

The first version of a MARC format for authority information was prepared by Lenore S. Maruyama of the Library of Congress, and published in 1976.[1] That format was used by the Library of Congress to distribute name authority records on a limited basis from 1976 through 1983.

The preliminary format was experimental in some ways, particularly in terms of record maintenance. All other MARC formats have always used full-record maintenance: when anything changes in a record, the complete record is redistributed, and the receiving agency can either replace the record blindly or compare fields to see what has changed and what actions should be taken. The preliminary Authorities format used a different method, based on what appeared to be most reasonable at the time. Each variable data field in an Authorities record contained a control subfield ‡w with 24 characters of information on that field; six of the 24 characters gave the date of last transaction. When changes occurred, a partial record was distributed, containing enough information to identify the record, and those fields that actually changed.

Those who suggested this method saw clear advantages to field-level change identification in maintaining authority files, particularly those files that directly control bibliographic information. When an update came in, a program could easily establish whether bibliographic changes would be needed (because the established form had changed) and, if so, whether those changes could be made by machine. Partial-record updates also reduce record size; if authority records were to be distributed electronically rather than on tape, this would reduce transmission costs.[2]

As use of MARC formats and the Authorities format grew, the partial-record updates became a problem. In order to process partial-record updates, an agency must already have loaded the relevant full records; further, any updates must be loaded in the exact chronological order in which they are received. New agencies trying to build authority files found it difficult to process the set of tapes. Some felt strongly that full-record updates would be easier to maintain.

**The Linked Systems Project**

Early in the 1980s, the Council on Library Resources (CLR) funded the Linked Systems Project (LSP), a joint project of LC, RLG and WLN to establish computer-to-computer linkages among bibliographic systems. The two early phases of LSP were the linkage system itself, establishing a standard set of protocols for computer-to-computer communication, and the first implementation, establishing direct exchange of Authorities information. When the implementation is fully established, selected RLIN and WLN participants will help to create authority records that can be made part of the national, LC-coordinated authorities system. As part of the Authorities phase of LSP (formerly known as the Linked Authority Systems Project or LASP), the Authorities format was studied and a number of recommendations were made; among them was a change from field-level status and update information to record-level transaction date/time information, and a change to full-record updates.

**Authorities: A MARC Format**

Josephine S. Pulsifer and Margaret Patterson of LC worked on a comprehensive revision of the Authorities format, with the assistance of Ann Ekstrom; after review by the USMARC advisory group and other interested parties, the first full edition of the format was approved in 1981.[3] The introduction to the first edition defines its scope:

The MARC authorities format provides specifications for the content and the content designation of authority records containing name, subject, and/or series authority information... The authorities format is designed to accommodate in a single record all of the authority information pertinent to the use of a given heading as a name and/or a subject and/or a series.[4]

The USMARC Authorities format has the same structure as all other USMARC formats. Figure 7.1 shows the coded and control areas of the Authorities format. Fields 020 and 022 can be used for sets and series; field 050 is only used when a single call number applies to a series. Fields 053 and 083 are not the same as the bibliographic 050 and 082;

### Figure 7.1 Authorities Format: 0XX Fields

```
001 Authority record control number
005 Date and time of latest transaction
008 Fixed-length data elements
    00-05     Date entered on file
    06        Direct/indirect geographic subdivision code
    07        Romanization scheme
    09        Authority/reference record code
    10        Cataloging rules code
    11        Subject heading system code
    12        Type of series code
    13        Numbered/unnumbered series code
    14        Heading use code--main or added entry
    15        Heading use code--subject added entry
    16        Heading use code--series added entry
    28        Type of government agency code
    29        Reference evaluation code
    31        Record update in process code
    32        Undifferentiated personal name code
    33        Status of authority heading code
    35-37     Language of heading code
    38        Modified record code
    39        Cataloging source code
```

```
010     LC authority record control number
014     Link to bibliographic record for serial or multipart item
020     International Standard Book Number (ISBN)
022     International Standard Serial Number (ISSN) (series)
035     Local system control number
040     Cataloging source
042     Authentication center
043     Geographic area code
045     Chronological code or date/time
050     Library of Congress call number (series)
052     Geographic classification code
053     LC classification number
083     Dewey Decimal Classification number
```

these fields contain classification numbers or ranges associated with an authority heading; for example, LC class "TH5281" is associated with "Scaffolding."

Figure 7.2 shows the Headings, References and Tracings fields for Authorities. There are deliberate parallels in content designation between the authorities and bibliographic families, making it feasible to use authority records to control bibliographic headings. These parallels are stated in the *Underlying Principles* (reproduced in Appendix A). For example, field 110 in Authorities establishes a corporate name heading which, depending on coded values, can control bibliographic fields 110, 410, 610, 710 and 810; within Authorities, fields 410 and 510 would provide See From and See Also From tracings for other corporate names, allowing systems to generate appropriate See and See Also references.

**Figure 7.2 Authorities Format: Fields 1XX-5XX**

```
HEADINGS
100     Heading - personal name
110     Heading - corporate name
111     Heading - conference or meeting name
130     Heading - uniform title
150     Heading - topical subject
151     Heading - geographic name

REFERENCES AND TRACINGS
260     General explanatory See reference (subjects)
360     General explanatory See Also reference (subjects)

400     See From tracing - personal name
410     See From tracing - corporate name
411     See From tracing - conference or meeting name
430     See From tracing - uniform title
450     See From tracing - topical subject
451     See From tracing - geographic name

500     See Also From tracing - personal name
510     See Also From tracing - corporate name
511     See Also From tracing - conference or meeting name
530     See Also From tracing - uniform title
550     See Also From tracing - topical subject
551     See Also From tracing - geographic name
```

The remaining fields in Authorities, shown in Figure 7.3, serve different functions and do not follow the patterns above. Fields 641 through 646 contain bibliographic description and local treatment information for series. Fields 663 through 682 contain a variety of information: definition, usage and scope; free-text references and tracings to explain complex relationships; and maintenance information, such as sources used to establish a heading or reasons for deleting a heading.

**Figure 7.3 Authorities Format: 6XX Fields**

```
SERIES TREATMENT INFORMATION
641     Numbering peculiarities (series)
642     Series numbering example
643     Place and publisher / issuing body (series)
644     Analysis practice (series)
645     Tracing practice (series)
646     Classification practice (series)

NOTES
663     Cataloger-generated See Also reference (names)
664     Cataloger-generated See reference (names)
665     Information or history reference (names)
666     General explanatory reference (names)
667     Usage or scope (names)

668     Characters in nonroman alphabets
670     Source data found
675     Source data not found
678     Epitome

680     Scope note (subjects)
681     Example under / Note under (subjects)

682     Deleted heading information
```

Figure 7.4 gives a few examples of heading/reference and heading/tracing pairs, all taken from *Authorities: A MARC Format*. Figure 7.5 shows a few note fields, with headings and tracings as needed for context.

**Uses for USMARC Authorities**

This is only a cursory review of the Authorities format. The format is used to build and maintain authority files for reference and for control. Authority files can be used to provide references for book and card catalogs, to suggest related headings, to maintain quality control in a bibliographic system, and even to make automatic changes as established headings change. Authority files can improve efficiency for an online catalog, by filtering searches through the authority system and, in some cases, by indexing bibliographic headings indirectly (through an authority file) rather than directly.

Authority files serve catalogers directly, and serve library patrons less directly but no less powerfully. One major function of cataloging and maintenance of catalogs (card, book or online) is guidance to related works. A patron looking for one book by an author should be able to find other books by the same author easily; a patron should be able to find those books even if that patron brings a different form of name to the search. Shared MARC authority files allow collocation on a national scale, increasing access to materials

**Figure 7.4 Authorities Examples: Headings, References and Tracings**

```
150  ♭0  ‡aTravel regulations
260  ♭♭  ‡isubdivision‡aOfficials and employees--Travel regulations
         ‡iunder countries, government departments, cities, etc; and
         subdivision‡aTravel regulations‡iunder special categories of
         officials, e.g.,‡aJudges--Travel regulations
```

```
100  00  ‡aAlexander‡bI,‡cEmperor of Russia,‡d1777-1825
400  00  ‡aAleksandr‡bI,‡cEmperor of Russia,‡d1777-1825

130  ♭0  ‡aBible‡xMusic
430  ♭0  ‡aBible.‡pO.T.‡pPsalms‡xMusic
```

```
100  00  ‡aPseudo-Brutus
500  10  ‡aBrutus, Marcus Junius,‡d85?-42 B.C.

150  ♭0  ‡aElectronic data processing‡xData preparation
550  ♭0  ‡aInput design, Computers
```

while reducing the cost of providing such access. The USMARC Authorities format is different from the bibliographic formats, but provides a powerful tool to aid in using those formats.

## HOLDINGS

USMARC provides only one field for storage or communication of holdings information: field 850. The bibliographic formats lack ways of storing extensive holdings data so as to allow manipulation of that data. Most implementations of USMARC have added local fields to accommodate holdings at various levels of complexity. Serial holdings have always been a problem in library automation, particularly in terms of automatic compression from piece-level holdings as used in a check-in system to summary holdings as needed for most displays.

Serial holdings change over time; new issues are received as pieces, collected and bound, and sometimes discarded or replaced by microfilm. Libraries control unbound serials differently than bound volumes: it is effectively impossible to circulate volume 13, number 5, of a periodical to one borrower, and volume 13, number 7, to another, once volume 13 has been bound—unless it has been bound in half-year, 6-issue bindings. A library must keep track of what issues are on hand, and of the current status of those issues. Even monograph holdings change over time, when the library considers physical condition and preservation information to be part of holdings information.

In October 1982, eight southeastern research libraries[5] received a Title IIC grant to begin developing a regional resource sharing system for serials. This group project, dubbed the "Southeastern ARL Libraries Cooperative Serials Project," worked with the Library

**Figure 7.5 Authorities Examples: Notes**

```
100 00 ‡aDe la
666 ⌷⌷ ‡aFor names beginning with a prefix, search under the prefix
        (under each element if the prefix is made up of multiple words)
        as well as under the name following the prefix.
```

```
667 ⌷⌷ ‡aNot to be confused with Smith, Sam.
```

```
100 10 ‡aAvery, Harold Eric
400 10 ‡aAvery, H. E.
670 ⌷⌷ ‡aHis Advanced physical chemistry calculations, 1971: t.p.
        ‡b(H. E. Avery, B. Sc., Ph. D., Dept. of Chem., Liverpool
        Polytechnic)
```

```
100 10 ‡aCalanques (France)
675 ⌷⌷ ‡aWeb. geog. dict., 1972;‡aE. Brit. micro.;‡aCol. Lipp. gaz.;
        ‡aTimes atlas, 1955
```

```
150 ⌷0 ‡aHoly Year
680 ⌷⌷ ‡iHere are entered works on the holy or jubilee years
        proclaimed by the popes.  For special holy years (regular or
        extraordinary) add date, e.g.‡aHoly Year, 1925
```

```
150 ⌷0 ‡aFruit processing
682 ⌷⌷ ‡iThis heading has been replaced by the heading‡aFruit--
        Processing,‡ia heading not printed in LCSH because it uses a
        freefloating subdivision controlled by a pattern heading.
```

of Congress to develop a proposal for a national format for holdings and locations. The result was Proposal 82-20, ''MARC Format for Holdings and Locations,'' first presented at the October 1982 USMARC advisory group meeting. Intensive discussion followed at the October 1982 meeting, at a special three-day conference in November 1982, and at the 1983 ALA Midwinter Meeting and September 1983 USMARC advisory group meetings.

The Southeastern group, LC, MARBI, and other USMARC advisory group participants worked to make the format useful for publications other than serials, and to make it easy to attach holdings information to a bibliographic record. Further, these groups worked to allow simple representation of holdings, recognizing that the complex representation allowed by the format is rarely needed or feasible. The Southeastern group contracted with SOLINET to develop program designs using the format, and to test the workability of the format. The years 1984 and 1985 will provide medium-scale tests of the format. Most involved agree that the format outlined below is more likely to meet detailed needs than any other methodology compatible with USMARC. Some who have worked on the format question its feasibility at the piece level, but all who have worked on it recognize the careful design and general consideration that have gone into it.

## USMARC Holdings Format

The proposed USMARC Holdings format is about 150 pages long, with detailed descriptions of subfield and field usage. This brief treatment gives some of the content designation and a few partial examples. Most monographic holdings segments are simple; serial holdings segments can become exceedingly complex.

The Holdings format is designed so that records can be maintained as independent USMARC records or attached to bibliographic records. When carried as independent records, Holdings records have the standard USMARC structure and include field 001, 005 and 008 (as would other USMARC records). Figure 7.6 gives the 0XX fields for the Holdings format. Fields 010 through 030 serve to link a holdings record to a bibliographic record. USMARC bibliographic records can be self-contained entities; Holdings records are meaningless unless linked to some bibliographic entity; it doesn't help to know that an institution has volumes 1–117 without knowing what they are volumes of. Field 004 provides an explicit link to a single USMARC record; other fields can link to records that may not be in USMARC form by providing unambiguous identifiers such as ISBN or CODEN.

### Figure 7.6 Holdings Format: 0XX Fields

```
001      Control number
004      Control number: parent bibliographic record
005      Date and time of latest transaction
007      Physical description fixed field (as in USMARC Bib)
008      Fixed length data elements
010      LC Card Number
020      ISBN
022      ISSN
023      International film number (SFN)
024      Standard recording number (SRN)
027      Standard technical report number (STRN)
030      CODEN
035      Control number
```

Figure 7.7 shows the remainder of the Holdings fields. Field 841 is used when a Holdings record is attached to a bibliographic record; it carries the Holdings type of record, descriptive cataloging form/level of description, and 008 values in three subfields. The rest of the format is comprised of three independent fields and three groups of fields, each containing three fields. Fields 843, 845 and 852 are independent; fields 853–855, 863–865 and 866–868 are groups in one respect, while the triplets 853, 863, 866; 854, 864, 867; and 855, 865, and 868 are groups in another respect. Figure 7.8 gives examples of some of the fields.

Field 843 describes the reproduction when the bibliographic record is for the original, but some (or all) of the holdings are for reproductions; a record may include multiple 843 fields. Field 845 is used to specify information on lending or reproduction of copies that

**Figure 7.7 Holdings Format: 8XX Fields**

```
841    Fixed length data elements (alternate storage)
843    Reproduction Note
845    Terms governing use
852    Location / Call Number

853    Definition of enumeration & chronology/publication pattern
854    Definition of enumeration & chronology/publication pattern :
         supplement or accompanying material
855    Definition of enumeration & chronology/publication pattern :
         index

863    Enumeration and chronology - basic bibliographic unit
864    Enumeration and chronology - supplement or accompanying mat.
865    Enumeration and chronology - indexes

866    Enumeration and chronology - bibliographic unit:
         alternative display
867    Enumeration and chronology - supplement or accompanying mat. :
         alternative display
868    Enumeration and chronology - indexes: alternative display
```

cannot be specified in coded fields 008/20 and 008/21. Field 852 provides location information for an item, and is the fundamental location and call number field. This field is typical of the newly defined Holdings fields in its wealth of subfields and extended description (9 pages). For some non-serial holdings, field 852 would be the single new field.

The first three related fields (853, 854 and 855) define enumeration and chronology or publication patterns. As with the other groups, the first field is for base publications; the second is for supplements or accompanying material; the third is for indices. These fields provide definitions and captions for holdings, but do not provide the holdings proper. Sequence numbers (‡6) link 853 to 863 or 866, 854 to 864 or 867, and 855 to 865 or 868. The discussion of 853 runs to 12 pages in the proposed format. Since fields 853 and 863 are the most critical fields for computer support of serials check-in and holdings compression, this level of detail is not surprising. The examples for fields 853 through 865 may not make much sense without the detailed content rules given in the format document.

Fields 853–855 and 863–865 are extensively subfielded to accommodate many levels of information; Figure 7.9 shows the subfielding for field 853. Where fields 853–855 contain the definitions and labels, using whole numbers in subfield ‡6, fields 863–865 contain the actual values, using decimal numbers in subfield ‡6. The format includes 14 pages of explanation for field 853, which can vary from one occurrence per physical piece down to a single statement for a long run. Subfields 863–865 also have subfields for information on physical condition at the piece level and preservation status of pieces, as shown in the second 863 example in Figure 7.8.

**Figure 7.8 Holdings Format: Sample Fields**

```
843 ƀƀ ‡aMicrofilm.‡bWashington,‡cLibrary of Congress,
     Photoduplication Service‡d[1954-    ]‡e5 reels. 35 mm.‡3v. 1-10.
843 ƀƀ ‡aMicrofilm.‡bNew Orleans,‡cRecordak Corp.,‡d[Dec. 8, 1969-
     ]‡e1 reel. 35 mm.‡fJapanese camp papers,‡3v. 1-2.

Two 843s for a single newspaper with split holdings:
843 ƀƀ ‡aMicrofilm.‡bNew York,‡cRecordak Corp.‡d[1962-   ]‡e328 reels.
     35 mm.‡3Feb. 4, 1883-Aug. 3, 1960
843 ƀƀ ‡aMicrofilm.‡bWinston-Salem, N. C.,‡cMann Film Laboratories,
     ‡d[1962-   ]‡e52 reels.  35 mm.‡3Sept. 1, 1960-Nov. 30, 1962
```

```
852 01 ‡aViBlbV‡bMain Lib‡bMRR‡kRef‡hHF5531.A1‡iN4273
852 01 ‡aDLC‡bSer Div‡hA123‡i.B456‡zSigned by author.
```

```
Examples of definition/value sets, 85X-86X
```

```
853 01 ‡61‡av.‡wa
863 51 ‡61.1‡a1‡p//
```

```
853 01 ‡61‡av.
863 51 ‡61.1‡a6‡p7312986‡qink spots‡rdiethyl zinc

[v. 6, acc. no. 7312986, has ink spots and has been preserved using
   diethyl zinc]
```

```
853 20 ‡61‡av.‡bno.‡u12‡vr‡x01‡wm‡tc.
863 40 ‡61.1‡a1-13‡t1
854 20 ‡61‡a(year)‡0Buyer's guide‡wa‡tc.
864 40 ‡61.1‡a1956-1962‡t1

[Library has v. 1-13, 1951-1963 with the Buyer's guide for 1956-1962]
Note: this pattern would NOT be used for a publication like Consumer
   Reports, where the Buying Guide is numbered as a regular issue.
```

```
855 ƀƀ ‡61‡av.‡i(year/year)‡oAuthor index
865 41 ‡61.1‡a21/25‡i1971/1976‡zin v. 25 of Emory law journal.

[Serial published as Journal of public law, v. 1-23; as Emory law
   journal, v. 23-  .  Holdings record for Journal of public law shows
   index location in note.]
```

The combinations of 853-855 and 863-865 are needed for the anticipated computer support of holdings compression and expansion. For those not using integrated serials check-in, for those who find the scheme too complex for implementation, and for those publications that can't be represented in such a scheme, the format includes a final trio of

**Figure 7.9 Holdings Field 853: Subfields**

```
‡6   Sequence control number (SCN)
‡a   Term designating first level of enumeration
‡b   Term designating second level of enumeration
‡c   Term designating third level of enumeration
‡d   Term designating fourth level of enumeration
‡e   Term designating fifth level of enumeration
‡f   Term designating sixth level of enumeration
‡g   Term designating alternative numbering scheme, first level of
       enumeration
‡h   Term designating alternative numbering scheme, second level of
       enumeration
‡i   Term designating first level of chronology
‡j   Term designating second level of chronology
‡k   Term designating third level of chronology
‡l   Term designating fourth level of chronology
‡m   Term designating fifth level of chronology
‡n   Term designating sixth level of chronology
‡t   Term designating copy
‡u   Bibliographic units per next higher level
‡v   Restart/continuous numbering code
‡w   Issues per year / frequency
‡x   Calendar change
‡y   Regularity pattern
‡3   Definition date span
```

fields. Fields 866, 867 and 868 allow free-text holdings strings, identified as ANSI Z39 notation or nonstandard notation. One or more such fields can replace a portion of the 85X/86X combinations for display purposes, can replace all of them, or can be used without 85X/86X fields.

**Outlook for Implementation**

The USMARC Holdings format represents years of work by the Southeastern ARL group, the Library of Congress (particularly Gary McCone) and USMARC advisory group. Most who have been involved with the design agree that, if any USMARC holdings format can serve serials check-in and other serials automation needs, this design can. Even the most pessimistic generally regard fields 852 and 866/868 as reasonable foundations for a national holdings reporting format. Fields 853–855 and 863–865 are far more difficult to establish, but are needed if computers are to generate piece predictions, establish missing-issue claims, and automatically recognize volume ends, compressing holdings at that point. Only experience will show whether the full USMARC holdings format can be implemented in a realistic, cost-effective manner. The design is a careful, thoughtful one; its future will depend on its workability.

## NOTES AND REFERENCES

1. Library of Congress. MARC Development Office. *Authorities: A MARC Format.* Preliminary edition. Washington, DC: Library of Congress; 1976.

2. These reasons for partial-record updates are the author's own, and probably do not reflect the full range of reasoning used in 1976; even in retrospect and knowing the problems of partial-record updates, the case for partial-record updates is a sensible one.

3. Library of Congress. MARC Development Office. *Authorities: A MARC Format.* Washington, DC: Library of Congress; 1981. [160] p.; updated June 1983.

4. Ibid., p. 2.

5. The eight members of the Southeastern ARL Libraries Cooperative Serials Project are Emory University, University of Florida, Florida State University, University of Georgia, University of Kentucky, University of Miami, University of Tennessee and Virginia Polytechnic Institute and State University (VPI). Most of this section, including all examples, is selected from Proposal No. 82-20 (August 1983).

# 8

# Links Within and Among USMARC Records

USMARC defines fields and records at a single level of significance. Each field within a record may be accessed independently from the directory, and (with few exceptions) each field functions as an independent data element or group of related data elements. Further, most USMARC records are independent, capable of being processed without reference to any other USMARC record. USMARC has not supported hierarchies of information, that is, records within records or fields within fields. Some non-USMARC formats do support subrecords or other hierarchical structures within records, but such support has never been part of USMARC.

While the formats have not had formal support for hierarchies, bibliographic data do involve hierarchical relationships, sometimes between elements within a single record, sometimes among various records. In recent years, USMARC designers have been looking at the problems of links and hierarchies, within a record and among records. While USMARC has always had some support for links and certain types of hierarchies, those links have been improved and broadened in recent years. USMARC still does not support formal subrecords, but now defines a sufficient variety of links within and among records to satisfy most bibliographic needs.

Linkage mechanisms fall into two broad categories: intra-record links, linking different elements within a single record, and inter-record links, linking different records. Some forms of inter-record linking support analytic cataloging of one sort or another; others support chronological relationships (successive entry cataloging), collocation, and authority control. Figure 8.1 lists links supported by USMARC; this chapter discusses some of those links.

**Figure 8.1 USMARC Linking Techniques**

| |
|---|
| INTRA-RECORD LINKS |
| Variant name fields<br>    Fields 87X    Variant form of name<br>    Subfield ‡j  Tag and sequence number of the field for which<br>                    this field is a variant |
| Alternate graphic representation  (Vernacular data)<br>    Field 066    Character sets present<br>    Field 880    Alternate graphic representation<br>    Subfield ‡6  Linking subfield |
| Materials specified<br>    Subfield ‡3  Materials specified |
| Sequence control<br>    Subfield ‡6  Sequence control number (Holdings) |
| ANALYSIS |
| Analytics of monographic and multipart series, using series note<br>    Fields 4xx    Series notes<br>    Fields 8xx    Series added entries |
| Display of parts in the notes area<br>    Field 505     Formatted contents note |
| Analytical added entries<br>    Fields 7xx    Other added entries |
| "In" analytics<br>    Field 773     Host item entry |
| OTHER INTER-RECORD LINKS |
| Linking entry fields<br>Control number links<br>Standard number links<br>Textual and authority links |

## INTRA-RECORD LINKS

Fields within a record are inherently linked to each other, in the sense that they all relate to the same overall record. Until 1976, LC MARC had no provision for explicit links between one field and another, or between groups of fields within a record.

**Variant Name Fields and Subfield ‡j**

In 1976, four fields were added to the Serials format which included explicit field-to-field linkage: the 87X "variant name" fields. These fields were used in pre-AACR2 CONSER records, where the ALA form of a corporate name would be recorded in field 871, while the AACR1 form was entered in field 110 (or 410, 610, 710 or 810). Subfield ‡j (Tag and sequence number of the field for which this field is a variant) contained a tag, a slash and a number: for example, ‡j710/1. This subfield (which could only appear in an 871) links this field to the first 710 in the record.

The 87X fields were added to all formats in 1979 and 1980, but were never implemented at the Library of Congress; when LC began using *AACR2*, it stopped using 87X fields in Serials. Though the fields are still defined, the subfield ‡j technique is not considered successful. Two problems limit the usefulness of subfield ‡j:

1. Maintenance of a record can disrupt the validity of the links through simple inattention. Inserting a 710 field (in the example above) without inspecting the 87X fields would leave the field with an incorrect link (the 871 would be treated as a variant form of the new "first 710").

2. The link is unidirectional. The 710 itself contains nothing to show that a variant form exists; thus, records with 87X fields could not be processed using normal field-by-field techniques.

The concept of an explicit field-to-field link is sound, and cases exist where such a link is valuable. A newer explicit intra-record link was approved by MARBI in 1982; its first major use in USMARC is to support storage of vernacular (nonroman) text.

**Vernacular Text**

USMARC never had formal facilities to store vernacular text (text in the nonroman character set of the publication, rather than translated or romanized text). When RLG was planning the RLIN CJK (Chinese, Japanese and Korean) enhancements, it was decided that all basic bibliographic fields should be available in romanized form as well as vernacular form. This required not only a technique for storing vernacular data, but a technique for linking the vernacular form to the romanized form and vice versa. The technique which was approved can actually be used for any alternate storage; it links a single field to another single field in an unambiguous manner that is not affected by subsequent changes to the record. This explicit linkage requires the definition of one new subfield, ‡6, in all variable data fields; it also requires the definition of a new field, field 880.

Storage of vernacular text actually required two new fields in USMARC. The first, field 066 (Character sets present), defines the nonroman character sets used in the record. Any character set outside of ALA Extended ASCII must be defined by a three-character "escape sequence," so called because the first character is always hexadecimal "27," the ASCII "escape" character. The second and third character of a sequence define the new character set. Field 066 contains the two-character completion for each character set used in a record; the field can be used to determine whether a local system is able to process all the text within a record. The field also indicates that the record may contain occurrences of Field 880, Alternate graphic representation.

Field 880 was recently approved and has been implemented within RLIN to support storage of records containing vernacular data in Chinese, Japanese and Korean. The field and its technique are equally applicable for other vernacular storage. The technique works as follows:

1. The romanized field (a 245, for instance) contains a leading ‡6 consisting of the string "<tag>-<no.>." The tag is always 880 for this function,¹ and the number (a two-digit whole number) is a neutral matching number. A typical subfield ‡6 might be "‡6880-03."

2. The 880 ‡6 contains the tag with which it is paired, and the same whole number. The number in field 880 ‡6 must match the number in the romanized field; the number has no other significance. The alternate graphic representation of the 245 field above would be in an 880 field beginning "‡6245-03." A variation is used when a vernacular field has no romanized equivalent: the 880 ‡6 contains the tag, a dash and two zeroes. The special number "00" can occur as often as needed; it signifies that there is no matching field. An example would be "‡6740-00," identifying the 880 field as containing a Uniform Title Added Entry which does not appear in romanized form.

3. Subfield ‡6 in field 880 contains three additional characters: a slash, and the last two characters of the initial escape sequence used in that field. The characters do not constitute an escape sequence, but indicate what the escape sequence will be.² For CJK records, the second and third characters are "$1" in RLG's initial implementation. Even though the subfield ‡6 has indicated the first alternate graphic representation to be used, the escape sequence must appear after the next subfield code and before any alternate graphics. Following a string of alternate graphics, another escape sequence returns to normal or, potentially, to yet another graphic representation.

Alternate graphic representations may not cross subfield or field boundaries. Proper data entry (or computer support) explicitly escapes back to normal Extended ASCII before the next subfield delimiter or field terminator. This practice is important; subfields are not always processed in the order in which they appear, and the escape sequence might otherwise not be interpreted properly.

Figure 8.2 is a simplified version of a CJK record, to show the use of subfield ‡6 and field 880. The record contains nine fields in roman characters; the 100, 245, 250, 260, 505 and 700 are all romanized versions which have vernacular equivalents, while the 300, 500 and 710 do not (these fields might not be romanized data). The last 880 field is an "orphan" vernacular field: as indicated by "‡6740-00," no romanized version has been entered. The technique illustrated by Figure 8.2 is stable; addition of other fields will not disturb the "sequence" of numbers, because there is no meaningful sequence. The "-22" for the 250 field is out of "sequence" in the example, which would make no difference for processing. The technique is also valuable for those programs incapable of handling the vernacular scripts; since all non-880 fields are romanized (or at least use Extended ASCII), all the program has to do is ignore ‡6 subfields and ignore field 880.

Figure 8.2 is a schematic representation but includes no text. Figure 8.3 is a tagged listing of part of an RLIN CJK record, showing the actual use of ‡6 subfields and escape sequences. (Escape characters are not normally printable; for this listing, the right arrow has been used to represent the escape character.) Unfortunately, 880 fields in Figure 8.3 appear to consist of meaningless groups of characters. This is because the CJK graphic representation includes a great many symbols, over 13,000 as of early 1984; the ASCII representation of these symbols requires three ASCII characters for each CJK character.

Figure 8.3 does not show actual CJK characters because of current hardware limitations. In RLIN, CJK records are stored using duplicate tag numbers for romanized and vernacular data; users are shown either or both sets of data depending on their terminal and their needs. Conversion to the USMARC 880 fields and establishment of linking subfields takes place when records are converted for batch processing. Unfortunately, printing devices available for batch processing at RLG do not support the CJK characters. Figure 8.4 shows the same record listed in Figure 8.3, as it would appear on an RLIN CJK terminal for editing; each group of three characters in an 880 field in Figure 8.3 now appears as a single character (or blank). Finally, Figure 8.5 shows the same record in a formatted bibliographic display; in this case, romanized equivalents are suppressed. (The same record displayed on a non-CJK terminal would suppress the vernacular fields.)

## Figure 8.2 Vernacular Data: Schematic Example

```
100 10  ‡6880-01‡aMain entry [romanized]
245 14  ‡6880-02‡aThe Title [romanized]
250 ƀƀ  ‡6880-22‡aEdition [romanized]
260 ƀƀ  ‡6880-03‡aImprint [romanized]
300 ƀƀ  ‡aCollation (no vernacular equivalent)
500 ƀƀ  ‡aNote (no vernacular equivalent)
505 ƀƀ  ‡6880-04‡aNote [romanized]
700 10  ‡6880-08‡aAdded entry [romanized]
710 10  ‡aUnlinked added entry (no vernacular equivalent)
880 10  ‡6100-01/$1‡aMain entry [vernacular data]
880 10  ‡6245-02/$1‡aTitle [vernacular data]
880 ƀƀ  ‡6250-22/$1‡aEdition [vernacular data]
880 ƀƀ  ‡6260-03/$1‡aImprint [vernacular data]
880 ƀƀ  ‡6505-04/$1‡aNote [vernacular data]
880 10  ‡6700-08/$1‡aAdded entry [vernacular data]
880 10  ‡6740-00/$1‡aUnlinked added entry [vernacular data with no
           romanized equivalent]
```

**Figure 8.3 Vernacular Data: Tagged Listing with Linking Fields**

```
066 ƀƀ ‡c$1
100 10 ‡6880-01‡aHs¨u, Shou-k'ai.
245 10 ‡6880-02‡aLi Li-weng ch¨u hua chu shih /‡cHs¨u Shou-k'ai.
250 ƀƀ ‡6880-03‡aTi 1 pan.
260 0ƀ ‡6880-04‡aHo-fei :‡bAn-hui jen min ch'u pan she :‡bAn-hui
        sheng hsin hu a shu tien fa hsing,‡c1981.
300 ƀƀ ‡a3, 3, 2, 171 p. ;‡c20 cm.
504 ƀƀ ‡aBibliography: p. 168-171.
600 10 ‡6880-05‡aLi, Y¨u,‡d1611-1680?‡xCriticism and interpretation.
700 10 ‡6880-06‡aLi, Y¨u,‡d1611-1680?‡tHsien ch'ing ou chi.
        ‡kSelections.‡f1981.
880 10 ‡6100-01/$1‡a→$1!=h!#  '8w'3H→)1.
880 10 ‡6245-02/$1‡a→$1!Cs!#  !Or!RK!#  !CQ'Xf!#  'XL']8!#  →)1/
        ‡c→$1!=h!#  '8w'3H→)1.
880 ƀƀ ‡6250-03/$1‡a→$1!Os→)11→$1!HJ→)1.
880 0ƀ ‡6260-04/$1‡a→$1⁵K!S/!#  →)1:‡b→$1!:g!=w°d!FM³K!JH!Na!#
        →)1:‡b→$1!:g!=w!MI!Be!U<!CU!<p'L{!WD→)1,‡c1981.
880 ƀƀ ‡6500-00/$1‡a"→$1!=h'8w'3H⁵C!=~'XL']8!M"i!T!Cs!Or!RK!CQ'Xfi!U
        !#  !C'i!T'^TK>[²6!;$i!U°4!M"°!!\k3=T→)1"--Pref.
880 14 ‡6600-05/$1‡a→$1!Cs!#  !He→)1,‡d1611-1680?‡xCriticism and
        interpretation.
880 10 ‡6700-06/$1‡a→$1!Cs!#  !He→)1,‡d1611-1680?.‡t→$1'^TK>[!!#
        ²6!#  !;$→)1.‡kSelections.‡f1981.
```

Subfield ‡6 represents a stable linking technique, and one which explicitly points to an alternative field; if there is an alternative version of field 245, you are told about it within the 245 field. The technique need not be limited to use for vernacular data; eight other fields beginning "88" are available for future uses and are reserved for such intra-record links. The definition of the completing element in subfield ‡6 is field dependent: within field 880, the completing element identifies an alternate graphic representation, but in another 88X field, the completing element could serve other purposes, even allowing a single 88X field to be used for a variety of functions. To date, no other 88X fields have been defined or proposed for definition.

**Materials Specified: Subfield ‡3**

Subfield ‡6 supports an explicit link between one field and one other field; as defined in the bibliographic formats, it cannot create a link among more than two fields. The bibliographic formats do not have any explicit, formal linking technique to link groups of fields within a record. RLG did develop an implicit linking technique in its implementation of the Archival and Manuscripts Control format; this technique will also be available within the Visual Materials format.The technique uses subfield ‡3, "Materials specified"; when used as part of a field, subfield ‡3 restricts applicability of the field to some portion of the record—to the materials specified. Subfield ‡3, defined in many descriptive and access fields, explicitly identifies a field as pertaining to part of the material covered by a record; when the same ‡3 value appears in several different fields, those fields can be treated as a group. For instance, field 583, "Actions," can form a history of processing for material; common ‡3 values link together the stages for a given set of material.

Figure 8.6 shows several fields from a hypothetical Archival and Manuscripts Control record, entered in chronological order as material was received and processed; these fields

**Figure 8.4 Vernacular Data: Tagged RLIN CJK Display**

```
TERMINAL: X03

BKS/TEMP  Books       FUL/BIB    CTY084-B1129        Catalog        CTYO-LOD
Record 28 of 342 - SAVE record
+
ID:CTY084-B1129   RTYP:c   ST:s   FRN:   NLR:      MS:  EL:  AD:03-16-84
CC:9114  BLT:am    DCF:a   CSC:   MOD:   SNR:      ATC:      UD:03-19-84
CP:cc      L:chi   INT:    GPC:   BIO:   FIC:0     CON:b
PC:s       PD:1981/        REP:   CPI:0  FSI:0     ILC:      MEI:1   II:0
010       82183552/ACN
020       ‡cRMBY0.60 (pbk.)
040       ‡cCtY‡dCtY
050 0     PL2698.L52‡bZ677 1981
066       ‡c$1
082       895.1/14
100 10    Hs"u, Shou-k'ai.
100 10    徐 寿凯.
245 10    Li Li-weng ch"u◊hua chu◊shih /‡cHs"u Shou-k'ai.
245 10    李 笠翁 曲话 注释 /‡c徐 寿凯.
250       Ti 1 pan.
250       第1版.
260 0     Ho-fei :‡bAn-hui jen min ch'u pan she :‡bAn-hui sheng hsin hua shu tien
          fa hsing,‡c1981.
260 0     合肥 :‡b安徽人民出版社 :‡b安徽省新華書店发行,‡c1981.
300       3, 3, 2, 171 p. ;‡c20 cm.
500       ‡6‡a"徐寿凯同志注释的《李笠翁曲话》 是《闲情偶寄》中的一部份"--Pref.


TERMINAL: X03

BKS/TEMP  Books       FUL/BIB    CTY084-B1129        Catalog        CTYO-LOD
Record 28 of 342 - SAVE record
+
504       Bibliography: p. 168-171.
600 10    Li, Y"u,‡d1611-1680?‡xCriticism and interpretation.
600 14    李 渔,‡d1611-1680?‡xCriticism and interpretation.
700 10    Li, Y"u,‡d1611-1680?‡tHsien◊ch'ing ou chi.‡kSelections.‡f1981.
700 10    李 渔,‡d1611-1680?.‡t闲情 偶 寄.‡kSelections.‡f1981.
```

**Figure 8.5 Vernacular Data: Formatted RLIN CJK Display**

```
TERMINAL: X03

BKS/TEMP  Books       LON      CTY084-B1129           Catalog        CTY0-LOD
FIN CTW 李 笠翁 - 1 cluster in BKS - SAVE record
UPD
徐 寿凯.
   李 笠翁 曲话 注释 / 徐 寿凯. -- 第1版. -- 合肥 ：安徽人民出版社 ：
安徽省新華書店发行, 1981.
   3, 3, 2, 171 p. ; 20 cm.


   "徐寿凯同志注释的《李笠翁曲话》 是《闲情偶寄》中的一部份"--Pref.
Bibliography: p. 168-171.


   1. 李 漁, 1611-1680?--Criticism and interpretation. I. 李 漁, 1611-1680?.
闲情 偶 寄. Selections. 1981. II. Title.

   LCCN: 82183552/ACN
   L.C. CALL NO: PL2698.L52.Z677 1981
   ID: CTY084-B1129              CC: 9114        DCF: a      [CJK]
   CALL: PL2698.L52Z9H74 1981
```

**Figure 8.6 Process Control Fields Containing Subfield ‡3**

```
541 ‡‡ ‡3Letters, 1890-1913‡aUnidentified collector.
541 ‡‡ ‡3Newspaper clippings, 1910-1945‡aJohn Sedgewick Ferwort
    Foundation
583 ‡‡ ‡3Letters, 1890-1913‡aAccessioned‡c11/06/83
583 ‡‡ ‡3Letters, 1890-1913‡aDeacidified‡c11/13/83
583 ‡‡ ‡3Newspaper clippings, 1910-1945‡aAccessioned‡c11/14/83
541 ‡‡ ‡3Letters, 1914-1919‡aJohn Sedgewick Ferwort Foundation
583 ‡‡ ‡3Letters, 1890-1913‡aTransferred to offsite storage‡c11/16/83
583 ‡‡ ‡3Letters, 1914-1919‡aAccessioned‡c11/16/83
583 ‡‡ ‡3Newspaper clippings, 1910-1945‡aDeacidified‡c11/16/83
583 ‡‡ ‡3Letters, 1890-1913‡aRemove restrictions‡c1/1/86
583 ‡‡ ‡3Newspaper clippings, 1910-1945‡aDeed of gift needed‡c1/1/84
583 ‡‡ ‡3Letters, 1914-1919‡aDeed of gift needed‡c1/1/84
```

make up the "process control" section of a record within RLIN. Figure 8.7 shows a possible display format, regrouping the fields based on contents of subfield ‡3. This technique works well for this particular situation, but it is not a formal linking technique, and is not explicitly supported by the format documentation. Subfield ‡3 links are informal and not restrictive. If a box of personal papers is processed as such through three stages, then split

**Figure 8.7 Display of Process Control Fields Using ‡3 Links**

```
Letters, 1890-1913. Source: Unidentified collector.
  Accessioned, 11/06/83.
  Deacidified, 11/13/83.
  Transferred to offsite storage, 11/16/83.
  Remove restrictions, 1/1/86.
Newspaper clippings, 1910-1945. Source: John Sedgewick Ferwort
  Foundation.
  Accessioned, 11/14/83.
  Deacidified, 11/16/83.
  Deed of gift needed, 1/1/84.
Letters, 1914-1919. Source: John Sedgewick Ferwort Foundation.
  Accessioned, 11/16/83.
  Deed of gift needed, 1/1/84.
```

into letters and diaries for further processing, the ‡3 values will not provide any link from the larger group to the smaller material groups. Subfield ‡3 is also defined for many added entry fields. There, as in other cases, it does not appear to be useful as a computer-supported link; rather, the subfield serves as an annotation. Subfield ‡3 is a textual subfield without a controlled vocabulary or controlled usage; it was not intended for computer-supported links, but has some value in such a role.

**Sequence Control Numbers: Subfield ‡6 in Holdings**

The proposed MARC Holdings format uses subfield ‡6 to link fields that contain different information relating to a portion of a serial run. This subfield ‡6 is entirely different from the subfield ‡6 used to support vernacular text. Within Holdings, subfield ‡6 is defined as a Sequence Control Number. Whole numbers in subfield ‡6s within fields 853–855 can be used to sort holdings into proper order overall; decimal numbers based on the same whole numbers appear in the subfield ‡6s within fields 863–865, subsorting holdings and relating actual holdings to patterns. Chapter 7 includes examples of subfield ‡6 as used in Holdings.

The ‡6 link is a formal one both for holdings and for vernacular data, since certain fields in the format do not make sense without reference to other fields. The two uses of ‡6 are mutually exclusive; vernacular data will not be carried in holdings fields, and holdings ‡6 values would only be used in the holdings fields. The two also have distinctly different formats. A holdings subfield ‡6 is restricted to numbers and a single decimal point, where the subfield ‡6 used with 88X fields must always contain a dash preceded by three digits and followed by two digits. Finally, the holdings subfield ‡6 actually links groups of fields, and the contents of subfield ‡6 are specifically intended for keeping fields in a given order; the bibliographic subfield ‡6 links one field to one other field, and the numeric portion has no sequential significance.

## INTER-RECORD LINKS

USMARC has a variety of means for indicating relationships among bibliographic records, ranging from contents notes to record number links. These links are discussed in two general areas, as shown in Figure 8.1: links that support analysis, and all other inter-record links.

## ANALYTICS

"Analysis is the process of preparing a bibliographic record that describes a part or parts of a larger item."[3] Analysis thus involves a smaller item, which can be called a "component part," within a larger item, which can be called the "host item." *AACR2* notes five methods of achieving analysis:

1. analytics of monographic series and multipart series, where the larger item is described in a series note;

2. display of parts in the note area, normally as a contents note;

3. analytical added entries, giving the part's main entry heading and uniform title;

4. "In" analytics, with full descriptive cataloging for the part and a brief citation (main entry, uniform title, title proper, edition and publication details) of the larger item in an "In" note; and

5. multilevel description, giving a relatively complete description of parts within a record for the whole.

### USMARC Support of Analysis: Pre-1984

USMARC has always supported the first three methods of analysis. Analytics of monographic series are supported by series notes and tracings, carried in fields 400–490 and 800–840. Figure 8.8 shows examples of series notes and tracings. These fields have worked well for those cases where the component part is also an independent bibliographic item, as it typically the case with monographic series.

**Figure 8.8 Series Notes and Entries: Examples**

```
110 10 ‡aUnited States.‡bDept. of State.
490 1ᵇ ‡aIts Publication 4107. European and British Commonwealth
    series,‡v17
810 1ᵇ ‡aUnited States.‡bDept. of State.‡tPublications‡v4107.
810 1ᵇ ‡aUnited States.‡bDept. of State.‡tEuropean and British
    Commonwealth series,‡v17.
```

Simple display of parts usually appears in field 505 (Formatted Contents Note). Analytical added entries appear in 7XX fields. Such entries provide access to component parts, while maintaining a coherent master record. Figure 8.9 shows examples of field 505 and of 7XX fields used as analytical added entries; other examples appear in several of the records illustrated in other chapters.

**Figure 8.9 Fields 505 and 7XX: Examples**

```
505 0ʙ ‡aSuite from Drottningholms-Musique, by J. H. Roman.--Ballet
    excerpts from Gustaf Wasa,a by J. G. Naumann.--Overture to Il re
    pastore, by F. A. Uttini.
```

```
700 12 ‡aFasch, Johann Friedrich,‡d1688-1758.‡tSymphony, string
    orchestra,‡rG major.
```

```
730 02 ‡aOil, paint and drug reporter.‡tBuyers directory.
```

Series fields, contents notes and added entries serve many requirements for analysis; all three are part in the core bibliographic formats, and all three have been heavily used in USMARC. There are limitations to the techniques; they are not suitable for some component parts and do not provide sufficiently detailed description for others. Added entries are unsuitable for articles within serials, because the number of potential entries is unlimited and 7XX fields have no specific place to indicate location within the serial. While added entries can be quite informative, libraries with special needs may wish to record more information on certain elements of a larger work; USMARC has not allowed for such detail. The USMARC formats did not allow for full analytic records.

**Analytic Records: Early Proposals**

The lack of USMARC support for full analytic records has bothered librarians in LC and elsewhere for years—since 1972 or earlier, by some estimates. In the early 1970s, a field was proposed which would link a full component-part record to a host-item record. At the time, the field was felt to be unsatisfactory. There was some feeling that a single record should accommodate full description for the host item and the component part. The 76X–78X linking entry field, after which the new field was patterned, had never been wholly satisfactory for indexing, partly because the main entry subfields failed to distinguish types of main entry. As a result, it was difficult to determine whether personal name indexing or corporate name indexing procedures should be used, and sometimes difficult to connect linking entries properly.

During the late 1970s, a number of different proposals were raised for consideration. A range of possibilities was presented at the 1980 ALA Annual Conference in New York, with some basic requirements appearing to gain acceptance. The requirements, as stated in Proposal 80-5.1, are as follows:

1. The technique must be capable of handling a variety of relationships including vertical, horizontal or chronological.

2. The technique must be consistent with the record structure standard as defined by ANSI Z39.2-1979.

3. All data fields must be directly accessible through the record directory.

4. All data fields should be fully content designated.

5. There should be no restriction on the data fields for the related item that can be selected for inclusion in a record.

6. The technique must be able to express relationships between bibliographic units within a single record and between separate records. The description of related bibliographic units may or may not reside in the same bibliographic record.[4]

Proposal 80-5.1 extended the directory, as allowed in ANSI Z39.2-1979: each directory entry may contain a fourth segment, an "implementation-defined portion." As proposed, the "implementation-defined portion" would add a thirteenth character identifying "fields belonging to one subrecord"; it also defined field 002, including a three-character "relationship code," the subrecord character and the legend of the subrecord. Given the set of requirements above, 80-5.1 appeared to be the best technique available; in May 1981, the technique was tentatively approved. Many other techniques had been considered, including ones that allowed entire fields to be imbedded within subfields, and ones that used fields to delimit portions of the directory.

The Library of Congress surveyed a number of federal agencies (and some other parties) to determine interest in the technique. Response, though interpreted by one participant as "favorable," was lukewarm. Most agencies did not use the MARC format and thought the method was "fine, if you use MARC." One agency that did use MARC, via OCLC, thought the proposal was fine, but outlined what OCLC would need to do to make the format work. The needed changes to OCLC, though well stated, would have been expensive to make and would have made OCLC or any similar system slower and more expensive to operate.

Representatives from OCLC and RLG had reluctantly acceded to the technique, but warned early on that it would be an expensive technique to implement. As they spent more time looking at it, the sheer expense and difficulty of the technique became more and more apparent. For the bibliographic services to support subrecords, online displays and data handling techniques would need to be changed drastically; the cost of software changes, documentation changes, and retraining appeared to be excessive. At the 1981 ALA Annual Conference in San Francisco, RLG and OCLC liaisons asserted that implementation of the subrecord technique would take several years and probably cost upwards of $2 million ($1 million for the bibliographic services alone).

Given this expense and difficulty, LC and others agreed that a less disruptive proposal might be reasonable, and that single-record multilevel storage might not be necessary. After further discussion and analysis, Sally McCallum of the Library of Congress prepared Proposal 81-13, which affirmed the existing Serials Linking Entry fields and extended the technique to provide for "In" Analytics.

**Analytic Records: Field 773**

Proposal 81-13, "Record-Linking Techniques," was prepared in October 1981, revised and approved in February 1982, and published in *Information Technology and Libraries* in September 1982.[5] The proposal is an excellent explication of analysis and other linking entry situations, and adds four new elements:

1. Two new values for Bibliographic Level: "a" for monographic (singly occurring) component parts and "b" for serial component parts (such as a running column within a periodical)

2. A new element in the Leader, position 19, "Linked-record code," to be used in those cases where the linked-to record is identified only by a control number;

3. A new subfield ‡7 for all linking entries, containing up to four one-character codes providing further information on the linked-to record; and

4. Field 773, "Host item entry," defined in all bibliographic formats.

The heart of MARC support for "In" analytics is Field 773, defined in Update 8 to *MFBD*. Field 773 is repeatable and is defined identically across all bibliographic formats, as shown in Figure 8.10. The field carries a suggested display constant, "In." Field 773 and the other elements of proposal 81-13 provide full support for the fourth method of analytic cataloging. Additionally, subfield ‡7 strengthens other linking entry fields by defining them more clearly for indexing and other manipulation.

Any MARC format can be used for an analytic record. If a music cataloger wishes to give a full description for a recording of Igor Stravinsky's *Zvezdoliki* on Side 2, Band 1 of "Stravinsky Conducts Stravinsky: Choral Music," a full USMARC music record can be created with legend "ja" (Sound recording, musical; component part, monographic). A continuing (serially appearing) column in a periodical can be cataloged with legend "ab" (Language material, component part, serial); an article in the same periodical would be "aa," since it is monographic.[6]

Figures 8.11 and 8.12 show portions of analytic records; both figures are derived from proposal 81-13. Both records are self-sufficient, and each has enough detail to allow access to the host item if needed. Figure 8.12 shows use of subfield ‡7; in this case, the four positions indicate the following:

**Figure 8.10 Field 773: Full Description**

---

773    Host Item Entry

Indicator 1: Specifies displaying of a note
0    Display a note
1    Do not display a note
Indicator 2 - Undefined

SUBFIELDS
‡7  Control subfield
     Character position 0 - Type of author name
     Character position 1 - Form of author name
     Character position 2 - Type of record
     Character position 3 - Bibliographic level
‡a  Main entry
‡b  Edition
‡d  Place, publisher, and date of publication
‡g  Relationship information
‡k  Series data for related title
‡r  Report number
‡s  Uniform title
‡t  Title
‡u  Standard Technical Report Number (STRN)
‡w  Control number
‡x  International Standard Serial Number (ISSN)
‡y  CODEN
‡z  International Standard Book Number (ISBN)

DESCRIPTION
   This field contains data that identifies the item that serves as
host for the component part for which the record was made (vertical
relationship).  Whenever this field is present in a record,
Leader/07 (Bibliographic Level) must be  set to value "a" (Component
part, monographic), value "b" (Component part, serial), or value "d"
(Subcollection).
   This field is provided in order to enable the user to locate the
physical piece that contains the component part.  Thus, only those
data elements required to assist in the identification of the host
item need to be included in the field, such as links to the
bibliographic record describing the item and/or descriptive data
that identify the host item.  In the case of host items that are
serial or multivolume in nature, information in subfield g that
points to the exact location of the component part within the host
bibliographic item is necessary.

**Figure 8.11 Analytic Record for Journal Article**

```
Cataloging record for a journal article:

Bryant, Keith L.
   Cathedrals, castles, and Roman baths; railway station architecture
in the urban south.
   ill.
   Grant St. Station (Aeck Assoc., archts.) and Decatur (Ga.) Station
(Stevens & Wilkinson, archts.).
   In Journal of urban history, February 1976, v.2, n.2, p. 195-230.
   1. Atlanta (Ga.)--Railroads--Stations.  2. Aeck Associates.  3.
Stevens & Wilkinson.
   LCCN: 75-3249                                              MARC
```

```
Partial MARC record for component part:

Legend: aa
001      ♭♭♭75003249
040  ♭♭  ‡aDLC
100  10  ‡aBryant, Keith L.
245  00  ‡aCathedrals, castles, and Roman baths;‡brailway station
         architecture in the urban south.
300  ♭♭  ‡bill.
500  ♭♭  ‡aGrant St. Station (Aeck Assoc., archts.) and Decatur (Ga.)
         Station (Stevens & Wilkinson, archts.)
651  00  ‡aAtlanta (Ga.)‡xRailroads‡xStations.
610  20  ‡aAeck Associates.
610  20  ‡aStevens & Wilkinson.
773  0♭  ‡tJournal of urban history‡gFebruary 1976, v.2, n.2,
         p.195-230.
```

1. ''p'': Subfield ‡a is a personal name;

2. ''1'': The name has a single surname;

3. ''am'': The host item is language material, printed or microform, monographic (a book). The third and fourth positions of subfield ‡7 contain the significant characters of the legend for the host item.

The Linked-record code is used only in the odd situation where a cataloger does not choose to enter a bibliographic citation to the host item. If field 773 (or any other linking

**Figure 8.12 Analytic Record for a Map in a Book**

Cataloging record for a map in a book:

Palliser, John, 1807-1887.
   A general map of the routes in British North America: explored by
the expedition under Captain Palliser, during the years 1857, 1858,
1859, 1860 / compiled from the observations and reports of Captain
Palliser and his offers, including the map constructed by Dr. Hector,
and other authentic documents. -- Glasgow : Robert MacLehose & Co.,
1968?
   1 map : col. ; 33 x 129 cm.
   Scale ca. 1:2,250,000
   Facsim. of 1865 ed. published by Stanford's Geographical Estabt.,
London.
   Relief shown by hachures.
   In Spry, Irene Mary (Bliss). The papers of the Palliser
expedition, 1857-1860. -- Toronto, Champlain Society, 1968.
   1. Canada--Exploring expeditions--Maps.  I. Hector, James, Sir,
1834-1907.  II. Robert MacLehose & Co. III. Stanford's Geographical
Estabt.
Map 78-690142                                                    MARC

---

Partial MARC record for component part:

Legend: ea
001    map78690142
100 10 ‡aPalliser, John,‡d1807-1887.
245 02 ‡aA general map of the routes in British North America :
       ‡bexplored by the expedition under Captain during the years 1857,
       1858, 1859, 1860 /‡ccompiled from the observations and reports of
       Captain Palliser and his officers, including the map constructed
       by Dr. Hector, and other authentic documents.
260 0ь ‡aGlasgow :‡bRobert MacLehose & Co., ‡c(1968?)
300 ьь ‡a1 map :‡bcol. ;‡c33 x 129 cm.
507 ьь ‡aScale ca. 1:2,250,000
500 ьь ‡aFacsim. of 1865 ed. published by Stanford's Geographical
       Estabt., London.
500 ьь ‡aRelief shown by hachures
651 ь0 ‡aCanada‡xExploring expeditions‡xMaps.
700 11 ‡aHector, James,‡cSir,‡d1834-1907.
710 21 ‡aRobert MacLehose & Co.
710 21 ‡aStanford's Geographical Estabt.
773 0ь ‡7p1am‡aSpray, Irene Mary (Bliss).‡tPapers of the Palliser
       expedition, 1857-1860.‡dToronto, Champlain Society, 1968.‡w(DLC)
       77574016

field) lacks any textual identification of the host item, a system must access the host record in order to prepare a meaningful note. The bibliographic services have implemented field 773 on the assumption that catalogers will choose to enter some textual identification. Some services do not allow Leader/19 to be entered; others allow it but make no effort to provide mechanical support. In practice, field 773 should almost always contain textual identification of the host item.

Textual reference has two limitations. First, it is less precise than a full representation of the host item. Second, it can become obsolete if the description of the host item is modified. When field 773 contains a record number and nothing else, those two limitations are replaced by other problems; full support of record number linkage in a network or distributed environment requires that the host record be communicated each time any analytic referring to it is communicated. Neither of the two largest bibliographic services provides such automatic support, and both urge that record number links not be used. For a processing system, record number linkage involves significant overhead in order to format a small note; a second record must be fetched and processed in the midst of processing the first record.[7]

Field 773 does not allow for multilevel description, the fifth form of analysis. USMARC has no provision for formal multilevel description, and it does not appear likely to add any such provision. Field 773 does not disrupt existing data, and it requires little new training for use; an analytic record is like any other USMARC record, with one new field. The technique is easy to implement without record number links and easy to use.

Only time will tell how heavily field 773 is used. The field appears to handle situations mentioned in other proposals with varying degrees of success. By stipulating that inter-record links are always from the smaller to the larger (whereas added entries can run from the larger to the smaller), field 773 simplifies (and narrows) the choices available for analysis. Field 773 uses a linking technique that has become familiar to serials catalogers. While linking fields have never been elegant or perfect, they have almost always worked in the real world.

## OTHER INTER-RECORD LINKS

USMARC has four other varieties of inter-record link, at varying levels of formality. Figure 8.13 gives examples of linking entries in the 760–788 range, in each case showing the linking field and the note that could be displayed from it. The first example includes subfield ‡7; the second includes an explicit control number link in subfield ‡w, providing precise access to a single linked-to record. The subfield ‡t gives sufficient information on the linked-to record for typical use.

The Holdings format requires explicit links to bibliographic records. Such links can be provided through control numbers or standard numbers. Control numbers normally link to a unique record, where standard numbers link to a unique bibliographic entity which may exist in any number of USMARC records. Control number and standard number links can

**Figure 8.13 Linking Entries: Examples**

```
760 0ḅ ‡7c1as‡aUnited States.   Geological Survey.‡tWater

    Main Series: United States. Geological Survey. Water.
```

```
762 0ḅ ‡tQuality of surface water of the United States
    ‡w(OCoLC)319778

    Has subseries: Quality of surface water of the United States.
```

```
767 0ḅ ‡tCofiec annual report‡x0304-6508

    Translated as: Cofiec annual report. ISSN 0304-6508.
```

```
780 00 ‡tJournal of the South African Logopedic Society‡x0081-2471

    Continues: Journal of the South Afican Logopedic Society. ISSN
0081-2471
```

```
785 02 ‡tJournal of polymer chemistry

    Superseded by: Journal of polymer chemistry.
```

also be used within the USMARC bibliographic formats: field 010 (LCCN) and standard number fields help to pull together different records for the same bibliographic item, and field 035 has some potential for tracing a single bibliographic description through various appearances on different systems.

All heading fields, main and added entries alike, serve to link bibliographic records containing common headings. Such links are directly supported by online indexing and by the filing order within card catalogs, and they represent the primary reason for authority control and establishment of uniform titles and controlled subject headings.

Links between bibliographic records and authority records, and between different authority records, are normally textual links; the USMARC Authority format does not generally provide for direct linkage from an authority record to a bibliographic record.[8] Several authority records may relate to a given bibliographic record, controlling different headings, and a single authority record may relate to tens of thousands of bibliographic records. Linkages from bibliographic headings to authority records are indirect in terms of the USMARC formats, but are direct in some system implementations of the formats. If a bibliographic heading is under authority control, that heading must match an existing established heading within an authority record.

Some systems store the record number of the authority record in place of the heading within the bibliographic record, reconstructing the record when it is displayed. This method of implementation adds to display overhead but makes changes in headings easy to implement; if the authority record changes, all controlled headings are automatically changed, without any system effort.

# NOTES AND REFERENCES

1. While no other 88X fields have been defined, the range of nine fields has been reserved for alternative fields. One potential use for an 88X field is to support "sorting forms," cases where a field cannot be properly sorted based on textual contents.

2. The final portion of subfield ‡6 as it appears in 88X fields (the characters following the slash) is defined based on the 88X field. For field 880, these characters always specify an alternate graphic representation. For another 88X field, the characters could have some other meaning, or might not be needed. In a sense, the completing portion of subfield ‡6 serves the same functions as indicator positions: whatever will help make the field more functional.

3. *Anglo-American Cataloguing Rules.* 2nd ed. Chicago: American Library Association; 1978: 270. 620 p.

4. *Proposal 80-5.1, MARC Subrecord Technique.* (Proposal for consideration by USMARC advisory group.) Washington, DC: Library of Congress; 1980 December 31.

5. McCallum, Sally H. "MARC Record-Linking Technique." *Information Technology and Libraries.* 1(3): 281-291; 1982 September.

6. "Monograph" tends to be interpreted as "book," but really means "nonserial" in USMARC usage. Most sound recordings are monographs, as are most films. Most articles in journals are monographic; continuing columns (for instance, Jaye Bausser's "Online Catalogs" in the *RTSD Newsletter*) are serial component parts.

7. An online system can function well using control number linkages. Bibliographic records in the Washington Library Network (WLN) are partially composed of links to authority records, which actually contain headings; the links are used to compose bibliographic displays as needed. In this case, the system was designed around such links, trading increased file accesses (to pull together records) for decreased storage and improved authority control. Independent-record and fully linked systems both have advantages; the point here is that an independent-record system may require some additional overhead to institute controlled links.

8. Field 014 in the Authorities format is an exception; this field links a series authority to the bibliographic record for the serial or multipart item.

# 9

# USMARC: Past, Present and Future

USMARC evolved from MARC II or LC MARC. MARC II emerged from years of effort and study, led by Henriette Avram of the Library of Congress and others. The Council on Library Resources provided early and continuing funding to encourage the development and spread of the formats. Courageous and innovative library leaders such as Frederick Kilgour of OCLC acted to build a massive and successful structure of shared bibliographic data on the solid foundation of the MARC formats. Innovators continue to expand uses of the format, while dedicated workers strive to make the formats more consistent and more useful.[1]

## THE BEGINNINGS: 1961-1965

The Library of Congress began to consider automation in the late 1950s.[2] The Council on Library Resources (CLR) paid for a study, published in 1963, which recommended a group within LC to design and implement automated procedures for cataloging, searching, indexing and document retrieval;[3] another CLR project considered methods for converting LC catalog card data to machine-readable form.[4] LC, CLR and the Committee on Automation of the Association of Research Libraries (ARL) cosponsored a conference in January 1965 to consider the two studies and their significance. The conclusions were as follows:

1. Availability of machine-readable catalog records produced and distributed by LC would help those libraries that have automated systems.

2. The machine-readable record should include all the data presently available on LC's printed card, plus additional information to produce a multipurpose record.

3. Agreement by a broad segment of the library community on the elements to be in-

cluded in the record was most desirable, and the design of the record at LC was probably the best means of achieving standardization.[5]

Henriette Avram, Ruth Freitag and Kay Guiles analyzed LC cataloging data and, in June 1965, prepared a proposed record format.[6] Many LC staff members and others in the library field commented on the proposal, which was followed by another CLR-sponsored conference in November 1965. Given the warm reception of the library community, LC sought and CLR provided funds for a pilot project. The pilot project needed a name, which was derived from *ma*chine-*r*eadable *c*ataloging: MARC was born.

## MARC PILOT PROJECT: 1966–1968

LC's pilot plan[7] was ambitious: the CLR grant of $130,000 was received in December 1965; by February 1966, contractors were chosen to write software and evaluate the project, and 16 libraries were selected as project participants from 40 who had expressed willingness.[8] Those contractors and participants met with LC staff on February 25, 1966: "the official opening of the MARC Pilot Project."[9] Expectations were that MARC I would be completed in April, with weekly tape distribution beginning in September 1966.

The project ran late, but only by two months. A test tape was distributed in October, and weekly distribution began in November 1966. The original plan called for eight months of distribution; interest and enthusiasm were high enough to extend it through to June 1968. LC was ready to extend the project almost from its inception: the extension announcement was made at the ALA Midwinter Meeting in January 1967, only two months after initial tape distribution. LC MARC staff began to evaluate the MARC I format in March 1967; a preliminary MARC II format was presented at ALA in June 1967. Another CLR-sponsored conference on December 4, 1967 considered the MARC II format and proposed bibliographic character set. At that time, four more libraries[10] were added to the pilot project, expanding the group of agencies cooperatively involved in evaluating and testing MARC.

The pilot project ended in June 1968; some 50,000 MARC I records were distributed in all. Twenty agencies evaluated the format and programs distributed with it, reporting back to LC.[11] Some of those agencies actually used the tapes for processing; others did not.

MARC I was intended as an experiment. The timing and scope were ambitious; the actual speed of implementation was little short of remarkable. In 1966, few libraries had significant automation, and computers available were barely capable of handling the most rudimentary library needs. Henriette Avram states in the MARC final report that "there is no doubt that eventually standards would have been designed for machine-readable bibliographic records, character sets, and codes for place and language."[12] Mrs. Avram's energy, enthusiasm and tenacity made such standards possible before most libraries saw any need or use for them.

The pilot program included distribution of computer programs to handle MARC I records. Given the severe limitations of the machines used, the programs had to be coded in language which was difficult to read and maintain; the programs were coded rapidly and with little overall success. Programs implemented at LC after the pilot project formed the basis for much of the batch processing software of the early and middle 1970s; "SKED" and "BIBLIST," two major programs, are familiar names to many involved in library automation at the time.[13]

The original format was different from MARC II, which was heavily influenced by the results of the experiment. The MARC Pilot Project established a common ground for machine-readable bibliographic data, and provided the basis for the success of MARC II. Reports from the participants show wide-ranging degrees of success or failure, but almost unanimous enthusiasm for the fundamental ideas behind MARC. MARC I established the feasibility; MARC II began the actual work of building a national system of shared cataloging.

## MARC II: 1968–1974

MARC I, an innovative format, is described in detail in the final report on the MARC Pilot Project. That report also outlines the original MARC II format for monographs, and compares the two formats.[14] Both formats are designed to carry information on monographs in a consistent form, but the two have little else in common. The separate directory, subfield codes and structured tags of MARC II are all innovations of the newer format. The structure of MARC II has remained essentially fixed since the original draft was issued in January 1968,[15] and has proven flexible and valuable, handling a range and volume of materials far greater than that of any similar development. The structure has survived for 16 years with no substantial change, while content designators and content continue to evolve.

The Library of Congress did not set out to provide software for MARC II. Instead, LC released detailed specifications for the new format as early as August 1968, in a publication originally titled *Subscriber's Guide to the MARC Distribution Service* (later *Books: A MARC Format*[16]). LC and ALA's Information Science and Automation Division (ISAD) launched a series of workshops to introduce MARC II. The MARC Institutes began in Seattle in July 1968 and continued for several years, introducing more than 2000 people to MARC II. MARC II became operational in March 1969, when the first MARC Distribution Service got underway. In 1969, and for many years thereafter, the primary role of MARC II was to distribute Library of Congress cataloging data in machine-readable form to other institutions. The Library of Congress and the American Library Association used a number of methods to publicize the formats and inform current and potential users. The MARC Institutes were one method; the MARC Users' Discussion Group within ISAD was another.

Weekly distribution of MARC records for English-language monographs began in March 1969. At first, the tapes only included U.S. imprints, about 1000 records per week. Coverage expanded rapidly to include other English-language monographs. Since then, other languages have been added; by the late 1970s, nearly all languages using the Roman alphabet were included in LC MARC tapes. With the Books format well on its way, the Library of Congress began work on other formats. Formats for serials[17] and maps[18] were published in 1970; a format for films[19] was published in 1971, and the original manuscripts format[20] was published in 1973. The last material format of the 1970s, and the final bibliographic format to be published as a separate production format, was for music:[21] the draft version of this format was published in 1973.

After MARC formats appeared, LC MARC distribution generally followed. Distribution of films cataloging began in 1972; distribution of serials and maps began in 1973. Since 1973, the Library of Congress has concentrated on a broader coverage of current formats, adding languages as funding permits. The Library of Congress never distributed manuscripts cataloging in MARC form; distribution of MARC records for scores and sound recordings began in 1984.

"The impetus given to standardization by LC/MARC is doubtless one of its most important results."[22] MARC has focused standardization efforts, while providing the means to allow diversity within standards. The early development of MARC II or LC/MARC contributed to standardization efforts and to the development of MARC formats in other countries. The structure of MARC was proposed as a national and international standard. ANSI standard Z39.2 was adopted in 1971;[23] the international equivalent, ISO 2709, was adopted in 1973.[24]

## Local Uses and Developments

Quite a few library automation projects began in the late 1960s and early 1970s. Many of these succeeded, and some are still in operation. Dozens of universities and other institutions began working with MARC during this period. The period from 1969 to 1974 was one of enormous growth in library automation.

Four projects which began in the late 1960s resulted in the four major bibliographic services of today. The Ohio College Library Center, now the Online Computer Library Center (OCLC), was founded in 1967, though provision of online services did not begin until 1971. At Stanford, Project BALLOTS (Bibliographic Automation of Large Library Operations Using a Time-Sharing System) also began in 1967; the project eventually resulted in an online multilibrary network in the 1970s, and was transformed into the Research Libraries Information Network (RLIN) at the end of that decade. Developments at the Washington State Library and the University of Toronto, both participants in the MARC Pilot Project, eventually led to the Washington Library Network (WLN) and University of Toronto Library Automation Systems (UTLAS).

## Use of MARC in 1972

In 1972, the Library of Congress contracted for a survey of MARC users, carried out by the firm of Becker & Hayes, Inc. and conducted and reported by Josephine S. Pulsifer.[25] There were 54 MARC subscribers as of August 8, 1972; 52 of these were doing or planning work with MARC. Those 52 included 12 research libraries, 15 other university libraries, 11 commercial firms, 4 special libraries, 6 national libraries, 2 state libraries, and

2 "library centers," namely, OCLC and the College Bibliocentre in Don Mills, Ontario. Most users had small development staffs; the largest group of librarians was six, the largest group of "computer people" seven. Nine subscribers had operational online systems, and 32 had operational offline (batch) systems; at least 11 had no operational systems at the time of the survey.

Figure 9.1 gives the number using each category of service set forth in the 1972 survey. One particularly significant use: the 52 subscribers provided LC MARC records in machine-readable form to at least 178 other agencies in 1972. In 1972, OCLC was serving 55 agencies. The largest single constituency appeared to be Richard Abel & Company, producing catalog products for 375 customers. Even in 1972, over 1000 agencies were using LC MARC data, directly or indirectly.

**Figure 9.1 MARC Users in 1972**

| Users | Service |
|---|---|
| 97 | Selection (lists for selection purposes) |
| 36 | Ordering |
| 514* | Catalog cards |
| 10 | Book catalogs |
| 63 | Union catalogs |
| 118* | Catalog products (spine labels, pockets, bookcards) |
| 10 | Machine-readable charge cards |
| 120 | New book lists |
| 159* | Bibliographies |
| 107* | On-demand searches |
| 134 | Selective dissemination of information (SDI) |
| 178* | Secondary distribution (tape, lists, online) |
| 265 | Microform distribution |
| 1148 | Apparent number of distinct users for all services |
| * | One commercial vendor did not release numbers of customers for these five services. Thus, each number is too low by some unknown factor. |

## FROM MARBI TO USMARC: 1974–1983

The American Library Association has several committees comprised of representatives from more than one ALA division; one of these, established prior to 1974 and noted in Chapter 1, is the Committee on Representation in Machine-Readable Form of Bibliographic Information, known as MARBI. This committee includes representatives from RTSD (Resources and Technical Services Division), RASD (Reference and Adult Services Division), and LITA (Library and Information Technology Association), formerly known as ISAD (Information Science and Automation Division).

The Library of Congress approached MARBI in 1973, suggesting that a MARC advisory committee be formed to work with LC on changes to the MARC formats; MARBI decided to make itself that advisory committee. At MARBI's request, LC drew up proposals and recommendations[26] which were adopted by MARBI at the ALA 1974 Midwinter Meeting. Later in the 1970s, LC began a series of quarterly meetings at which liaisons from the bibliographic services and national libraries considered MARC changes. The network group and MARBI were brought together in the late 1970s.

Henriette Avram served as the Library of Congress liaison to MARBI from 1974 until April 1976; during this time, she was assisted by Kay Guiles, Lenore Maruyama and Josephine Pulsifer. Various LC staff members (Kay Guiles, Josephine Pulsifer and Pamela Andre) worked with MARBI between April 1976 and 1978, reflecting organizational changes within LC during this period. Mary Kay Daniels Ganning was the LC liaison to MARBI from 1978 to May 1980, with Lenore Maruyama serving from June to December 1980. Margaret Patterson was appointed MARC Communications Format Specialist in 1981 and, in that capacity, became the MARBI liaison; she has been assisted by Phyllis Bruns and Gary McCone in working with MARBI and the USMARC advisory group.

If the early 1970s were years of major new undertakings, the late 1970s were years of consolidation, cooperation and growth. No new material formats were developed, but the old ones were refined, with better explanations and more explicit detail. Use of the formats grew rapidly during the 1970s, and continues to grow as systems become more available and more sophisticated. The middle 1970s were the start of explosive growth for the bibliographic services. The smallest of the four major bibliographic services in 1983 has some four times the users that OCLC had in 1972; OCLC itself has at least 30 times as many.

The middle 1970s saw the development of the preliminary Authorities format, discussed in Chapter 7. This format was initially designed so that LC could share its authority control information with the library world; as with other MARC formats, the Authorities Format quickly took on significance beyond its original purpose.

Specifications for shared records were established during the decade with the publication of the National Level Bibliographic Record (NLBR) documents for various materials. NLBR uses MARC as a base and common vocabulary, specifying essential and recommended data elements for various levels of completeness.

CONSER, a project for CONversion of SERials, began in 1974 with CLR funding.[27] A cooperative project based at OCLC, CONSER has built a database of hundreds of thousands of serials records.

The Linked Systems Project (LSP) began in 1980. Funded by the Council on Library Resources, with the Library of Congress, Washington Library Network and Research Libraries Group as initial participants, the project involves an online communications link and intersystem data retrieval and maintenance facility to support a shared authority file (and, later, bibliographic interchange).[28] LSP is establishing standards for telecommunications protocols, and is firmly based on use of MARC, which is the principal format for transmission of records. This three-way project, which has recently included OCLC as an observer, uses MARC as a telecommunications format to permit same-day coordination of databases.

## The MARC Formats for Bibliographic Data

A cooperative project involving the Library of Congress and the Research Libraries Group yielded a major new publication in 1980, the *MARC Formats for Bibliographic Data (MFBD)*. LC combined and edited the individual MARC formats and entered them into a special database designed and implemented at RLG. The product of this database, *MFBD*, turned six format documents into one massive looseleaf publication. *MFBD* has columns for the formats, identifying validity of fields and subfields and applicability of descriptions and examples. Placing all six formats side-by-side clarified the inconsistencies and the common core of the formats. LC and MARBI were now confronted with the set of formats whenever change arose. Many more in the library community began to think of MARC as a single format with variations, and wondered why the variations were as extensive as they were.

*MFBD* also accelerated a tendency that had already begun. Users of one MARC format would begin exploring the other formats, and see fields for which they had applications. New fields would be proposed by one special interest group, and adopted in a single format. After that adoption, other groups would come to LC and MARBI and suggest that the same field be added to other formats, often with minor changes in details of content designation, terminology or application. Since 1980, MARBI and LC have worked steadily to bring the formats closer together. Approval of an existing field for a new format has become almost automatic; in some cases, MARBI or LC simply recommends that a new field be adopted "across formats" when it is first proposed.

## The Weisbrod Study

At LC's request, David Weisbrod of Yale University studied the MARC formats and, as a result, wrote *Principles of MARC Format Content Designation*[29] in early 1981. That document raised a large number of questions about the formats and suggested some answers, projecting some proposed principles for the future. As a result of Weisbrod's study, two MARBI projects began in 1981 and continued through 1982.

The first was a long list of potential areas for future consideration, including those raised by Weisbrod's report and others raised during discussion. Over the course of a year's analysis, the bulk of the list was eliminated (either because the problems had been solved or were being worked on, or because the issues were determined to be insignificant or outside the scope of MARBI). A final short list of a dozen or so topics included "Format Integration" as one of the highest priorities, noting that "several encoding problems would be solved if the *MFBD* were integrated across formats and codes/subfields/fields could be assigned as appropriate without concern for their validity within a particular format."[30]

The second project, which also began as a result of Weisbrod's report, resulted in a written set of underlying principles for content designation. Those who founded and developed LC MARC worked from a largely implicit set of principles. However, while there were articles on the design principles of MARC, no codified set of principles was available for use by the USMARC advisory group or those advocating changes in MARC.

John Attig of Pennsylvania State University prepared a discussion paper, based partly on Weisbrod's study, setting forth the principles of LC MARC as determined from the actual formats. During 1981 and 1982, this draft was thoroughly examined by the USMARC advisory group and other interested parties. A preliminary version was published[31] and an open hearing was held at the 1982 ALA Annual Conference in Philadelphia.

After further changes and review, the document was approved on October 29, 1982, in a meeting of the USMARC advisory group at the Library of Congress. The resulting document, *The USMARC Formats: Underlying Principles,*[32] appears with annotations as Appendix A.

## MARC Standards Office

During this transitional decade, the Library of Congress established a MARC Standards Office. This office provided a crucial focus for developments in the MARC formats. Relations between LC, MARBI, the bibliographic services and other interested parties were in flux during these years; in addition to the work required to organize agendas, prepare proposals and keep communications flowing, the LC liaisons also spent much of their energy encouraging agencies to work with, rather than against, one another. The early 1980s involved enormous growth and change in USMARC, much of it related elsewhere in this book. Some of the major changes are the revised Authorities format, a format for Machine-Readable Data Files, the new Archival and Manuscripts Control format, the Visual Materials format, and support for analytics and vernacular data.

## USMARC TODAY

USMARC is certainly not perfect, and probably not ideal. It is, however, a success— of a magnitude which must surprise even the foresighted group that designed MARC in the late 1960s. Started for a single major purpose, USMARC has become the common language of library automation and serves thousands of libraries for a multitude of purposes. USMARC is the vehicle for distribution of Library of Congress cataloging in machine-readable form. USMARC is the basis for the major bibliographic services in the United States, and for processing done by networks within the framework of OCLC. Book jobbers and specialized vendors rely on the consistency of USMARC for transmitting, receiving and transforming bibliographic records. USMARC is the basis for massive retrospective conversion, a key step in making online catalogs work as replacements for card catalogs. By providing a flexible, consistent, efficient communications (and processing) format, USMARC has encouraged rational growth and extension of library automation.

The following notes on current use of USMARC are necessarily incomplete. For example, for-profit vendors are not included. We will look at the Library of Congress and the four main bibliographic services as major providers of USMARC services. Statistics given are the latest available—generally, the end of 1983.

## THE LIBRARY OF CONGRESS

Library of Congress cataloging has always had a special place in the American library community; it represents a large body of consistent application of cataloging rules. Many other agencies conform to Library of Congress practice. While distribution of LC cataloging is no longer the only major role of USMARC, it is still a vital factor in the health of shared cataloging in the United States. Most library use of LC MARC records is indirect, through bibliographic services or other agencies. As of March 1984, the Library of Congress maintained the USMARC distribution services shown in Figure 9.2.

### Figure 9.2 LC USMARC Distribution Services

| Service | Subscribers as of 12/83 | Transactions 4/83 - 3/84 | File Size 3/84 |
|---|---|---|---|
| Books (all) | 40 | 301,692 | 1,801,109 |
| Films | 22 | 3,512 | 67,710 |
| Maps | 21 | 9,773 | 83,021 |
| Serials | 26 | 124,125 | 214,448 |
| Name Authorities | 10 | 255,143 | Note 1 |
| Books-Canada | 5 | 30,600 | 181,493 |
| Books-English Language | 13 | 199,647 | 1,218,932 |
| Books-U.S. | 5 | 140,236 | 803,191 |
| Minimal-Level Cat. | 1 | Note 2 | 86,208 |
| CONSER | 2 | 45,373 (Note 3) | 216,375 |
| GPO | 16 | 21,932 | 173,824 |

NOTES: Transactions include new records, changes, and deletions.
1. The Name Authority Master File had 532,209 records as of 3/81.
2. File size: backfile. Distribution had not begun as of 3/84.
3. Distributed 4/83-3/84; file size is total for 8/81-3/83.
   The CONSER snapshot file to 7/81 included 339,327 records.

## OCLC

The Online Computer Library Center (OCLC) is the largest online bibliographic service in the world, and it maintains one of the largest terminal networks in the world. OCLC provides well over 3000 libraries with USMARC records on archive tapes, either directly or through cooperative agencies. Online cataloging in OCLC is based firmly on USMARC, with some extensions to accommodate limited holdings and card-related information. OCLC provides a number of USMARC-based services in addition to cards and tapes. Among these services are an interlibrary loan network, retrospective conversion services for libraries, union listing services for groups of libraries, and acquisitions and serials check-in services. OCLC also produces a local library system based on the National

Library of Medicine's Integrated Library System. This MARC-based system is intended to be a total library system supporting all library functions including circulation, online public access catalog, and cataloging maintenance including authority control.

OCLC provides services through networks, which are separate agencies. Several of these networks, such as AMIGOS in the Southwest and SOLINET in the Southeast, provide their own USMARC processing services of various sorts. At the end of 1983, OCLC was serving 3784 libraries and processing agencies. Many of these libraries were receiving OCLC archive tapes, either directly or through networks and consortia. As of December 1983, OCLC had 753 tape subscriptions in all. In 1983, OCLC produced 8762 OCLC MARC tapes, containing a total of 44,376,051 records.

Figure 9.3 shows the activity and total sizes for the OCLC files. OCLC is a "master record" system; there is theoretically only one record per bibliographic entity, with multiple holdings symbols for various libraries holding the item. As a result, OCLC file sizes are not directly comparable to file sizes of UTLAS and RLIN, which are not master record systems, though they are directly comparable to file sizes at WLN.

**Figure 9.3 OCLC: Size and Activity, Calendar 1983**

| OCLC | End of Calendar 1983 | | | |
|---|---|---|---|---|
| Format Designation | Records 1983* | Total | Holdings Symbols 1983* | Total |
| Books | 886,739 | 8,589,345 | 22,383,778 | 146,291,030 |
| Films(AV) | 31,207 | 248,057 | 154,163 | 677,477 |
| Maps | 13,467 | 121,433 | 31,926 | 176,192 |
| Manuscripts | 6,693 | 40,667 | 7,162 | 43,935 |
| Scores | 15,230 | 208,045 | 233,272 | 1,305,901 |
| Recordings | 39,873 | 276,346 | 433,537 | 1,816,819 |
| Serials | 77,827 | 656,045 | 1,010,142 | 5,235,910 |
| Authorities | 203,595 | 1,016,123 | ------ | -------- |
| All Formats | 1,284,631 | 11,156,061 | 24,243,980 | 155,547,264 |

*January 22-December 30 1983 only, except for Authorities, which include the entire calendar year 1983.

## THE RESEARCH LIBRARIES GROUP, INC. (RLG/RLIN)

The Research Libraries Group (RLG) is a consortium of universities and independent research libraries, involved in a number of cooperative ventures. Not all of these ventures are based on USMARC. The programmatic ventures of RLG include preservation, collection development, a number of specialized databases, and other areas outside the normal role of a "bibliographic utility." RLG maintains a large computer system and online network to support its goals. That network, the Research Libraries Information Network (RLIN), includes major USMARC-based files and provides cataloging, acquisitions and interlibrary loan services to its members and to other users of RLIN. Tapes produced as a result of RLIN processing are called "transaction tapes."

RLG had 46 members as of the end of 1983, but RLIN served more than 545 libraries at that point. Many libraries receive RLIN transaction tapes; in 1983, over 2300 tapes were produced, containing a total of 2,262,351 records. As with some other services, RLIN uses USMARC for cataloging and acquisitions, adding a substantial number of local extensions to store processing and control information. Batch services within RLG are all based on USMARC, though the online database is not USMARC in any structural sense.

The RLIN database grew phenomenally during 1983, partly as a result of the batch "Archive load," in which records of RLG members cataloged elsewhere were added to the database. This process alone added more than 4 million records to the RLIN database. The RLIN database is not a master record database: each institution has a separate record for each bibliographic item. Figure 9.4 shows records added during 1983, separating batch loads (Archive loads and records distributed by LC) from online activity. The numbers for "batch loads" also include some portion of the 597,253 Acquisitions records added during calendar 1983, specifically those records that were not also cataloged during the year. "Holdings symbols" are not relevant within RLIN, given the structure of the data. The numbers are not directly comparable to OCLC, since the databases differ in structure. RLIN includes between 4.5 and 5 million different bibliographic editions in its Books file.

**Figure 9.4 RLIN II: Size and Activity, Calendar 1983**

| RLIN II | Calendar 1983 | | |
|---|---|---|---|
| Format Designation | Records Added in 1983 Batch | Online | Total File Size |
| Books | 3,698,475 | 1,299,487 | 11,226,126 |
| Films | 3,346 | 2,521 | 71,993 |
| Maps | 5,440 | 2,926 | 89,132 |
| Scores | 31,095 | 19,641 | 112,547 |
| Sound Recordings | 15,455 | 10,504 | 51,223 |
| Serials | 223,296 | 95,706 | 1,316,744 |
| Authorities | 103,201 | ------- | 2,345,055 |
| Total | 4,080,308 | 1,430,785 | 15,212,760 |

## UNIVERSITY OF TORONTO LIBRARY AUTOMATION SYSTEMS (UTLAS)

UTLAS is the only major Canadian bibliographic service, but does have some library customers within the United States. UTLAS maintains a large online network, but does much of its work by batch processing. While OCLC and WLN maintain master record files, and RLG maintains a file in which all records are available as copy, UTLAS maintains a series of private files. UTLAS users may allow others to use their records as source records, but are not required to do so. UTLAS maintains full authority control as an option, and provides a full range of services to its customers. These include acquisitions, cataloging, tapes, cards and book or microform catalog production.

As of the end of 1983, UTLAS had over 250 customers in Canada, the United States and Japan who were directly linked to its facilities; the total end-user population (customers and libraries served by them) was over 2000. Forty users were receiving MARC tapes, with a total of 2,505,930 transactions distributed during 1983. Figure 9.5 shows total file sizes for UTLAS at the end of 1983; because of the nature of the system, reliable counts of records added or of records by format are not available.

**Figure 9.5 UTLAS: File Sizes, End of 1983**

| UTLAS | End of Calendar 1983 | |
|---|---|---|
| Source bibliographic records (LC, NLC, UK, etc.) | | 5,268,200 |
| User bibliographic records | | 14,161,598 |
| Source authority records | | 1,813,524 |
| User authority records | | 684,354 |

## WASHINGTON LIBRARY NETWORK (WLN)

The Washington Library Network (WLN) is a regional bibliographic service that has developed a sophisticated set of software, including full authority control. WLN provides services to libraries in the Pacific Northwest; WLN software has been licensed to a number of other libraries in various parts of the United States and the world (WLN software is the basis for the Australian national bibliographic network, for instance). A private vendor also licenses the software and, in turn, sublicenses it to groups of libraries or individual libraries as a local library system.

WLN provides acquisitions, cataloging and the other usual services, and produces microfiche and microfilm catalogs. WLN provides a MARC tape subscription service to its participants. The tapes are not archive or transaction tapes. Rather, they are snapshot tapes of the current version of (1) database records to which a library has added holdings during a specified period of time, and/or (2) database records that include holdings for that library and that have been updated during the specified time period. WLN tape subscribers receive updates to apply to their local files, allowing them to take full advantage of maintenance work done to the WLN Authority and Bibliographic files. Most subscribers receive biweekly tapes with new holdings and update records.

WLN, like OCLC, is a master record database; the holdings of many libraries are added to one record, rather than maintaining multiple records for different libraries. WLN participants play an active role in cooperative maintenance of the database: any participant may initiate changes to upgrade existing records. All changes and new records are reviewed by WLN staff before master records are added or modified. All participants benefit from cooperative maintenance in the online catalog, COM catalogs,[33] and WLN MARC tapes.

As of the end of 1983, 120 WLN libraries were using the Washington Library Network, not including users of other WLN-software installations. Seven of these libraries received WLN MARC tapes, accounting for a total of over 220,000 records during 1983. Figure 9.6 shows records added to each format in WLN during 1983, LC MARC records loaded, and the total size of the files; total file size by bibliographic format was not available.

**Figure 9.6 WLN: Size and Activity, Calendar 1983**

| WLN | End of Calendar 1983 | |
|---|---|---|
| Format | Records Added in 1983 | Total |
| Books - WLN Input | 88,375 | ---- |
| Serials - WLN Input | 6,281 | ---- |
| Films - WLN Input | 3,627 | ---- |
| Books, serials, films - LC | 179,847 | ---- |
| Total bibliographic records | 278,530 | 2,846,542 |
| Holdings | 172,562 | 1,356,190 |
| WLN Authorities | 341,893 | 3,256,478 |

## THE FUTURE: LIBRARY USE OF USMARC

Most libraries involved in automation today use USMARC indirectly, through a bibliographic service. Most libraries with local systems use USMARC as a communications format. An online system that cannot use USMARC tapes as input data is at a severe competitive disadvantage, and most other local systems of any size are designed to accept USMARC as input. At least one commercial system allows libraries to do in-house cataloging in USMARC format, with the LC MARC database on hundreds of floppy disks as a resource file; this system, and some other local systems, are designed to generate USMARC as well as accept USMARC.

Use of USMARC for local processing is so widespread and so diverse that it would be impossible to give a fair summary. Back files of the *Journal of Library Automation* and its successor, *Information Technology and Libraries,* show frequent mentions of new systems based on USMARC. In the last few years, USMARC has become the assumed basis for such systems; those that are not based on the national format are exceptional and usually small or designed to serve special needs. RLG uses its heavily extended RLIN MARC for all batch processing, finding it to be an efficient and flexible processing format. North-western University's NOTIS system uses a version of USMARC as a structural format for batch processing, as does the University of California, Berkeley. A number of other local systems do the same. Maintenance of an online file in the MARC structural format is much less frequent; normally, a structural transformation takes place into the structure of the database management system being used.

As card catalogs decline and online catalogs grow, and as economics encourage further cooperation, use of USMARC is sure to increase both as a communications and as a processing format. Libraries and other agencies recognize the resilience of the format for changing library needs, and also recognize the virtue of maintaining that resilience in processing.

Through its history, USMARC has served as a format for communication from one to many, and as a format for local use. USMARC is unusual among standards; by establishing a common basis, it allows and even encourages diversity to meet local needs. When a public library can derive 96% of its cataloging and can manipulate those records, cataloging time and talent is freed to add entry points that meet the needs of the community.

It seems fitting to close this brief historical discussion, largely based on Henriette Avram's work, with the final paragraphs from *MARC, Its History and Implications*. Mrs. Avram speaks specifically of standards; her hopes for the future are being realized largely because of the success of LC MARC and USMARC.

The benefits that accrue to a library and its clients from the establishment of and the conformity to standards are many. Products from different sources will mesh. Records from different libraries will be interchanged. Machine systems will be more easily developed and shared. Union catalogs will be possible without costly editing for consistency, thus facilitating interlibrary loan. Cost of local changes to catalog records will be minimized. It will be advantageous for vendors to manufacture hardware to handle the requirements of libraries. The process of ordering, cataloging, etc., will be more uniform. Therefore, less searching and bibliographic verification will be necessary and duplication of effort will be avoided. Networking will be facilitated. Various data bases will be accessible through the use of standard protocol. Service to the user will be improved and that is really what MARC is all about.[33]

## MAINTAINING AND REVISING USMARC

The USMARC formats are published by the Library of Congress. LC is responsible for the maintenance of the formats and has final authority over the contents of the formats. The Library of Congress does not act unilaterally; changes in USMARC are discussed thoroughly in open sessions involving the Library of Congress; the MARBI committee; and liaisons from the bibliographic services, other national libraries, and other interested parties.

Many proposals for USMARC revisions originate in the Library of Congress; most originate in other agencies and associations, or are submitted by interested librarians. The bibliographic services take an active role in proposing USMARC revisions and in discussing such proposals. Some proposals arise directly out of discussion at MARC review sessions, and some proposals result from special projects. Proposals are channeled through the Library of Congress. A full-time MARC Format Specialist gathers and coordinates proposals, ensures that proposals reach the appropriate parties within LC, and sees that proposals ready for open discussion are copied and sent to interested parties.

**Role of the Library of Congress**

The Library of Congress initiates some proposals and reviews others prior to open discussion. Internal review at LC can help to assure that proposals are consistent with USMARC, can coordinate multiple proposals, and can raise issues that need to be resolved. LC internal review can also eliminate proposals that have already been dealt with, proposals clearly outside the scope of USMARC, and proposals that are not ready for open discussion. The Library of Congress puts proposals into a standard format, assigns proposal numbers, and copies and distributes the proposals to a wide mailing list. LC also prepares agendas for the quarterly review sessions, and establishes the dates for the spring and fall sessions. Following revision and approval of changes, LC acts on the changes as the publisher of the MARC formats. Editorial changes are made online to the MARC fields database on the RLG computer; once each quarter, RLG generates sets of revised format pages and sends them to LC. The revised pages are printed by the Government Printing Office (GPO) and distributed by LC's Catalog Distribution Service (CDS) to those who subscribe to the *MFBD* quarterly update service.

The Library of Congress does not make most changes to USMARC immediately after approval. Some changes require more editorial effort than others, and post-approval review sometimes turns up problems with approved revisions. On occasion, the Library of Congress has returned to the review sessions with proposed changes in approved USMARC revisions.

**The Quarterly Review Sessions**

A review session is held at the American Library Association Midwinter Meeting and the Annual Conference each year. These two sessions are actually MARBI committee meetings, and are open to all ALA members. Two other MARC review sessions take place in spring and in fall. These spring and fall review sessions are held at the Library of Congress, are two or three days long, and involve some MARBI members and other active participants. Major changes in USMARC are always discussed at least once during Midwinter Meeting or Annual Conference MARBI meetings, and final review of major changes usually takes place at those meetings.

Divisions differ in the amount of publicity provided for MARBI work. Recently, summary reports on MARBI activity have been appearing in the three divisional newsletters with good regularity. MARBI members represent themselves, their institutions and their divisions. They are appointed for two-year terms and can be reappointed once, as with other ALA committee appointments.

Each of the four major bibliographic services sends one or two liaisons to the four review sessions. These liaisons are expected to gather the views of staff and to represent the needs of their services. Liaisons are also invited from the National Agricultural Library, the National Library of Medicine, and the National Library of Canada. Liaisons do not have votes but do have voices. The importance of the bibliographic services and national libraries is well known, and objections raised by the bibliographic service liaisons are rarely ignored.

Each bibliographic service has an ongoing program to maintain MARC within the system. The liaisons work to assure that MARC is workable and meets their needs, which are generally the needs of the library community. Because the services are involved in review, they usually have some advance knowledge of upcoming changes in the formats, though the gap from approval to publication can be anywhere from three months to three years or more. Once changes are published, teams of analysts, programmers, testers, trainers and writers must work to make the changes part of the bibliographic service's operation, and to reflect the changes in documentation.

USMARC review group meetings air the difficulties with USMARC, generate useful changes in the formats, and generally work to keep the formats contemporary and useful. In some ways, the machinery of USMARC may seem cumbersome; however, compared to typical standards organizations, USMARC maintenance is streamlined and effective. MARBI members and liaisons give up nearly half of ALA conference time to meetings, and those who continue with MARBI do so because they believe in the benefits of USMARC and wish to improve the formats. The combination of LC's editorial work and leadership and the careful analysis and discussion typical of the quarterly review sessions makes USMARC a living, vital standard for recording and manipulating bibliographic data.

**Format Integration: An Ongoing Project**

Publication of *The USMARC Formats: Underlying Principles* did not change USMARC but did articulate the conceptual bases for the formats. One obvious deduction from the statement of principles is that all bibliographic formats are based on common assumptions and work in a similar manner; the Principles make no distinctions among bibliographic formats and apply equally to all. The Principles identify a group of individual formats within the "bibliographic family." The family was continuing to grow, and more people involved with MARC were thinking of the family as a single organism.

Several members of the USMARC advisory group took action to increase discussion of format integration during 1983. John Attig published an article in March 1983[35] which proposed merging USMARC bibliographic formats into a single format and considering revision of the legend. Attig later prepared a discussion paper for MARBI[36] suggesting a strategy for format integration, beginning with a statement of intention and objectives and ending with re-evaluation of the legend.

Attig's discussion paper reached the USMARC advisory group agenda in September

1983; in one form or another, format integration will probably stay on the agenda until the issues are resolved. The first stage in Attig's strategy was reached when the following statement was approved by MARBI at January 1984 meetings in Washington, DC:

*Statement of Intention and Objectives:*
In its discussions of format integration, MARBI has agreed on the following definition of an integrated format. The USMARC bibliographic formats are considered a single integrated format. Content designation defined therein is valid in any record in which it is appropriate.

In order to begin the process of format integration, MARBI has agreed to identify inconsistencies among the various existing formats and to evaluate the advantages and disadvantages of eliminating these inconsistencies (including the impact of such changes on existing systems). Where the advantages predominate, the inconsistencies will be removed. Any inconsistencies that remain will be clearly labeled in the format documentation.

Work toward these objectives accelerated during 1984. The Research Libraries Group liaisons to the USMARC advisory group (Kathleen Bales and Walt Crawford) prepared two omnibus proposals, contributed to the Library of Congress for its own internal work on format integration. The first proposal, 84-1, identified a number of specific inconsistencies among existing formats and suggested possible ways of eliminating the inconsistencies. The second proposal, 84-3, proposed a method of carrying information on seriality in other material formats and recommended extending a large number of fields from the Serials format to other formats. Those concerned with USMARC at the Library of Congress are studying these proposals and others that have been prepared over the past few years. At LC and elsewhere, people are considering the problems of change and the problems of retaining the existing set of formats.

There are definite costs associated with maintenance of multiple formats; these costs are most noticeable when a new format is proposed. On the other hand, any change in the formats has associated costs; a major shift in the appearance or substance of the USMARC formats could be disruptive. For these and other reasons, the process of format integration and the addition of seriality elements to other formats will be time consuming. Those involved are attempting to maximize the potential benefit while minimizing the present cost.

Potential benefits include a more compact *MFBD*; more straightforward addition of fields to formats; the ability to enter full information on serially issued maps, films, sound recordings and other materials; less maintenance and validation overhead for computer systems handling USMARC; and, generally, greater consistency of practice within USMARC bibliographic formats. Potential costs, which must be avoided or minimized, include the extensive changes in the files of LC, the bibliographic services and others; need for retraining of catalogers and those who enter data; and possible situations in which existing records become invalid. Those working on format integration are aware of the costs, and recognize the probable need for compromise in order to avoid disruption of existing systems. With skill, care and time, many of the benefits can probably be achieved with few of the costs.

## NOTES AND REFERENCES

1. Some of the sources named as references serve for further study. Most of this chapter is derived from those sources, particularly Henriette Avram's *MARC, Its History and Implications* (see note 2) and *The MARC Pilot Project* (see note 7).

2. Avram, Henriette D. *MARC, Its History and Implications.* Washington, DC: Library of Congress; 1975: 3. 49 p.

3. King, Gilbert W. [and others]. *Automation and the Library of Congress; A Survey Sponsored by the Council on Library Resources, Inc.* Washington, DC: Library of Congress; 1963. 88 p. (Not consulted for this work.)

4. Buckland, Lawrence F. *The Recording of Library of Congress Bibliographical Data in Machine Form; A Report Prepared for the Council on Library Resources, Inc.* Washington, DC: Council on Library Resources, Inc.; 1965. 54 p. (Not consulted for this work.)

5. Avram, op. cit., p.3.

6. Avram, Henriette D.; Freitag, Ruth S.; Guiles, Kay D. *A Proposed Format for a Standardized Machine-Readable Catalog Record: A Preliminary Draft.* Washington, DC: Library of Congress; 1965. (Not consulted for this work.)

7. All of the information and references in this particular section came from: Avram, Henriette D. *The MARC Pilot Project: Final Report on a Project Sponsored by the Council on Library Resources, Inc.* Washington, DC: Library of Congress; 1968. 183 p.

8. The initial participants were as follows: Argonne National Laboratory, Georgia Institute of Technology, Harvard University, Indiana University, Montgomery County Public Schools, Nassau (County) Library System, National Agricultural Library, Redstone Scientific Information Center, Rice University, University of California Institute of Library Research (Los Angeles), University of Chicago, University of Florida, University of Missouri, University of Toronto, Washington State Library and Yale University.

9. Avram, *The MARC Pilot Project,* p. 5.

10. The four additional participants were as follows: California State Library, Illinois State Library, Cornell University Library, and SUNY Biomedical Communications Network.

11. Avram, *The MARC Pilot Project,* pp. 91–173.

12. Ibid., p. 1.

13. Ibid., p. 44–45.

14. Ibid., pp. 77–82.

15. Avram, Henriette D.; Knapp, John F.; Rather, Lucia J. *The MARC II Format: A Communications Format For Bibliographic Data.* Washington, DC: Library of Congress; 1968. 167 p.

16. Library of Congress. MARC Development Office. *Books: A MARC Format; Specifications for Magnetic Tapes Containing Catalog Records for Books.* 5th ed. Washington, DC: Library of Congress; 1972. 106 p.

17. Library of Congress. Information Systems Office. *Serials: A MARC Format; Specifications for Magnetic Tapes Containing Catalog Records for Serials.* 2d ed. Washington, DC: Library of Congress; 1974. 104 p. Preliminary edition, 1970.

18. Library of Congress. Information Systems Office. *Maps: A MARC Format; Specifications for Magnetic Tapes Containing Catalog Records for Maps.* Washington, DC: Library of Congress; 1970. 45 p.

19. Library of Congress. MARC Development Office. *Films: A MARC Format; Specifications for Magnetic Tapes Containing Catalog Records for Motion Pictures, Filmstrips, and Other Pictorial Media Intended for Projection.* Washington, DC: Library of Congress; 1970 [i.e., 1971]. 65 p.

20. Library of Congress. MARC Development Office. *Manuscripts: A MARC Format; Specifications for Magnetic Tapes Containing Catalog Records for Single Manuscripts or Manuscript Collections.* Washington, DC: Library of Congress; 1973. 47 p.

21. Library of Congress. MARC Development Office. *Music: A MARC Format; Specifications for Magnetic Tapes Containing Catalog Records for Music Scores and Musical and Non-musical Sound Recordings.* Draft. Washington, DC: Library of Congress; 1973.

22. Avram, *MARC, Its History and Implications,* p. 21.

23. American National Standards Institute. *American National Standard Format for Bibliographic Information Interchange on Magnetic Tape.* New York: ANSI; 1971. 34 p. (ANSI Z39.2-1971).

24. International Organization for Standardization. *Documentation—Format for Bibliographic Information Interchange on Magnetic Tape.* 1973. 4 p. [ISO 2709-1973(E).] (Not consulted for this work.)

25. Library of Congress. MARC Development Office. *MARC User Survey, 1972.* Washington, DC: Library of Congress; 1972. 58 p.

26. Avram, Henriette D. "The Library of Congress View on Its Relationship to the ALA MARC Advisory Committee." *Journal of Library Automation.* 7(2): 119–125; 1974 June. Also in: *Library of Congress Information Bulletin.* 33(9) Appendix II: A60–A65; 1974 March 1.

27. Maruskin, Albert F. *OCLC: Its Governance, Function, Financing and Technology.* New York: Marcel Dekker; 1980: 36. 145 p.

28. Davison, Wayne E. "The WLN/RLG/LC Linked Systems Project." *Information Technology and Libraries.* 2(1): 34–46; 1983 March.

29. [Weisbrod, David.] *Proposal No. 81-4. Principles of MARC Format Content Designation.* Washington, DC: Library of Congress; 1981 May 1. 66 p.

30. [Woods, Elaine W.] *Discussion Paper No. 5.* Numerous versions with differing pagination produced during 1981 and 1982.

31. Attig, John. "The USMARC Formats—Underlying Principles." *Information Technology and Libraries.* 1(2): 169–174; 1982 June.

32. "The USMARC Formats: Underlying Principles." *LC Information Bulletin.* 1983 May 9.

33. WLN produces some 225 COM catalogs a year, replacing one major use for MARC tapes created by other bibliographic services. COM catalogs always reflect the most current version of database records held by a library.

34. Avram, *MARC, Its History and Implications,* pp. 31–32.

35. Attig, John. "The Concept of MARC Format." *Information Technology and Libraries.* 2(1): 7–17; 1983 March.

36. Attig. John. *Integration of USMARC Bibliographic Formats.* 1983 August. 9 p. (MARBI discussion paper no. 7.)

# 10

# MARC Extensions: OCLC MARC and RLIN MARC

USMARC is unusual in that the definition explicitly allows for extensions. The Library of Congress distributes pure USMARC records, by definition; other agencies that generate USMARC tapes tend to add extensions to the format as defined in *MFBD*. Even the Library of Congress maintains extensions to USMARC in its own internal format. Proper extensions to USMARC are supersets of USMARC; any pure USMARC record will fit into the extended format, but some of the extended format's information won't fit into pure USMARC. The tape formats used by the two largest bibliographic services in the United States are both proper supersets of USMARC.

Extensions to USMARC do not change the format itself; they consist of additional content designation: subfields, indicator values, characters and fields. Other bibliographic services and other agencies also extend USMARC. OCLC MARC and RLIN MARC are used in this chapter as the two most prominent examples of extended USMARC formats, and as formats that, in some cases, use different means to achieve similar ends.

## OCLC MARC

OCLC bases its content designation and cataloging standards firmly on USMARC as defined in *MFBD*. Online displays show full USMARC content designation, and OCLC has historically been the only bibliographic service to implement every USMARC format. OCLC has defined three types of extensions to USMARC content designation: additional subfields, additional fields for general local use, and additional fields reserved for use by national libraries.

### Subfield Extensions

OCLC has defined additional subfields for USMARC fields in two cases. One of these cases affects a single field; the other is defined for a great many fields.

*Subfield ‡b in Field 035.* Field 035 contains Local system numbers. Use of the field is not well controlled. As defined by OCLC, "Field 035 may be used by a participating institution for its own control number."[1] The current USMARC definition includes only ‡a, Local system number, consisting of an NUC code (in parentheses) followed by a local system number. OCLC defines ‡b as "Institution code," the OCLC symbol rather than the NUC code. When ‡b is used, the NUC code is not entered in ‡a.

*Subfield ‡w: AACR2 verification.* "Subfield 'w' contains a two-character code that: (1) verifies that the field contains the AACR2 form of name heading, and (2) indicates the verification's source."[2] This subfield is directly related to OCLC's massive reconstruction of its database in 1981, changing headings to conform to AACR2 whenever possible. Subfield ‡w is explicitly labeled as an extension to USMARC. Subfield ‡w is defined for this purpose in all fields subject to name authority control and a few others: 100, 110, 111, 130, 240, 400, 410, 411, 600, 610, 611, 630, 651, 700, 710, 711, 730, 800, 810 and 811. The subfield is also defined for OCLC's local subject entry fields 691, 692, 693, 694 and 695.

## Field Extensions

OCLC defines a number of fields that are not part of USMARC. Most of these fields carry local call numbers, local holdings and local subject headings. One field is provided for any desired local use, without definition or restriction. Figure 10.1 shows the OCLC extended fields for coded and control fields (Figure 10.3 shows other OCLC extended fields for general use). Some OCLC extensions are widely thought of as part of USMARC. Since OCLC is by far the largest provider of online bibliographic services and USMARC tapes, this confusion may be understandable. Understandable or not, the confusion is not fostered by OCLC. OCLC extensions are clearly labeled as such in OCLC publications: "Field XXX has been defined by OCLC and is not part of the standard LC-MARC formats."

Field 019 contains OCLC Control Number(s) for duplicate records that have been deleted. The field is useful for processing agencies in tracing a record that has disappeared.

Field 049 contains location, copy and volume information for an item. Groups of libraries have frequently established explicit guidelines for coding 049, so that holdings can be manipulated easily. In addition to the wealth of subfields, OCLC has provided structure within and among the subfields. The primary subfield ‡a can include text to be printed above or below a call number, with each line of text surrounded by square brackets and the position of lines given by the position of text within the subfield: text before the holdings symbol appears above the call number, and text after appears below. Subfield ‡d · defines a sequence of other subfields, as does subfield ‡m.

Subfield ‡a of 049 is used by OCLC to control catalog card generation. Most other subfields are provided so that OCLC users can record holdings in a meaningful way, and so that networks and other processing centers can manipulate them. The field can be complex; OCLC devotes 10 single-spaced pages to "general guidelines" for its use. Field 049 allows complex and sophisticated storage of holdings. Figure 10.2 is an example (taken from OCLC's field guides) of what is possible using field 049:

**Figure 10.1 OCLC Extensions: 0XX Fields**

| | |
|---|---|
| 019 | OCLC control number cross-reference |

| | | |
|---|---|---|
| 049 | | Local holdings |
| | ‡a | Holding library code; text associated with call number |
| | ‡c | Copy statement |
| | ‡l | Local processing data |
| | ‡o | Local processing data |
| | ‡d | Definition of bibliographic subdivisions |
| | ‡v | Primary bibliographic subdivision |
| | ‡p | Secondary bibliographic subdivision |
| | ‡q | Third bibliographic subdivision |
| | ‡r | Fourth bibliographic subdivision |
| | ‡s | Fifth bibliographic subdivision |
| | ‡t | Sixth bibliographic subdivision |
| | ‡u | Seventh bibliographic subdivision |
| | ‡y | Inclusive dates of publication or coverage |
| | ‡m | Missing elements |
| | ‡n | Notes about holdings |

| | | |
|---|---|---|
| 090 | | Locally assigned LC-type call number |
| | ‡a | LC class number |
| | ‡b | Cutter number or book number |
| | ‡e | Feature heading |
| | ‡f | Filing suffix |

| | | |
|---|---|---|
| 092 | | Locally assigned Dewey call number |
| | ‡a | Dewey Decimal Classification Number |
| | ‡b | Book number |
| | ‡e, ‡f | Same as 090 ‡e, ‡f |

| | | |
|---|---|---|
| 096 | | Locally assigned NLM-type call number |
| | ‡a, ‡b | Same as 060 ‡a, ‡b |
| | ‡e, ‡f | Same as 090 ‡e, ‡f |

| | | |
|---|---|---|
| 098 | | Other classification schemes |
| | ‡a | Call number, one printed line (repeating) |
| | ‡e, ‡f | Same as 090 ‡e, ‡f |

| | |
|---|---|
| 099 | Local free text call number |
| | Subfields defined as in 098 |

**Figure 10.2 OCLC: Field 049 Example**

```
049 ƀƀ ‡aXXXr‡c2‡d[‡vser.‡pvol.‡qno.]‡vI‡p1‡q1-2‡p2‡q1-4‡d[‡vser.
    ‡pvol.‡qpt.]‡vII‡p1‡p2‡q1-3
```

Holding library XXXr holds one copy, numbered 2. The publication has two customary numbering schemes: (1) "series" divided into "volumes" divided into "numbers," and (2) "series" divided into "volumes" divided into "parts." Series I consists of volume 1 in two numbers, and volume 2 in four numbers. Series II consists of volume I in one physical volume, and volume 2 in three parts.

OCLC's field 090, which contains only LC-type call numbers, is a local extension. OCLC defines the same subfields for 090 as for 050: ‡a, LC class number, and ‡b, Local cutter number (book number). OCLC adds two new subfields to support classified catalogs: ‡e, Feature heading, and ‡f, Filing suffix. Subfield ‡b in OCLC's 092 is not the same as subfield ‡b in the standard Dewey call number field 082, and it has special rules for specifying line breaks on a printed card.

Field 098 represents an attempt by OCLC to represent all known standard schemes for classification. As stated in the field's scope note, "Classification schemes defined in this field are generally available in printed form, but are neither major schemes (such as LC or Dewey) nor completely local schemes." The special nature of field 098 is in its indicators, which specify the classification scheme used. Both indicators are taken together,[3] carrying a number from "00" (National Center on Educational Media and Materials for the Handicapped) to "24" (Swank Classification for State, County and Municipal Documents). Other numbers are reserved, and added as required. Field 099 contains call numbers that don't fit elsewhere, such as local systems unique to a given library, text used in place of call numbers, and call numbers which can't be formatted properly from other fields. Like field 098, field 099 has a repeatable ‡a, where each subfield contains a printing line of the call number, and also contains ‡e and ‡f. Unlike field 098, the indicators in 099 are undefined.

Field 590 is used for notes that pertain only to a single library or single copy of an item. The field can be used for any note which a library wishes to place in the notes section of a catalog card. Examples could be "Library retains latest 3 years only" or "Copy is missing pages 300-325." Field 690 contains a topical subject heading that is not based on a standard thesaurus. It has the same subfields as field 650, and is used in the same way. Field 691 is comparable to field 651; the same notes apply as for field 690. Fields 692, 693, 694 and 695 are local equivalents for fields 600, 610, 611 and 630, respectively, and have the same subfields. These fields were defined for CONSER, and are only used in Serials; in that format, they are used for subject headings not assigned by national libraries.

Field 910 contains information of local interest; the first 21 characters of ‡a can be used as a footnote on catalog cards. Field 936 is used when serial cataloging is based on something other than the first issue published.

Field 949 is open for any desired use. To quote OCLC's documentation, "this field may be defined in any manner by any OCLC participating library or affiliated network, according to its needs for local processing information." The field is repeatable, and may contain any indicators and any subfields. Provision of field 949 is another attempt by OCLC to allow libraries and networks to meet their own needs; OCLC does not do any validation of the field or its internal content designation. Any user is free to use the field for any purpose whatsoever. Figure 10.3 lists fields 590-949, together with their definitions.

**Figure 10.3 OCLC Extensions: 590-949 Fields**

| | |
|---|---|
| 590 | Local note |
| 690 | Local subject added entry - topical heading |
| 691 | Local subject added entry - geographic name |
| 692 | Local subject added entry - personal name |
| 693 | Local subject added entry - corporate name |
| 694 | Local subject added entry - conference / meeting |
| 695 | Local subject added entry - uniform title heading |
| 910 ‡a | User-option data |
| 936 ‡a | Dates or volume designations of pieces used for cataloging |
| 949 | Local processing information |

While OCLC extensions for local data only include a few fields, the fields allow for a moderately wide range of local data. The Local call number fields offer unique capacity for specifying use of lesser-known classification schemes, and field 049 allows well-structured specification of holdings. Field 949 is an essential conduit, allowing libraries to "talk to themselves" and to processing agencies. Field 949 is of no use to OCLC itself, but can be valuable if well defined within a library or group of libraries.

**Field Extensions for National Libraries**

OCLC has defined several fields that are not present in USMARC and are not available for use by most libraries. Most of these fields, shown in Figure 10.4, are used in the CONSER project for records entered by the National Library of Canada or by the Library of Congress. Some fields are equivalents for fields in Canadian MARC (CANMARC), and some provide for LC internal needs. Field 680 appears to be a candidate for addition to nationally defined USMARC, allowing libraries to use PRECIS as an additional means of subject access. OCLC currently considers field 680 to be an OCLC extension.

### RLIN MARC

RLG also produces tapes in a superset of USMARC, with additional subfields and additional fields. RLIN MARC has an unusually wide range of additional fields, including a number of fields with alphabetic tags.

**Subfield Extensions**

RLIN MARC includes one new subfield for USMARC fields, and another locally defined subfield that was originally used in nationally defined fields, but is now limited to RLIN field extensions.

**Figure 10.4 OCLC Extensions: Fields Reserved for National Libraries**

| Tag | Description |
|-----|-------------|
| 012 | Terminal Display |
| 680 | PRECIS Descriptor String |
| 886 | Foreign MARC Information |
| 890 | Holdings (Local LC) |
| 900 | Personal Name Equivalence or Cross-reference |
| 901 | Numbered Copy Information |
| 911 | X-copy Information |
| 920 | Corporate Name Equivalence, Cross-reference, History Note |
| 921 | Conference/Meeting Name Equivalence, Cross-reference, History Note |
| 930 | Uniform Title Heading Equivalence or Cross-reference |
| 940 | Uniform Title Equivalence or Cross-reference |
| 980 | Series (Personal Name) Equivalence or Cross-reference |
| 981 | Series (Corporate Name) Equivalence or Cross-reference |
| 982 | Series (Conference or Meeting) Equivalence or Cross-reference |
| 983 | Series (Title) Equivalence or Cross-reference |
| 990 | Link to Equivalence, Cross-references, and History Notes |

Subfield ‡9, which can appear in any field subject to authority control, contains a single character. If present, the character is an assertion and request: that the field in question is controlled by the authority file designated by the character, and that it should continue to be so controlled. When RLG implements authority control, subfield ‡9 will be used to identify and, if necessary, modify controlled fields.

*Subfield* ‡% contains coded values to identify special tracings, such as tracings for fine printers, special bindings and the like. Currently, ‡% is only used in local added entry fields. In RLIN, these fields represent those added entries that are strictly local in form or of strictly local interest. The RLG-defined local added entry fields are shown in Figure 10.5 together with their USMARC equivalents.

**Figure 10.5 RLIN Extensions: Local Added Entries**

| RLIN | USMARC | RLIN | USMARC | RLIN | USMARC |
|------|--------|------|--------|------|--------|
| 690 | 650 | 796 | 700 | 896 | 800 |
| 691 | 651 | 797 | 710 | 897 | 810 |
| 696 | 600 | 798 | 711 | 898 | 811 |
| 697 | 610 | 799 | 730 | 899 | 830 |
| 698 | 611 | | | | |
| 699 | 630 | | | | |

## Field Extensions

In addition to the local added entry fields shown in Figure 10.5, RLIN MARC adds a large number of other fields to USMARC. None of the others are displayed as MARC tags in RLIN online. All other extensions are tagged with mnemonics, and translated to fields and subfields for RLIN MARC tape transmission. RLIN MARC extensions can be broken down into three groups: call numbers and holdings; miscellaneous local information and errors; and acquisitions information.

## Holdings and Call Numbers

RLIN provides extensive holdings support, but has no single field with the sophistication of OCLC's field 049. RLIN does include an implementation of the ANSI Serials Holdings at the Summary Level standard, field "SHS" (RLIN MARC 930). Three RLIN MARC fields, shown in Figure 10.6, provide for three levels of call number, holdings and card-related information. Figure 10.6 also shows the mnemonics for the subfields. Figure 10.7 shows field 930, the summary holdings statement, and gives an example of its use.

Many of the elements in 090, 950 and 955 govern card production. Others, specifically 950‡u, 955‡q, 955‡r and 955‡u, are provided to allow libraries to pass information to local systems. RLIN local information is retained and displayed in the online system, and a history of transactions is maintained. Copy fields (955) are always related to location fields (950), and all 955s related to a given 950 follow that 950 in the directory. The ‡1 subfield is repeated in field 955 to serve as a safeguard for 955-950 links.

Field 930 is specifically designed to contain holdings statements recorded according to ANSI summary standards. RLIN field guides include an extensive discussion of the subfields and their relation to the ANSI standard. Coded values, subfields ‡f, ‡g and ‡h, use the codes defined by the standard. The field appears to accommodate the requirements of the summary holdings standard without requiring excessive work, and is being used by several RLG members. The example in Figure 10.7 shows:

A serial held in location NAT at institution MiU (NUC code), copy 1, with call number SH11. A45. The library holds volumes 1–23 published from 1881–1903. The report was created in July 1980. Completeness is not known; the serial is not currently received and is permanently retained.

## Other RLIN MARC Extensions

RLG has defined 14 more fields, not including acquisitions data. More than one-half of these fields are equivalents to OCLC's Field 949: fields reserved for libraries to define and use as they see fit. Figure 10.8 lists the 14 fields.

Fields 901–907 all carry the same definition and the same rules. "LDx is used for information needed by a library that is not provided by existing fields. Each library may use LDx for its own purposes."[4] Each field is repeatable, and a library may define indicators and subfields to suit its own needs. RSN, field 910, is used to record variant practice from

**Figure 10.6 RLIN Extensions: Call Numbers and Holdings**

| RLIN MARC | Mnemonic | Description |
|---|---|---|
| FIELD 090 | | RECORD LEVEL INFORMATION |
| 090 ‡a‡b | CALL | Call number |
| 090 ‡v | VOL ‡v | Volume statement of holdings |
| 090 ‡y | VOL ‡y | Date statement of holdings |
| 090 ‡z | VOL ‡z | Retention statement |
| 090 ‡n | ANT | Additional local notes |
| 090 ‡f | FNT | Footnote |
| 090 ‡p | PTH | Pathfinder code |
| 090 ‡t | FSP | Field suppression |
| 090 ‡i | INS+EXT | Output transaction instruction, extra card control statements |
| 090 ‡h | HST | Previous INS+EXT values |
| FIELD 950 | | LOCATION LEVEL INFORMATION |
| 950 ‡l | LOC | Permanent shelving location |
| 950 ‡a‡b | LCAL | Location level call number |
| 950 ‡d | LCAL ‡d | Stamp above call number |
| 950 ‡e | LCAL ‡e | Stamp below call number |
| 950 ‡vyz | LVOL | Location level volume information |
| 950 ‡n | LANT | Location level additional notes |
| 950 ‡u | LANT ‡u | Non-printing notes |
| 950 ‡w | LANT ‡w | Subscription status code |
| 950 ‡f | LFNT | Location level footnote |
| 950 ‡p | LPTH | Location level pathfinder |
| 950 ‡t | LFSP | Location level field suppression |
| 950 ‡i | LINS | Location level instruction |
| 950 ‡h | LHST | Previous LINS values |
| FIELD 955 | | COPY LEVEL INFORMATION |
| 955 ‡l | <LOC> | System-generated from 950 ‡l |
| 955 ‡a‡b | CCAL | Copy level call number |
| 955 ‡c | COP + | Copy information |
| | MDES | Material designation |
| 955 ‡q | SHNT ‡q | Acquisitions control number |
| 955 ‡r | SHNT ‡r | Circulation control number |
| 955 ‡s | SHNT ‡s | Shelf list note |
| 955 ‡u | SHNT ‡u | Non-printing notes |
| 955 ‡i | CST | Copy status |
| 955 ‡h | CST | Copy status (previous date) |

RLG standards. The primary use for RSN is to note changes that a library has made in the bibliographic content of LC data, either MARC or non-MARC. The note serves as a guide and warning to other users. RLG has defined field 936 to conform to OCLC's definition of 936, which does appear on distributed CONSER records.

**Figure 10.7 RLIN Extensions: Field 930, Summary Holdings Statement**

```
930    Summary Holdings Statement
   ‡a    Institution code - location data
   ‡b    Sublocation identifier - location data
   ‡c    Copy identifier - location data
   ‡d    Call number - location data
   ‡e    Date of report - general holdings data
   ‡f    Completeness code - general holdings data
   ‡g    Acquisition status code - general holdings data
   ‡h    Retention code - general holdings data
   ‡i    Local notes - general holdings data
   ‡j    Enumeration - specific holdings data
   ‡k    Chronology - specific holdings.

930  ƀƀ  ‡aMiU‡bNAT‡cCopy 1‡dSH 11. A45‡j1-23‡k1881-1903‡e8007‡f0‡g5‡hƀ
```

RLG has placed series control information in bibliographic records rather than in series authority records. With implementation of the contemporary authorities format, RLG will allow series control information in either location. SPT, field 948, is used to specify the part designator for a series. The field consists of a subfield ‡a containing a caption such as "v." or "no." An institution may use ATN, field 94a, to record details of its own analysis, classification or tracing practices for a monographic series, multivolume monograph or the like. The field is repeatable. RLIN provides coded data elements for some of this information in ATC, field 94b; field 94a is used when the coded values do not provide enough information. Note the alphabetic third character in the tag. Figure 10.9 gives examples of field 94a. Field 94b contains two coded subfields; ATC, ‡a, consists of three one-character codes specifying Analysis practice, Classification practice, and Tracing practice for a bibliographic entity that can be analyzed. SNR, ‡s, is a single code stating that a series is numbered, unnumbered or variously numbered and unnumbered.

RLIN provides PVT, field b99, to allow libraries to store confidential local information, such as data on donors of rare books. Libraries may define indicators and subfield codes for PVT as needed. The field differs from other local data elements in terms of display: PVT is only displayed to the library that owns a record.

ERF and ERR, fields 01e and 89e, are used to store coded and variable fields that do not pass RLIN edits. Such fields may be created when records are loaded from tape; errors occurring during online record entry must be corrected before record entry can be completed.

**RLIN Acquisitions Data**

USMARC has never included tags containing alphabetic characters, but such tags have always been legitimate possibilities. When RLG implemented an acquisitions system and decided to integrate acquisitions data with bibliographic data, initial analysis showed

**Figure 10.8 RLIN Extensions: Local and Error Fields**

| | | | |
|---|---|---|---|
| 901 | | LDA | Local data element A |
| 902 | | LDB | Local data element B |
| 903 | | LDC | Local data element C |
| 904 | | LDD | Local data element D |
| 905 | | LDE | Local data element E |
| 906 | | LDF | Local data element F |
| 907 | | LDG | Local data element G |
| 910 ‡a | | RSN | RLG standards note |
| 936 | | PUC | Piece used for cataloging |
| 948 ‡a | | SPT | Series part designation |
| 94a | | ATN | Analysis treatment note |
| | ‡a | | Copy designation |
| | ‡b | | Analysis treatment |
| | ‡c | | Classification treatment |
| | ‡d | | Miscellaneous treatment information |
| | ‡e | | Numbering treatment |
| 94b | | | Treatment codes |
| | ‡a | ATC | Analysis treatment codes |
| | ‡s | SNR | Series numbering |
| 998 | | | Local control information |
| | ‡a | UD | Update date |
| | ‡b | OID | Operator initials |
| | ‡c | CIN | Cataloger initials |
| | ‡d | AD | Date added to file |
| | ‡i | | Current transmission date, form yymmdd |
| | ‡h | | Previous tape transmission dates |
| | ‡l | LID | Library ID, RLG form |
| | ‡n | NUC | Library NUC code |
| | ‡q | QD | Queueing date for preservation microfilming |
| | ‡s | CC | Cataloging category |
| | ‡t | RTYP | Record type |
| | ‡w | LINK | Source of record within RLIN (if any) |
| b99 | | PVT | Private local information |
| 01e | | ERF | Error in coded field |
| 89e | | ERR | Error in variable data field |

that the 9XX range of locally defined tags would become overcrowded if all acquisitions data was defined as 9XX fields. RLG chose to place all acquisitions data in fields having tags beginning 'u,' and at the same time began using alphabetic characters in some other extended fields (such as b99, 94a and 89e).

**Figure 10.9 RLIN Extensions: Field 94a Examples**

```
94a ♭♭ ‡bVols. 1-10 classed together and unanalyzed.‡cVol. 11-
    classed separately.‡dSeries traced vol. 11-
```

```
94a ♭♭ ‡aCopy 1, Music‡bAnalyzed and series traced v. 15 (1975)-
    only.‡cAll vols. classed together.
```

RLIN defines "units" to contain acquisitions data: a single unit reflects one order or other acquisition. A single bibliographic entity can have as many as 99 units, each identified by a one- or two-digit number. Data relating to a specific unit is grouped by indicators; all acquisitions fields carry the UID, or unit identification number, in the indicator positions.[5]

Figure 10.10 shows RLIN acquisitions fields from u01 through u11, making up the unit codes and status and notification information. The CPST gives the current status of

**Figure 10.10 RLIN Extensions: Acquisitions Fields u01-u11**

| RLIN MARC | Mnemonic | Description |
|---|---|---|
| FIELD u01 | | UNIT IDENTIFICATION AND TYPE |
| u01 ‡a | UID | Unit identification |
| u01 ‡d | UAD | Date unit added |
| u01 ‡s | UST | Unit status |
| u01 ‡t | UTYP | Unit type |
| u01 ‡i | CPST | Current processing status: latest |
| u01 ‡h | CPST | --Previous values (repeating ‡h) |
| u01 ‡f | FPST | Future processing status |
| FIELD u02 | | STANDARD NUMBER |
| u02 ‡2 | -- | Name of number: ISBN, ISSN, etc. |
| u02 ‡a | ISxx | Standard number, ‡a |
| u02 ‡b‡c | --‡b‡c | ‡b and ‡c (if any) of Standard Number |
| FIELD u08 | | ADDITIONAL CODED INFORMATION |
| u08 ‡r | RUSH | Rush status for order |
| u08 ‡p | DP | Display permit |
| u08 ‡n | LSI | Local system identifier |
| u08 ‡o | SID | Selector identification |
| FIELD u10 | | REQUESTER FIELD |
| u10 ‡s | REQ ‡s | Requester output selection |
| u10 ‡a | REQ ‡a | Requester, coded value |
| u10 ‡b | REQ ‡b | Requester name |
| u10 ‡cde | REQ ‡cde | Requester address, lines 1-3 |
| u11 ‡a | DRR | Departmental report request |

an acquisition: being ordered, being claimed, partially received, cataloged, and so on. Field u02 can contain an ISBN, ISSN or other standard number. "DP" is used online to determine whether other libraries can see detailed acquisitions information for the unit. "LSI" will be used as the order number on all communications, with the record ID and unit ID

**Figure 10.11 RLIN Extensions: Supplier, Claim and Extended Fields**

| RLIN MARC | Mnemonic | Description |
|---|---|---|
| FIELD u20 | | SUPPLIER NAME AND ADDRESS |
| u20 ‡a | SUPN ‡a | Supplier code |
| u20 ‡b | SUPN ‡b | Supplier name |
| u20 ‡cde | SUPN ‡cde | Supplier address, lines 1-3 |
| u20 ‡x | SUPN ‡x | Standard Address Number (SAN) |
| FIELD u21 | | LIBRARY CODES FOR VENDOR AND ORDER |
| u21 ‡a | SHIP | Ship-to address (coded form) |
| u21 ‡b | BILL | Bill-to address (coded form) |
| u21 ‡c | DAC | Deposit account number |
| u21 ‡n | LSAC | Library supplier account number |
| FIELD u22 | | SUPPLIER CODES AND CATALOG INFORMATION |
| u22 ‡a | SICO ‡a | Supplier instruction codes |
| u22 ‡b | SICO ‡b | nonprinting instruction codes (history) |
| u22 ‡c | SCAT | Supplier catalog reference |
| u25 ‡a | SRPT | Supplier report |
| FIELD u30 | | CLAIM INTERVALS |
| u30 ‡m | MCI | Material claim interval |
| u30 ‡i | ICI | Invoice claim interval |
| FIELD u31 | | CLAIM COUNTS |
| u31 ‡a | NCC | Number of claims to cancellation |
| u31 ‡b | NCS | Number of claims sent |
| FIELD u33 | | INVOICE CLAIM |
| u33 ‡a | ICL | Invoice claim request & date |
| u33 ‡d | ICAD | Invoice claim action date |
| FIELD u34 | | EXTENDED PROCUREMENT CLAIM & REVIEW |
| u34 ‡a | EPCL | Extended procurement claim date |
| u34 ‡r | ERI | Extended review interval |
| FIELD u40 | | EXTENDED PROCUREMENT CODES |
| u40 ‡s | EPST | Extended Procurement Status |
| u40 ‡d | EPDT | Date associated with EPST |
| u40 ‡t | ETYP | Extended procurement type |
| u40 ‡f | EFRQ | Frequency |

used if no LSI is given. The "requester output selection" code can cause automatic genera-tion of notices when an item is ordered, received or cataloged. The requester can be iden-tified by code or a full name and address can be entered.

Figure 10.11 shows acquisitions fields u20 through u40. Most of these elements are self-explanatory. SICO values are codes for notes to print on orders, claims and cancella-tions. The ‡b subfield allows a library to retain codes that are no longer appropriate (for instance, certain notes would make sense on an order but not on a claim).

Figures 10.12 and 10.13 show the remaining RLIN MARC acquisitions fields. The subfield ‡b in field u52 and u53 serves the same function as in u22, allowing a library to keep track of notes which are no longer appropriate. Most elements are self-explanatory. Field ufi allows libraries to enter fiscal information for transmission to their own system, or for use in RLG-produced reports of encumbrances and expenditures during a given period.

## WHY EXTEND USMARC?

OCLC and RLIN both extend USMARC as nationally defined; so do most other agencies. Extensions are needed because USMARC is designed as a communications for-mat for bibliographic data. Local extensions support local processing needs; in this sense, even OCLC is a "local" system. Extensions serve functions not handled by USMARC, such as:

1. *Holdings:* OCLC, RLIN and many others have supported storage of holdings data

**Figure 10.12 RLIN Extensions: Acquisitions Notes**

| RLIN MARC | Mnemonic | Description |
|---|---|---|
| u50 ‡a | AQNT | Acquisitions note |
| u51 ‡a | SLNT | Selection note |
| FIELD u52<br>u52 ‡a<br>u52 ‡b | <br>SINT<br>SINT ‡b | SUPPLIER INSTRUCTION NOTES<br>Supplier instruction note (textual)<br>Nonprinting supplier instruction note |
| FIELD u53<br>u53 ‡a<br>u53 ‡b | <br>CLNT<br>CLNT ‡b | CLAIM NOTES<br>Claim note<br>Nonprinting claim note |
| u54 ‡a | SRNT | Serials note |
| u55 ‡a | CTNT | Cataloging note |
| u5f ‡a | ACNT | Accounting note |

for many years, long before USMARC took up the issue. Holdings information is vital for resource sharing and for local systems; bibliographic services must provide holdings support to serve their members and users.

2. *Acquisitions:* Information on acquisitions can serve cooperative collection development programs; some of the bibliographic services also provide specific acquisitions services. Most acquisitions data is of strictly local interest, and technically inappropriate for a national communications format. Since much USMARC communications is from a library to itself (using a bibliographic service as an intermediary), such data still need a place.

Extensions to USMARC allow support for functions beyond the scope of USMARC, and make it possible to experiment with functions not yet standardized in USMARC. USMARC's explicit provision for extensions, reserving ranges of tags, makes it possible for designers to add local functions without fear of conflict when USMARC changes. This explicit provision protects the generality of the formats and reduces the need for extensions that violate the normal structure of USMARC.

**Figure 10.13 RLIN Extensions: Item, Price and Fiscal Fields**

| RLIN MARC | Mnemonic | Description |
|---|---|---|
| FIELD u70<br>u70 ‡1<br>u70 ‡a<br>u70 ‡b | <br>MLOC<br>QTY<br>MAT | ITEM CONTROL ELEMENTS<br>    Original expected shelving location<br>    Quantity: number of copies<br>    Material description |
| u71 ‡a | FUND | Library fund identification code |
| FIELD u75<br>u75 ‡a<br>u75 ‡1<br>u75 ‡i<br>u75 ‡h | <br>ITEM<br>SLOC<br>IPST<br>-- | ITEM DETAILS<br>    Material description<br>    Expected shelving location<br>    Item processing status, latest<br>    -- Previous (repeating ‡h) |
| FIELD u7f<br>u7f ‡a<br>u7f ‡b<br>u7f ‡p | <br>LPRI<br>CURR<br>LPD | PRICE INFORMATION<br>    List price<br>    Currency code<br>    List price display permit |
| FIELD ufi<br>ufi ‡a<br>ufi ‡b<br>ufi ‡c<br>ufi ‡d<br>ufi ‡e<br>ufi ‡f<br>ufi ‡g<br>ufi ‡h<br>ufi ‡n | FI<br>FI ‡a<br>FI ‡b<br>FI ‡c<br>FI ‡d<br>FI ‡e<br>FI ‡f<br>FI ‡g<br>FI ‡h<br>FI ‡n | FISCAL INFORMATION<br>    Fund<br>    Fiscal year<br>    Encumbrance amount<br>    Date of encumbrance<br>    Invoice number or identification<br>    Number of items paid for<br>    Payment amount<br>    Date of payment<br>    Note |

# NOTES AND REFERENCES

1. OCLC, Inc. *Serials Format*. Columbus: OCLC, Inc.; 1980.

2. Ibid.

3. Use of both indicators to represent a single value is a violation of the *Underlying Principles*. These principles were not yet codified when OCLC defined field 098, and the violation does no damage to the general format; this special case also provides a real capability.

4. All citations in this section are from various RLIN Field Guides or from RLIN internal documentation.

5. As with OCLC's field 098, indicators as used in RLIN acquisitions fields are in violation of the *Underlying Principles*. Both indicators are used together to make up a single value. These fields were defined prior to approval of the *Underlying Principles*.

# 11

# MARC Compatibility

Few library automation systems use pure USMARC; most records, and most systems, are MARC-compatible. MARC compatibility has become a stock term in library automation; the term does not have a precise meaning, and may be used in a way that is misleading.

There are two fundamental uses of the phrase "MARC-compatible." The first use is in relation to computer programs, hardware or full systems; a "MARC-compatible" system should be able to process USMARC records directly. The second use relates to data formats other than pure USMARC; a "MARC-compatible" format is, realistically, one that is "somehow related to" USMARC. The direct implication of the term, however, is that "MARC-compatible" records can be processed using the same programs that process pure USMARC records.

USMARC was designed as a communications format. Since it was never designed for online use, transformations for such use are natural and proper. USMARC is used extensively for batch processing though here, too, some transformation may take place. "MARC-compatible" *systems* and "MARC-compatible" *formats* are two different things, although they will be discussed together for convenience. No single meaning for MARC compatibility will suffice, but a clear distinction can be made between full compatibility and partial compatibility: fully compatible formats and systems are those that can accept pure USMARC records and, as needed, regenerate the same USMARC records without loss of content, content designation or structure. Properly, the term "MARC-compatible" should be reserved for systems and formats that can accept and regenerate USMARC records. The extensions, transforms and Level I systems and formats in this chapter are all MARC-compatible. Other formats and systems are partially compatible at best; in practice, most systems and formats called "MARC-compatible" are only partially compatible.

## THE SIGNIFICANCE OF COMPATIBILITY

Why is MARC compatibility important? A circulation system doesn't require a full bibliographic record, and can store a limited record more efficiently; acquisitions records need not be comprehensive: you don't need tracings for orders. MARC compatibility means flexibility, and allows a library to move towards an integrated system. A brief record may suffice for a circulation system, but will reduce access in an online catalog. If you can use an existing bibliographic record to produce an order, you'll do less keying than you would to enter even the most minimal acquisitions record—and the item will be cataloged, needing only call numbers and locations to complete processing. MARC-compatible systems are designed for the future. With full compatibility, a library can provide data for regional union lists, can use new programs to provide new services, and can take advantage of advances in library automation. MARC provides a common ground for sharing data; without compatibility, a library is foreclosing such sharing.

## PRECISE COMPATIBILITY: LC MARC

The highest level of USMARC compatibility is identity. Identity normally results from common implementation of a single comprehensive standard by more than one agency. Identity implies that all processes working on one case will work the same on other cases. It requires that the character set, record structure, content designation, data element identification, coded values, and rules for content be the same in all cases.

An implementation of USMARC would be identical to USMARC if it included all (and only) data elements contained in the *MARC Formats for Bibliographic Data,* stored in ALA Extended ASCII, using the structural definitions given in *MFBD,* and using ISBD punctuation and AACR2 cataloging rules as used in *MFBD.*[1]

The citation above is an overly strict interpretation of precise compatibility. In fact, non-*AACR2* cataloging can still be LC MARC in its purest form, as can records with non-ISBD punctuation, as long as all content designation was precisely as stated in *MFBD.* The problem with identity is that the only fields allowed are those fully defined in *MFBD.* While those fields allow comprehensive descriptive cataloging and access points, they do not allow for local call numbers, locations or other local data. Library practitioners tend to include fields in USMARC which are not actually part of the national formats, such as OCLC fields 049, 949 and 090–099. You should distinguish between full compatibility and strict identity. A fully compatible format is one that can accept pure USMARC records and regenerate them without loss of data or content designation. Such a format need not be identical to LC MARC.

### Tape Blocking

One aspect of pure LC MARC is tape blocking. The Library of Congress and WLN use a moderately sophisticated method of arranging records on tape, which avoids any wasted space due to records of varying length. This special blocked and spanned format, which follows current ANSI and ISO standards, was initiated in 1977 and is used in all MARC Distribution Service tapes. The LC MARC tape format makes each physical record exactly 2048 characters long. Each physical record contains one or more record segments;

each record segment begins with a segment control word, which contains the length of the segment and a single numeric control character. The control character assigns one of four possible meanings to the record segment:

1. Complete logical record, beginning and ending within the physical record;

2. Initial segment, beginning in this physical record but continuing to at least one more;

3. Terminal segment, the conclusion of a logical record which began in an earlier physical record;

4. Intermediate segment, a physical record that neither begins nor completes a logical record; each intermediate segment must, by definition, fill a complete physical record.

An average MARC Distribution Service record will be around 800 characters; the record will be longer for serials and shorter for books. Many records will be much shorter, perhaps as short as 250 characters, and some records will be much longer, potentially well over 10,000 characters. The tape blocking method described above saves input/output processing for shorter records, and can result in more records fitting on a reel of tape.[2] OCLC and RLG produce tapes using the pre-1977 LC MARC format. This format always uses at least one physical block for each logical record, and carries no special control words; multiblock records are recognized by their length, the first five characters of the leader. This "unblocked spanned" format requires more tape and more input/output operations, but does allow simpler software to read the records, and allows systems to add more records to an existing tape. Since OCLC and RLIN do not use the LC tape format, neither bibliographic service produces pure LC MARC/USMARC tapes.

**Transforms and Extensions**

Fully compatible formats and systems differ from pure USMARC in two ways: extensions and transforms. Extended formats, generally called simply USMARC in this book, use the pure USMARC structure and incorporate all *MFBD* fields, but add additional information. A pure USMARC record can be converted to the extended format and restored intact, but some extended records can't be converted to pure USMARC without loss of data. Transformed formats carry the same information as USMARC, but carry it in a different way. Pure USMARC records can be mechanically converted to the transformed format and mechanically restored to pure USMARC, again without loss of content or content designation. Extended formats can be processed using standard USMARC software, but transformed formats usually can't; as a result, transforms are better thought of as MARC-equivalent than as USMARC.

## EXTENSIONS

The most common USMARC formats are actually supersets of USMARC: A is a superset of B if all of B is contained in A, but not all of A is contained in B. A superset of MARC can accommodate all elements of USMARC, and can restore a full USMARC record intact, but a superset format can't always be transformed to pure USMARC without loss of content. Supersets imply extensions: the elements of the superset that are not present in USMARC. At least three different forms of extension are possible: character set extensions, structural extensions and content designation extensions.

**Character Set Extensions**

USMARC uses a much larger character set than is standard for most computers: ALA Extended ASCII (American Standard Code for Information Interchange) contains over 170 printable characters, including the special characters and diacritical symbols needed for most languages that use the roman alphabet. Materials in nonroman languages require other graphic displays; at the moment, addition of such graphics constitutes an extension to USMARC. Standard notation is now provided in USMARC to accommodate such extensions, but the extensions themselves are not yet defined.

The New York Public Libraries began adding Cyrillic and Hebrew characters to MARC records years ago, using their own techniques to identify character strings as nonroman; the Research Libraries Group now supports data entry in Chinese, Japanese and Korean, using the MARC-defined notation and an alternate character set definition that has not yet been adopted by the American National Standards Institute. These character set extensions are proper supersets. USMARC records containing only ALA Extended ASCII characters are stored alongside records with additional characters, and the extended records can be transformed to records that do not contain character set extensions.

**Structural Extensions**

Database management systems typically store USMARC records in a different structure; that structure may contain elements that assist in processing and that constitute extensions to USMARC. Unlike character set extensions and content designation extensions, structural extensions cannot usually be communicated in USMARC communications format. One structural extension uses hierarchical structures for location and copy information, where copy information is contained within location structures. USMARC does not allow for hierarchical structures; an internal system that uses such structures for data entry and storage typically establishes a methodology for representing the structures within the linear format of USMARC, using content designation extensions.

**Content Designation Extensions**

The most common extensions to USMARC add content designation and content; USMARC provides considerable flexibility for locally defined fields and subfields. Since certain fields and subfields are explicitly reserved for local definition, it is always possible to distinguish between USMARC and the extensions. It is possible to add locally defined subfields to fields defined within USMARC, using the 22 subfield symbols reserved for local use. While such extensions do exist, they are less common than field extensions and somewhat more difficult to use.

Bibliographic services usually define extensions to USMARC; libraries that use MARC locally may use the extensions defined by a bibliographic service, and may add their own local extensions. The University of California Division of Library Automation adds a sophisticated multilevel structure to USMARC to store location, call number and holdings information. Other agencies also add local content designation to USMARC.

Most of this chapter, and most of this book, includes such extensions as part of USMARC. As noted below, a system that can't store or handle proper format extensions may limit interchange of records. For the purposes of this discussion, a fully compatible system is one that can accommodate USMARC records, including those with properly defined local extensions.

## TRANSFORMS

A reversible format involves one or more transforms that distinguish it from pure USMARC. The four transforms discussed below are samples of possible transforms; all four are actually used in the United States in one way or another. All four types of transforms have two key aspects in common. First, they can be converted back to pure USMARC by computer, without human intervention, and without loss of content or content designation. Second, they make processing easier for some reason. Otherwise, the work of doing the transform would be unnecessary overhead.

### Character Set Transforms

USMARC uses an extended version of ASCII, the American Standard Code for Information Interchange; ASCII is simply a standard set of binary representations for characters. Regular ASCII uses seven binary digits for each character; ALA Extended ASCII, used for USMARC, uses an eighth binary digit. There are 94 printable characters in ASCII; adding another digit doubles the number of printable characters to 188, and ALA Extended ASCII uses nearly all of the 188 possible character positions.

ASCII is the standard representation for most computer manufacturers in the United States; the one major exception, IBM, bases its larger systems on EBCDIC, Extended Binary Coded Decimal Interchange Code. Since IBM computers are widely used in large-scale library automation, many systems use an extended version of EBCDIC to store MARC data. An informal 1981 survey suggests that most large operations, including OCLC, RLIN, and WLN, use extended EBCDIC internally;[3] the Library of Congress uses extended EBCDIC for internal processing. Whatever character set is used internally, all normal transmission of MARC records on tape is in extended ASCII. There are two good reasons for this:

1. Extended ASCII is part of the communications standard;

2. There is no single definition for extended EBCDIC; there are at least two distinct versions of extended EBCDIC in common use.[4]

Use of extended EBCDIC for internal processing is generally transparent to the user; if your system can read ALA Extended ASCII, you needn't be concerned with the character set chosen for internal operations.

## Communications Transforms

USMARC is specifically designed as a tape communications format, and functions well in that role; certain systems may modify the structure of USMARC for online communications, without loss of information. One communications transform is used by RLIN to support the "PASS command," in which a record is passed from an RLIN terminal to some other system. The "PASS command" uses a transform for two reasons: the transform reduces the number of characters that must be transmitted, and it is simpler to convert the RLIN internal form into the "PASS" form than into extended MARC form. The "PASS" transform takes the content-carrying elements of the leader and attaches fields, beginning each field with its tag and ending each field with a field terminator. Figure 11.1 shows the record for *A Manual of AACR2 Examples Tagged and Coded Using the MARC Format* in "PASS" form. In this form, the record shrinks from 745 to 611 characters, a savings of 18%.

The "PASS" format is only useful for compressed communications. It lacks the validation capabilities built into USMARC, and would be much slower to process, but can be transformed back to USMARC form using a simple program. The Linked Systems Project, communicating MARC records directly from system to system, will not use a PASS-like format, but will transmit full MARC records. Does a PASS-like format represent a "more efficient" or "better" format than full USMARC for telecommunications? The Linked Systems Project designers didn't think so. In those cases where direct transmission of USMARC is sensible, transmission would typically involve small numbers of records at any given time. The 15%–20% overhead of full MARC appears to be minor in the overall scheme of telecommunications needs; the loss of error-checking and the need to restore full USMARC would appear to counterbalance any efficiency in transmission time.

### Figure 11.1 USMARC Transforms: PASS Format

```
Offset   Text
    0    namƀƀƀƀƀ001CRLG82-B33509◊00519821119081042.0◊00882
   50    1119s1982ƀƀƀƀmnuƀƀƀƀƀƀƀƀƀ00000ƀengƀd◊020ƀƀ‡a0936
  100    996137◊040ƀƀ‡aCU‡cCU◊10010‡aBlixrud, Julia C.,‡d19
  150    54-◊24512‡aA manual of AACR2 examples tagged and c
  200    oded using the MARC format /‡cby Julia C. Blixrud
  250    and Edward Swanson.◊2600ƀ‡aLake Crystal, Minn. :‡b
  300    Soldier Creek Press,‡c1982.◊300ƀƀ‡aiii, 116 p. ;‡c
  350    28 cm.◊500ƀƀ‡a"An adjunct to the series of manuals
  400     illustrating cataloging using the Anglo-American
  450    cataloging rules, second edition, prepared by the
  500    Minnesota AACR2 Trainers."◊650ƀ0‡aCataloging.◊7001
  550    0‡aSwanson, Edward,‡d1941-◊71020‡aMinnesota AACR2
  600    Trainers.◊‖
```

## Storage Transforms

USMARC as a structure is well suited to sequential processing; it is not as well suited to direct access, as in an online catalog. (USMARC as a format was never designed for direct online use and, in fact, was not designed for processing use at all.) Many online implementations transform USMARC data into a different structure which is better suited to direct access. In some cases, the data structure must suit the needs of a database management system; no known commercial database management system can handle USMARC directly. As with character set transforms, storage transforms are usually transparent to the user. A system will typically convert USMARC into its internal storage format when records are read, and convert records back to a USMARC structure for batch processing or communications.

## Content Designation Transforms

A system need not store USMARC records with three-digit tags. The BALLOTS II system at Stanford used mnemonics to identify each field, both in data entry and in the database itself. What USMARC calls the 100 field, BALLOTS II called "MEPN" for Main Entry Personal Name. BALLOTS II transformed the content designation of USMARC, reversing the transform when producing tapes. Quite a few library automation systems, including WLN, use mnemonics for entry and display of MARC variable fields; even more systems use mnemonics for entry and display of elements within the leader and variable control fields. Figure 11.2 shows a sound recordings 007 field as a field, and as two different sets of mnemonics: the first, the set designed for this book; the second, the

**Figure 11.2 MARC Transforms: Mnemonics for Coded Fields**

```
007    sd|bsmennmpln


Sound Recordings 007


GMD:s          SMD:d          Orig/Rep:|      Speed:b        Sound:s
Groove:m       Dimens:e       Width:n         Config:n       Kind:m
Material:p     Cutting:l      RepChar:n


Same information with mnemonics defined for this book


RMD:d  OR:|  SPD:b  SND:s  GRV:m  DIM:e  WID:n  TC:n  KD:m  KM:p  KC:l  RC:n


Same information with RLIN mnemonics
```

set used on RLIN, lacking the initial "s" which is supplied by the system. Systems can be implemented using mnemonics to define and store elements, or using them as aliases for entry and display; for instance, RLIN actually stores the 007 as a single field. Another possible transform uses dummy subfield codes to make single-character codes easier to recognize: OCLC uses this technique for field 007.

Mnemonics were more popular in the early years of MARC II, when many analysts felt that numeric MARC tags were too foreign for easy acceptance by librarians. Mnemonics were designed to ease the way into computer-supported systems, though some systems (specifically OCLC) implemented tags for data entry at an early stage. In the last few years, USMARC tags and subfields have become a common language; OCLC's success has contributed to this situation. The brevity and clarity of tags also helped make them known and used: "111" is easier to say and write than "Main Entry—Conference or Meeting Name," and "x11," when understood, is a particularly brief way of saying "Conference or Meeting Name in any use, including Main Entry, Subject, Series, or Other Added Entry."

## LEVELS OF MARC COMPATIBILITY

As emphasized above, not all "MARC-compatible" systems and formats are wholly compatible. There have been, and still are, systems and formats that claim MARC compatibility but cannot store and regenerate all USMARC records without some loss of information. Figure 11.3 lists a number of known and possible levels of MARC-compatible systems; some of these levels are purely theoretical, but most refer to real systems. The figure generally lists systems in order of decreasing desirability: Level I systems are more powerful and flexible than Level II systems, and so on. Within a given level, the arrangement is arbitrary. This arrangement of compatibility levels is suggested as a starting point for comparing those systems that are less than wholly compatible.

## LEVEL I: FULLY REVERSIBLE WITH MINOR RESTRICTIONS

Level I compatibility is full compatibility for most practical purposes. Most existing systems, including those of most major bibliographic services, fall into this category. Level I systems and formats can accept and store nearly all USMARC records and, as needed, regenerate those records without loss of content, content designation or structure. However, Level I systems may not be able to accept certain fields or records due to special characterstics of those fields or records; these restrictions are known and documented. If the restrictions are minor, the system is a Level I system, and is "MARC-compatible" in most practical senses.

### Type IA: Record Length Restrictions

A Type IA system can accept and reconstruct USMARC, as long as the record does not exceed a certain length. If Type IA is taken as a "very compatible" type, the shortest reasonable length limit is 2000 characters. In systems handling a wide variety of materials, anything less than 8000 characters will be too short for a significant number of records.

**Figure 11.3 MARC Systems: Levels of Compatibility**

```
LEVEL I       Fully reversible, record or field restrictions
    IA           Record length restrictions
    IB           Field length restrictions
    IC           Format restrictions
    ID           Miscellaneous restrictions
    ID1             Limits on character extension handling
    ID2             Limits on content extension
    ID3             Explicit record form restrictions
    ID4             Explicit field restrictions


LEVEL II      Outdated systems

LEVEL III     Proper subsets of USMARC
    IIIA         Character set subsets
    IIIB         Field subsets

LEVEL IV      Formats which can read but not restore USMARC
    IVA          Selective field retention
    IVB          Lack of output facilities
    IVC          Loss of internal content designation
    IVD          Loss of field specificity
    IVE          Extreme character set limitations
    IVF          Extreme record or field length limitations

LEVEL V       Incompatible systems and formats
```

LC MARC records average 800 characters or so; probably less than 1% of records distributed by LC are over 2000 characters. Addition of extensions for holdings and other local data can change this dramatically, as can the special nature of some formats. For instance, RLIN MARC records average 1200 characters, and about 2% are over 2000 characters; the average record in the RLIN Archival and Manuscripts Control implementation is over 3500 characters, and some records have had more than 16,000 characters.

Most commercial database systems impose a Type IA limitation; for systems popular in library automation, this limit can be as low as 3000 characters. Most bibliographic services have had, or continue to have, length limits. When BALLOTS was still used primarily by Stanford, the tape output program had a length limit of 2048 characters; RLIN II has a tape limit of 30,000 characters, but a smaller database limit of around 20,000 characters. Both OCLC and the Library of Congress have length limits on output records, though both are nearer to 10,000 characters.

**Type IB: Field Length Restrictions**

Some systems can handle long records, but have problems with long fields; such systems may be Type IB systems, depending on how long fields are handled. The Library of Congress has distributed at least two different USMARC records with contents notes (field 505) in excess of 1500 characters. Online systems can have problems with such fields, because the single field may run to more than one screen. One system with a field length restriction automatically splits longer fields into multiple occurrences of shorter fields. If the longer field is nonrepeatable, the shorter fields can be combined on output to eliminate any incompatibility.

A system that limits field length to 1500 characters will seldom have problems; if it handles those problems automatically, there is no real loss of compatibility. A system that limits fields to 500 characters is much less compatible. Intervention is required to handle what will be fairly frequent errors. A system that limits fields to anything less than about 300 characters is so restrictive that it should probably not be considered Type IB; such a system will reject or truncate so many fields that record-loading will always be problematic. Such a system is getting in the way of USMARC.

### Type IC: Format Restrictions

Does a local system handle USMARC perfectly, but not if the records are in the Maps format? That's a Type IC system. RLIN II never accommodated the Manuscripts format; WLN did not implement the Music format until January 1984. Some local systems can only handle Books, or Books and Serials, or some other combination. Format restrictions are quite reasonable under some circumstances. To the extent that USMARC formats become integrated, format restrictions should disappear.

### Type ID: Miscellaneous Restrictions

Some systems may impose other restrictions on USMARC records; as long as the restrictions are well defined, and do not significantly limit acceptability of USMARC records, the systems are still Level I systems, as they still provide full compatibility for most situations. A few of the possible restrictions:

1. *Character Extensions:* Few systems or formats are prepared to handle nonroman representations of text, such as Chinese, Japanese, Korean, Cyrillic, Hebrew or Arabic. USMARC now has standard methods for storing such text; the methods allow systems that can't handle the characters to discard them without damaging the rest of the record. If a system retains nonroman text without displaying it, the system may be considered fully compatible. If the system strips 880 and 066 fields and leading subfields ‡6s when data is loaded, the system is a Type ID system: records will be meaningful, but some records will lose data. If a system is simply unable to deal with records containing nonroman text, the system is in a lower category. Most probably, it is out of date.

2. *USMARC Extensions:* Some systems cannot store or handle the added fields defined in OCLC MARC or RLIN MARC. Such systems may be wholly USMARC compatible in a technical sense. However, a system that can't handle format extensions may not be able to play a full role in the emerging national complex of bibliographic interchange.

3. *Explicit Record Restrictions:* A system could restrict entry of certain forms of records, such as those not cataloged to *AACR2* standards, or those not showing complete descriptive cataloging. Some systems restrict record entry based on authority control, by deliberate design. It seems likely that any such restriction would be well known to a system's users, and might well be considered desirable.

4. *Explicit Field Restrictions:* A system might have deliberate restrictions on certain obscure fields; if such restrictions do not affect most records, do not affect usefulness, and are well known to users, the system may be considered a Type ID system.

A clear distinction should be made between Level I systems and lower level systems. As previously noted, most present-day systems fall into Level I, with some minor restrictions on field or record acceptability, and should be considered MARC-compatible. Lower-level systems pose greater problems; generally, any system below Level I should be considered partially compatible at best.

## LEVEL II: OUTDATED SYSTEMS

Many MARC-compatible systems and formats become outdated, as USMARC changes to meet new needs. Maintenance of format currency requires significant professional support, from library professionals and computer professionals. If a system is to maintain current compatibility, staff must be assigned to keep the system up to date. Major bibliographic services use the equivalent of at least one full-time highly skilled employee in maintaining USMARC formats. This full-time equivalent might be composed of continuing part-time work by two or more people who are responsible for USMARC updates, augmented by others who prepare and implement actual changes at quarterly intervals.

If a system is a year out of date, but the system developers are working on upgrades, it may still be workable, and may be restored to Level I; if a system is not being maintained at all, it will tend to drift down to lower levels of compatibility and usefulness with time, as more and more records are not handled properly or at all.

## LEVEL III: PROPER SUBSETS OF USMARC

Some formats can handle all or most USMARC records; these are Level I formats. Other systems and formats retain the content and content designation, but lose portions of quite a few records. They are called Level III systems. These systems can regenerate a USMARC record that will pass USMARC validity tests, but that may be missing known categories of information from the original record. A proper subset record will contain at least the core fields for any USMARC record accepted, retaining all standard ASCII characters and providing ASCII substitutions for extended alphabetic characters. Figure 11.4 shows the variable data fields for *The Brandenburg Concerti* as it might be stored in a Level III form. Fifteen of the original 32 fields have been eliminated, together with some important information, but the record is still useful and meets general USMARC standards.

**Figure 11.4 Sound Recordings Record, Minimal Level IIIB Equivalent**

```
040  ƀƀ  ‡aRPB‡cRPB‡dWaBeW
100  10  ‡aBach, Johann Sebastian,‡d1685-1750.
240  10  ‡aBrandenburgische Konzerte
245  14  ‡aThe Brandenburg concerti‡h[sound recording] / ‡cJohann
         Sebastian Bach.
260  0ƀ  ‡aWashington, D. C. :‡bSmithsonian Institution,‡cc1978‡e(New
         York :‡fColumbia Special Products).
300  ƀƀ  ‡a3 sound discs (97 min.) :‡b33 1/3 rpm ; ‡c12 in.
440  ƀ0  ‡aSmithsonian collection of recordings
500  ƀƀ  ‡aTitle on container: The six Brandenburg concerti.
500  ƀƀ  ‡a"Performed and recorded on original instruments for the
         first time in America."
500  ƀƀ  ‡aThe concerti "occupy five sides of the three discs in this
         set...The sixth side ... is blank, save for a spiral groove
         designed to protect your turntable."
500  ƀƀ  ‡aManual sequence.
500  ƀƀ  ‡aProgram notes by Albert Fuller ([12] p. : ill. ; 30 cm.) and
          notes on the recordings by James Morris ([1] p. ; 26 cm.) laid
          in container.
650  ƀ0  ‡aConcerti grossi.
700  11  ‡aFuller, Albert.‡4prf
710  21  ‡aAston Magna Foundation for Music.‡4prf
740  40  ‡aThe six Brandenburg concerti.
```

## Type IIIA: Character Set Subsets

Most USMARC records do not have any diacritics or special characters, and most library processes do not require such characters, even if present. Type IIIA systems usually discard diacritics; special characters can be handled one of two ways. Well-designed Type IIIA systems translate special characters to standard ASCII equivalents: a slashed O becomes a regular O, a superscript 2 becomes a regular 2. Poorly designed Type IIIA systems simply discard all characters outside of normal ASCII. If records containing special characters are fed into these systems, the results can be peculiar, because words may be missing letters.

Type IIIA systems are likely to be with us for some time. Many fully compatible systems use standard ASCII for display or listing, and most inexpensive display devices are restricted to standard ASCII. Libraries must determine how crucial storage of diacritics and special characters is for their future needs. For large research libraries and libraries with extensive non-English holdings, loss of extended characters may well be quite important; for other libraries, the loss may be unimportant. A system should at least prepare equivalents. "Kai Friis Moller" is understandable as a name, even with the slashed o replaced by a regular o. "Kai Friis Mller," the result of dropping the special characters, is useless for retrieval or alphabetic sorting, and is nearly useless for any purpose: how would a user know what letter was dropped between the "M" and the "l"?

## Type IIIB: Field Subsets

Quite a few systems can read USMARC records and can regenerate records in USMARC format, but can only store selected fields. If the selected fields constitute reasonably complete bibliographic records, these systems are Type IIIB: reversible with known losses. Some systems allow a library to make its own decisions regarding completeness. In this case, the system itself may be fully USMARC-compatible; the reduction to Type IIIB compatibility is at the library's option. Using the levels and types given here, a library could choose its own level, anywhere from full compatibility (all fields retained), through Type IIIB (all core fields retained), down to Type IVA (USMARC format, but with limited field retention). Some systems may allow for partial record retention for an online database with full retention offline; such systems can provide short-term efficiencies without reducing a library's long-term flexibility.

## LEVEL IV: CONVERTIBILITY

A format is convertible from another format if it is possible to convert records from the second format to the first by program, but not to reverse the process without loss of information. Convertibility may also be called unidirectional compatibility. Technically, Level III systems are convertible rather than fully compatible. The distinction between Level III and Level IV is in a system's ability to restore a record to correct USMARC format and substantially complete content. In the past, many systems called "MARC-compatible" have actually offered convertibility. Unidirectional compatibility is the most unclear area of USMARC compatibility, and the area most open to abuse.

Some Level IV systems can produce records that are in USMARC format, but that lack some content or content designation. Other Level IV systems, probably the majority of systems called "MARC-compatible," can accept USMARC as input, but make no effort to generate it as output. A Level IV system must be able to accept pure USMARC records in machine-readable form, through some communications medium, and should generally be able to accept extended USMARC records as well. Otherwise, the system is simply not MARC-compatible, and belongs at Level V. Typical Level IV systems include circulation systems and some online catalogs. A number of Level IV types may exist, and existing systems are likely to fall into more than one type; the examples given here are by no means exhaustive.

### Type IVA: Selective Field Retention

Bibliographic records can be compact or lengthy, depending partly on what fields are used; if a circulation system only uses the 1XX, 245‡a and 260 ‡c, why should the system store all the other fields? Figure 11.5 shows the record for the *Brandenburg Concerti,* also used in Figure 11.4, transformed to a minimal Level IVA version. This record saves an enormous amount of storage; even with USMARC overhead, it would run to around 110 characters, rather than the 1500 or more characters of the original. The record doesn't distinguish the version clearly, as there were quite a few *Brandenburg Concerti* recordings in 1978, but it does identify the item in a rudimentary way (although, without access to the legend, this record could even be for printed music rather than for a recording). Most selective field retention is less extreme. A library could eliminate most 0XX fields (except for call numbers, LCCN and standard numbers) without damaging bibliographic access in most situations. A system might suppress most notes and all linking entries and still retain fairly complete information.

**Figure 11.5 Sound Recordings Record: Level IVA Version**

```
100 10 Bach, Johann Sebastian
245 14 The Brandenburg concerti
260 0ҍ  ǂc1978
```

### Type IVB: Lack of Output Facilities

Many library systems are not designed to generate machine-readable records for use by any other system. Such systems could store USMARC records in a manner that would allow regeneration but would be unable to carry out the regeneration. If a system lacks machine-readable output facilities but stores data in a fully compatible manner, it can be upgraded to full USMARC compatibility with a small development effort. Most systems that lack machine-readable output facilities also change USMARC data on input, for a variety of reasons.

### Type IVC: Loss of Internal Content Designation

Some systems retain most content from USMARC records, but eliminate indicators and subfield codes as overhead. Such systems retain full information for searching or display, and may seem to be fully compatible. Problems may arise when libraries attempt to add other functions, because of reduced flexibility of record use and machine manipulation. This reduced flexibility is not matched by a savings in storage. There are savings (no more than 5% to 10%), but they are not sufficient to balance the loss of specificity. In fact, systems that discard internal content designation are likely to do so for reasons other than storage, such as difficulty in suppressing subfield codes on display. The problem is that the information is lost forever. A well-designed library automation system can suppress subfield codes on display with little trouble; once the subfield codes are gone, they cannot be restored.

### Type IVD: Loss of Field Specificity

The next step after dropping subfield codes is dropping field specificity. A typical record includes author, title, imprint and notes: a system could store all this in four fields. Going a bit further, a system could store a record as Main Entry, Imprint and Notes: three fields in all. Such a scheme simplifies data handling and may well work better with a database management system, but it has all the disadvantages noted above, and more. Collapsed fields compromise access as well as flexibility; acceptance of a Type IVD system severely limits future use of a database.

**Type IVE: Extreme Character Set Limitations**

A good case can be made for translating USMARC records from ALA Extended ASCII to standard ASCII, using character conversions. When a character set is even smaller than standard ASCII, the damage to the data is much greater. A typical Type IVE system stores all information as upper-case letters, numbers and punctuation; such systems are also likely to drop subfield codes and are unlikely to be up-to-date on USMARC changes. Early library automation systems were frequently limited to upper case characters by the equipment available at the time. To the extent that such systems survive today, they may be warmly regarded as library history, but should be shunned as library practice.

**Type IVF: Extreme Data Limitations**

It is one thing for a system to limit fields to a maximum length of 1000 characters; it is quite another to limit authors to 50 characters, titles to 40 characters, and publishers to five characters. A system with such extreme data limitations could not reconstruct records with any true semblance of USMARC quality. The emergence of powerful and inexpensive microcomputers probably heralds a temporary re-emergence of such extremely limited systems, because microcomputers have tended to be short of storage space. For larger systems, storage space is a diminishing cost, leaving little justification for extreme truncations of data fields.

## LEVEL V: INCOMPATIBILITY

There have been cases where a system or format was called MARC-compatible even though it could neither accept USMARC records nor generate USMARC records. At best, these systems represent marketing ploys or mistakes. A system or format is incompatible with USMARC if records in either format cannot be algorithmically converted into the other format in any useful manner. If a system uses MARC tags or something resembling MARC tags but can neither accept USMARC input in machine-readable form nor generate USMARC output in machine-readable form, it may well be "MARC-like," but is simply not MARC-compatible.[5]

## THE CASE FOR PARTIAL COMPATIBILITY

Complete bibliographic records are longer than they need to be for many applications. Full USMARC records are even longer than complete bibliographic records. Portions of USMARC records would never be displayed for public services or most technical processing, and USMARC content designation carries sophistication that is not needed for many processes. Long records require more storage than short records; complex records require more sophisticated programming than simple records. Storage costs money, programming costs money, and complex programs sometimes run slower than simple programs.

Money and time are the primary justifications for lower-level compatibility. During the first year of operation, a well-designed system that stores only those data elements needed for the application, and that eliminates most content designation, will almost certainly be cheaper than a similarly well-designed system that maintains full USMARC compatibility. If a system is being custom-built by programmer/analysts who have not done complex MARC processing, the system will probably be operational sooner if the designers are allowed to reduce USMARC to a format with which they are familiar. Money and time argue against full USMARC compatibility.

Many existing systems were designed when full USMARC compatibility was considered unrealistic. Such systems continue to function, and the lack of full USMARC compatibility does not make them useless or obsolete. If a local system maintains full USMARC in offline files, reflecting the current state of the bibliographic records, there is no good reason why a specific online system should carry full USMARC records. The records can always be retrieved from offline storage for any new function or change in needs, while the online system can operate with smaller storage and simpler programs.[6]

## THE CASE AGAINST PARTIAL COMPATIBILITY

The needs of a library change, and the desires and expectations of library users change. Costs of storage and computers also change, and the changes are in different directions. Needs, desires and expectations almost always rise, while storage and computing costs have fallen rapidly for quite a few years.

The compact record that suits today's circulation system will restrict access in tomorrow's online catalog; the moderately complete record that provides access in tomorrow's online catalog may restrict a library's capacity to offer sophisticated special retrieval or listings in the years to come. A short-term savings of lower-level compatibility may be paid for by long-term lack of flexibility. People who deal with full MARC become aware of the two fundamental rules of USMARC compatibility:

1. You don't need to process or display all the information just because it's there.

2. Once you discard information, don't expect to restore it. When it's gone, it's gone.

## NOTES AND REFERENCES

1. Crawford, Walt. "Library Standards for Data Structures and Element Identification: U.S. MARC in Theory and Practice." *Library Trends.* 23(4): 265–281; 1982 Fall. This chapter is loosely based on pages 273–277.

2. Tapes consist of physical blocks separated by inter-record gaps. The gaps are 0.5 inches for tapes written at 1600 characters per inch, and 0.3 inches for tapes written at 6250 characters per inch. In the latter case, any standard method of writing MARC records to tape uses almost as much tape for inter-record gaps as for records; smaller blocks mean that less information can be written to a single tape.

3. Two brief reports discussed use of Extended EBCDIC: "EBCDIC Bibliographic Character Sets— Sources and Uses: A Brief Report." *Journal of Library Automation.* 12(4): 380–83; 1979 December, and "Programmers Discussion Group Meets: PL/I, MARC, and Holdings." *Journal of Library Automation.* 14(3): 236–237; 1981 September.

4. "EBCDIC Bibliographic Character Sets . . .", op. cit.

5. Some library automation systems are not MARC-compatible and make no claims of compatibility. This discussion is not an attempt to belittle such systems. A system which is non-MARC and says so is at least on firm ground. Level V systems that are mislabeled, refers only to those systems that claim MARC compatibility but do not deliver it.

6. See Chapter 12 for a discussion of the dangers of relying on archival storage on magnetic tape, and for some notes on the possibilities of retrieving full records from partial records.

# 12

# Using MARC in the Library

So far, the discussion has centered on USMARC formats: their structure, how they work, what they include, how they were developed, and what may be meant by "MARC-compatible." This chapter works from the other direction: USMARC as a tool to meet library needs.

When a library uses MARC, it needs to consider three major areas, which usually involve dealing with vendors or other outside agencies:

1. *Acquiring USMARC records* from the Library of Congress, the major bibliographic services, agencies that provide USMARC as a byproduct or directly, or through retrospective conversion;

2. *Processing USMARC records* to maintain them for later use, and to provide needed services such as catalog cards, union lists and acquisitions products;

3. *Using USMARC in local systems,* either turnkey systems provided by an outside agent, locally developed systems, or local extensions to purchased systems.

The final area is outside the scope of this book; USMARC records can be used for any library automation that involves bibliographic materials, and for many which do not. However, processing services and local systems do have common aspects in terms of reading and maintaining MARC records, no matter what the source of the records or the purpose of the systems.

This chapter will discuss the acquisition and processing of MARC records, including problems that can arise and how to prevent and/or correct them.

## SOURCES OF USMARC

The Library of Congress provides subscriptions to various classes of USMARC records such as books, serials or films. LC's MARC Distribution Service offers large quantities of original cataloging, all done to a common set of guidelines, at a low price per record. Records from LC are a major source of cataloging for all the bibliographic services, most commercial agencies providing cataloging data, and a few large libraries. Most libraries will not find MARC Distribution Service to be the most appropriate source. The tapes include more records than most libraries need, do not include local data, and require a powerful processing system in order to extract needed records, add local data, and build a library's own database.

OCLC, RLIN, UTLAS and WLN provide millions of MARC records each year to thousands of libraries, and provide only the records that libraries have requested. The bibliographic services allow various levels of local data in the records, and give libraries access not only to LC cataloging but to contributed cataloging from many other libraries. Records from bibliographic services cost more per record than MARC Distribution Service subscriptions, but are more likely to meet a library's needs. Each bibliographic service also provides many of the processing services needed by libraries, including catalog cards and various other products.

Other agencies including commercial vendors provide USMARC records in various ways. One company sells a microcomputer-based local cataloging and card-production system that includes LC MARC on hundreds of diskettes. Several book vendors offer to provide cataloging along with the books, in card form or as MARC records; such vendors may be useful for smaller libraries. Some of the cooperative library agencies, including some of the networks that broker OCLC services, provide additional sources of USMARC records or record processing.

## RETROSPECTIVE CONVERSION

When a library converts to an online public catalog or any catalog based on machine-readable files, library users and staff may be confronted by a split collection: materials cataloged in the last few years are in the online catalog, but older materials are not. Studies of online catalog use show that most people don't go past the first catalog; if something isn't in that catalog, it may as well not be in the library. Consider your own habits in using a library; most of us spend as little time at a card catalog as we possibly can. A split catalog and people's natural tendency to stop after the first lookup result in loss of access to much of the library's collection, including most serious literature and older works in the humanities. If weeding takes place based on use studies, valuable material may be discarded because lack of access has resulted in low circulation.

The solution to this problem is retrospective conversion. In this case, "conversion" refers to the creation of machine-readable cataloging records by converting manual records such as catalog cards, and "retrospective" indicates that the process is only needed for older records. Current acquisitions are cataloged directly in machine-readable form.

Retrospective conversion can yield a complete online catalog, but it is neither simple nor inexpensive, and no single method is ideal for every library.

**Types of Retrospective Conversion**

Five major types of retrospective conversion appear to be in use in American libraries; while some conversion projects do not result in USMARC records, each of the five types can result in USMARC records.

1. *Online conversion using large source databases* is usually done using one of the major bibliographic services. Library staff take catalog cards and look for records that match, adding local holdings and call numbers when records are found. If no match is found, material will be converted to machine-readable form, possibly working to a lower than usual standard, since the material is usually not in hand. In some cases, libraries will enter unmatched records directly into their local system (as in type 4 or 5 below), rather than entering them into the major bibliographic service.

2. *Batch conversion using unique keys* may involve a commercial agency, a library network, or a bibliographic service: the library submits lists of keys in paper form or machine-readable form, and the service matches those lists against its database, returning matched records. In some cases, local holdings are submitted along with the keys, and added to the retrieved records. Unique keys can include LC Card Number, ISBN, ISSN or numbers assigned by an agency. Microcomputers have made batch conversion more feasible, by making it easy and relatively inexpensive for libraries to enter keys in machine-readable form. Unique-key batch conversion is typically done in combination with the next method, used where unique keys are not available.

3. *Batch conversion using author/title search* is similar to the method above, but it is used where no unique key is available or the key is ambiguous. The library prepares lists of brief entries and matching local data, on paper or in machine-readable form; the conversion agency attempts to match those entries, and returns records that are found. This method requires more keyboard work and may be more prone to error, but it does not require the additional searching that may be needed for unique-key conversion.

4. *Contract keying* has been used for years, with varying degrees of success. The library photoreproduces its catalog cards and ships the film to an agency; that agency has the catalog cards keyed into machine-readable form, and converts the text strings into USMARC. In some cases, fields and subfields are assigned during keying; in others, the agency attempts conversion by automatic format recognition (AFR) programs. Automatic format recognition has always been controversial. The University of California had a large project in the early 1970s using such techniques; there have been many others, and some libraries are still using such techniques. Some of the largest retrospective conversion projects use AFR techniques.

Ideally, AFR combined with special symbols during keying can result in MARC records that are usable without later editing and that can be upgraded to full MARC with minor editing. The ideal is rarely achieved; given the complexity of a full catalog card and the sophistication of USMARC content designation, AFR is generally only partially successful. Some contract conversion operations use less sophisticated means, including overseas keying and nominal conversion routines. The resulting records may be adequate for circulation systems, but are unlikely to be anywhere close to full MARC. At worst, this method of conversion can yield records that cost more to edit than a library would have spent on online conversion with full cataloging for records not found. Those planning retrospective conversion should be aware that the worst case is not unknown in the history of library automation.

The problems with contract keying and AFR may also affect batch conversion, if the database used was partly or wholly created by AFR techniques. One technique that can be used in an attempt to make AFR more workable, and to cut costs, is to scrap portions of the catalog card. However, while the resulting records may well be useful for circulation systems and some other functions, they represent a degradation of the catalog in terms of intellectual content if not access, and must be viewed with considerable caution.

Some contract keying does not use AFR techniques or uses them with substantial editing; it is possible to achieve excellent results through such keying.

5. *Full local record entry in MARC form* is the final possibility. A library may choose to do local entry for records not found through batch processing, particularly if the library does not use a bibliographic service. If retrospective conversion is only for brief-record entry, full local entry may be useful for small and medium-sized libraries. If libraries are looking toward more extensive local systems requiring more extensive records, full local entry is likely to be too labor-intensive to be justified. As with contract keying, local record entry made more sense when bibliographic service databases were smaller; it may still make sense for specialized collections, where the likely percentage of found records will be small. Combinations of online or batch conversion from large databases and local record entry may well be cost effective, if the "large database" includes a high percentage of needed records.

### Solving Retrospective Conversion Problems

Retrospective conversion can involve small companies and new ones; the first few contracts may reveal fundamental difficulties in MARC software. A library should evaluate the results during a test phase, and attempt to solve problems if the vendor seems to be doing a good job otherwise. Structural errors should not happen with established vendors, but many structural errors can be corrected easily; the difficult aspects of retrospective conversion are content and content designation.

Some major retrospective conversion projects have deliberately omitted portions of catalog cards, thus eliminating content. Any omission of this sort should be established, and agreed to, in advance. If libraries are relying on source records that were converted in such a manner, they must be aware of the loss of information. Other conversions include all the content from catalog cards, but fail to designate the content properly; depending on the nature of the failures, this may be a minor nuisance or it may render the records useless.

A library must have experienced MARC users, preferably catalogers, available to evaluate the quality of conversion. A library must also establish its minimum standards, and determine how much postconversion editing it can afford to do. Retrospective conversion contracts are usually made on the basis of price, but the price of a conversion is not the cost of the conversion. If records are incomplete or scrambled, the cost of conversion in terms of required editing or lost information may be much higher than the direct price. A trial conversion may be the only way to evaluate the quality of an agency's work. This is true for list-matching agencies, where hit rate and quality of retrieved records are both important, and for record-conversion agencies, where accuracy of data entry and quality of content designation are critical.

Retrospective conversion is more likely to require significant compromise than any other source of USMARC records. The highest quality conversions are typically those with the highest direct price: online searching on a bibliographic service and entry of records not found. Such projects typically cost more and take longer in the short run, but over the long run they increase the quantity of shared cataloging available for other libraries and assure a desired level of record quality. For a library with extensive future plans for use of MARC records, the long-term costs of "expensive" conversion may well be less than those of "cheap" conversion. Postconversion editing is more expensive and time consuming than checking at time of entry, and postconversion editing is less likely to be needed if the conversion process is carefully planned.

## PROCESSING AND LOCAL USE

Once USMARC record sources are identified, the records must be processed and used. Vendors and processing agencies provide a number of processing services, including:

1. *Tape checking and maintenance:* OCLC MARC subscriptions and RLIN transaction tapes need to be checked promptly, and need to be refreshed periodically to be sure no deterioration has occurred. Some vendors provide such services, possibly combined with elimination of duplicates, for libraries that are building toward local systems;

2. *File maintenance:* Vendors who check and maintain tapes may also maintain MARC files. This involves sorting the records on the tapes into some predetermined order, then replacing records with newer versions as they appear. Some vendors also apply authority control to existing records, validating and updating bibliographic headings based on authority files;

3. *Conversion to other formats:* Some vendors convert USMARC tapes into formats required for local circulation systems or other systems, when those systems can't accept USMARC directly;

4. *Product generation:* A number of vendors prepare printed or microform products

from databases made up of MARC tapes submitted by a library. Such products can include full catalogs, lists of new holdings, and specialized access lists;

5. *Union list generation:* Vendors can combine tapes for several libraries into unified databases and products.

If a vendor, agency or local system is to make use of USMARC records, the tapes must be correct, and they must be processed correctly.

## PROBLEMS WITH MARC TAPES

Any supplier of USMARC records, whether commercial, bibliographic service, or the Library of Congress, will occasionally supply a bad tape. Tape problems fall into a number of distinct categories:

1. *Incorrect or blank tapes.* No agency can guarantee that every tape will be labeled and shipped correctly. While LC, shipping multiple copies of the same tape, is quite unlikely to ship incorrectly, bibliographic services that ship hundreds of different unique tapes each week or month will occasionally put the wrong tape in the wrong package. Any recipient of LC MARC Distribution Service tapes should read the tapes as soon as possible to verify that the tapes actually contain the data indicated in the accompanying list of record numbers; other tapes should also be verified as soon as possible. Bibliographic services may have time limits for replacing defective and incorrect tapes.

2. *Tapes with defective records.* Magnetic tape is a somewhat imperfect medium; flaws in the creation, shipping or reading process can yield one or more records unreadable.

3. *Incorrect records.* The chance of invalid MARC structure from LC or the bibliographic services is actually quite low; any such case would probably be caused by physical tape defects. Newer vendors may have problems that have not been identified or resolved, but such problems can usually be straightened out once they are apparent. Records from any source may sometimes have incorrect content designation or contents.

Records with incorrect contents may or may not be the supplier's problem. Bibliographic services are usually sending records directly requested by a library back to that library, and the service may not be responsible for data errors that are in the online record and faithfully reflected on the tape. LC records will occasionally have misspellings, incorrect subfields, or implausible choice of entry; no institution is perfect. Other USMARC vendors may present a different problem, particularly in a retrospective conversion project. If the cataloging received is consistently poorer than seems reasonable, the library needs to work with the vendor to clarify expectations; if poor-quality records continue, a library may have no choice but to terminate the contract and find another source.

4. *Misunderstandings.* Agencies receiving MARC Distribution Service tapes may expect that LC will implement all MARC format changes exactly on schedule, and that any current tape will contain cataloging that follows current interpretations. Neither expectation is based on LC assertion or on reality; LC's distribution of MARC format changes is based on the wider needs of the library community as well as its own needs. For instance,

field 005 (date/time stamp) was published quite a few months before LC intended to implement it; the field was more important for other creators of MARC records than for the Library of Congress.

Misunderstandings may also arise with bibliographic services when changes are made in tape format or content. It is the bibliographic service's responsibility to document its practices and identify the date when practices change, but it is the library's responsibility to read that documentation and pass it on to processing agencies. Misunderstandings with other vendors may arise through documentation problems, contractual problems, simple communication problems, or failure to perform. In every case, careful attention to the promises made and services actually received should avoid some problems and resolve others.

## READING MARC RECORDS

Whether you do your own processing or a vendor does it for you, the first step is to read the tapes; even if a vendor is archiving tapes for you until you're ready to use them, the vendor must read the records to assure proper maintenance of the tapes.

### Physical Structure

The physical structure of a MARC tape includes the number of tracks, the density of information expressed in bits per inch (BPI), the labeling, and the character set. Most USMARC tapes are nine track, though some suppliers may offer seven-track tapes as an alternative. Three tape densities are widely used: 800 BPI, 1600 BPI and 6250 BPI. Some USMARC suppliers offer libraries a choice of 800 BPI or 1600 BPI; others offer 1600 BPI or 6250 BPI, and some may offer all three. Higher densities are generally preferable, if processing vendors can handle them. 6250 BPI puts almost four times as much data on a reel of tape as 1600 BPI, and tapes written at 6250 BPI tend to be more reliable than those written at 1600 BPI. However, some processing agencies may not be able to read 6250 BPI tapes.

All standard MARC tapes use half-inch wide standard reels, and all standard MARC tapes have standard internal ANSI labels and are written in ALA Extended ASCII. Other tapes represent alternative transmissions, but may well be used in certain cases. Alternative labeling schemes include unlabeled tapes, IBM OS labels, and IBM DOS labels; the only alternative character set in wide use is EBCDIC (see Chapter 11). Any tape that doesn't have ANSI labels and isn't written in ASCII isn't a standard MARC tape. Tapes with no internal labels may be rejected by processing centers, because they pose serious handling problems.

### Logical Structure

Standard USMARC tapes come in two different logical structures, as discussed in Chapter 11. Some vendors may be unaware that two structures exist, and others may have a cloudy picture of what the two structures are. Computer processing agencies that have not previously handled MARC data will almost certainly not recognize either structure.

Special tapes may use other structures, particularly variable blocked or "VB," in which large variable-length physical records, up to 32,768 characters in length, carry as many complete logical (MARC) records as will fit. VB structures are not directly allowed for ANSI tapes, but can result in extremely efficient tape usage and machine processing. If your vendor or processing agency is aware that OCLC or RLIN records are unblocked spanned, the vendor is probably able to deal with long records; if the vendor can state the difference between LC and OCLC structures, the vendor can probably handle both. If a vendor is further willing to accept specially produced VB tapes, the library may have extra flexibility.

## Tape Checking and Reporting

You need to know what your vendor or processing center will do to make sure a MARC tape is valid and correct, particularly if the vendor is handling tapes for a library with no current local capabilities. Tapes do get mislabeled and can be damaged in shipping; without prompt checking, it may be difficult or impossible to replace a bad tape. Vendors should be willing to describe their checking procedures. The tape should at least be read and records should be counted, with the final count compared to the tape log. While such a process will show that the records are readable, and having the right number of records generally suggests that the correct tape is in hand, this process may not turn up minor tape problems. More thorough testing can include some or all of the following steps:

1. Counts should be kept by bibliographic format, as determined from the leader. In some cases, these counts will also be on the tape log. The length of each record should be stored, with a running total kept; some tape logs include a figure for total length. If the number of records and total length match the log, you can be almost certain that the log and the tape are for the same records.

2. The leader and directory of each record should be checked, to determine that the required constant characters are present in the leader, that the directory has only numbers in the fourth through twelfth positon of each entry, and that the directory ends with a field terminator at a position one less than the base address in the leader.

3. Each bibliographic record should contain an 001, an 008 and a 245 field. If 005 fields are present, the date ranges can be checked for reasonableness. Library identifiers, whether NUC codes or service-assigned codes, should be present in defined positions in the records, and can be checked to make sure that the right library's tape is in hand.

4. A more exhaustive scan can go through the directory field-by-field: for each field, the position pointed to by adding the base address, field offset and length of field, and subtracting one, should contain a field terminator. For each field except those with tags beginning "00," the position pointed to by adding the base address, field offset and two (that is, third position of the field) should contain a subfield delimiter. All tags beginning with a given character should appear together in the directory, and the first characters should be in ascending order according to ASCII sequence; letters, if any, come after numbers.

5. In the process of an exhaustive scan, the program might list the first and last record number or even a sampling of record numbers; these can also be checked against the tape log to assure receipt of the correct tape.

6. Conceivably, an initial check could also validate fields and subfields according to *MFBD* rules for existence and repeatability. Such elaborate validity checking is usually only appropriate when a vendor is building a database for a library, and is more appropriate when the records have been created in some unusual manner, for instance, by retrospective conversion.

7. Validity checking should not test to see that tags are in absolute ascending order: they need not be, and there may be good reasons why they are not. Testing to see that fields appear in the same order as in the directory is also improper. Except for the control fields, fields may appear anywhere within a record, without regard to the order of the directory.

The vendor or processing center should report back if errors are encountered, and this report should be timely and include specific information on the nature of the errors. Record suppliers may need this information, and may require that the defective tape be returned so that they can investigate the problem.

### Mixed Bibliographic Formats

A vendor that processes records may not be able to handle all formats. What does a vendor do with records that can't be handled? A vendor should be able to read tapes containing a mixture of bibliographic formats. If the vendor is processing your records into format-specific files, the reading process should route records to the correct files. Some vendors may be able to process CANMARC and other MARC formats in addition to USMARC. While you may not need such flexibility, a vendor's recognition of non-USMARC formats may also suggest a knowledgeable approach to USMARC.

### Handling MARC Extensions

You probably won't provide a vendor with pure USMARC tapes; almost all USMARC tapes for individual libraries contain extensions to MARC, defined by bibliographic services, vendors or the libraries themselves. Can the vendor handle the tapes you provide? If you change sources for records, will the vendor be able to handle the change? MARC extensions are more difficult for processing than for tape maintenance, but RLIN MARC may prove difficult even for tape maintenance, if a vendor's reading programs assume that all tags are numeric. There are vendors that make no distinction between USMARC and OCLC MARC. Such vendors will have great difficulty in handling any tapes other than those produced by OCLC.

If you're an OCLC user, you might not worry about a vendor that can only process OCLC MARC. This could be a mistake. Are you sure you'll always use OCLC, and that you'll never want to use MARC records from other sources such as retrospective conversion or union list projects? Are you willing to assume that OCLC will never add new extensions to OCLC MARC? (Certainly, RLG is likely to add more extensions to RLIN MARC; OCLC may well add new extensions to OCLC MARC.) This last question suggests one problem with vendors that are restricted to OCLC MARC: such restriction tends to imply specialized programs and limited MARC expertise. A vendor that only handles OCLC MARC may well be handling "OCLC MARC as we understood it when the programs were written," with processing getting more and more outdated as time goes on.

A vendor may deliberately restrict processing to OCLC tapes for business reasons, while showing clear evidence of familiarity with other MARC extensions. If the vendor is satisfactory on all other counts, this restriction may be reasonable. If a vendor is willing to handle other MARC extensions, how are they handled? Does the vendor maintain current awareness of practices of suppliers, or is the library expected to inform the vendor of changing needs? Either method can work, though the latter places a heavier load on the library.

A full-service vendor might be expected to handle OCLC MARC, RLIN MARC, UTLAS MARC, WLN MARC and LC Distribution Service tapes. If a vendor can handle that mix, chances are that the software is flexible enough to be able to add new extensions. Processing a mix of MARC extensions is moderately difficult and requires flexible software. Integrating a mix of extensions into a common database or list is even more difficult, but certainly not impossible. Vendors that can process multiple extensions into a common form without loss of information protect a library's future flexibility.

## Keeping Up with USMARC Changes

Changes in MARC affect a vendor's ability to read and process records. The mid-1980s are dynamic years for USMARC, with new material formats, analytics, holdings and new ways of thinking about MARC. The major bibliographic services have staff assigned to monitor and analyze changes in USMARC, so that changes can be implemented smoothly and rapidly. The *MARC Formats for Bibliographic Data* are updated quarterly, and changes should normally be implemented within three months of an update. (LC normally waits at least three months after publishing an update before distributing records which follow the update.) Will a vendor keep up with changes in USMARC? Will the vendor actively pursue such changes, or handle them passively as client libraries request them?

Tape maintenance programs and simple processing systems may go for years without requiring change. Agencies may be using programs written elsewhere, or written by programmers no longer available to do maintenance. Vendors may not have staff with the library and computer background needed to analyze changes in USMARC. If a vendor has internal MARC expertise, you can probably get the name of at least one staff expert. If there is some doubt as to a vendor's actual knowledge, a brief discussion with that expert should resolve your questions. One difficulty with this approach is that you need to know enough about MARC to ask the right questions; by the end of this book, you should be off to a good start.

Can you work with a vendor or agency that lacks USMARC expertise? Possibly so, if you can do your own analysis and the vendor will act on your suggestions. If you're rely-ing on bibliographic services to keep you up to date on USMARC, as most libraries do, you can't expect those services to help out your vendors on a regular basis; some services may be willing to provide consultation on a fee-for-service basis, but none of the bibliogra-phic services are in the business of supporting commercial vendors.

A vendor may assert that it maintains current MARC handling, even if it doesn't maintain internal expertise. You should satisfy yourself that the vendor is able to make good on that assertion. How did the vendor implement analytics? Has the vendor im-plemented analytics at all? If you mention Field 773 and Subfield ‡7, does the vendor re-spond intelligently?

Smaller vendors may rely on libraries to bring them up to date on MARC. If you're willing to take on this task, you should be sure that you can deal with the vendor on changes. Must you learn programming jargon to communicate with the vendor's program-mers, or will the vendor meet you halfway? Remember that the language of libraries is also a jargon, and the language of USMARC is an unusually extensive jargon.

To some people's thinking, "Biblish," the language of libraries, and "MARClish," the language of USMARC, are even more arcane than "computerese." Some dedicated library programmer/analysts have become versed in all three dialects; some librarians working with programmers or computers have also become multilingual in library and computer jargon. If you can work with such a person and agree on an appropriate dialect, MARC changes and updates will be easier to discuss.

The problem with this approach is that it is usually not needed. If a vendor has such people on staff, the vendor probably has enough internal MARC expertise to maintain cur-rent processing. Most probably, the "multilingual" staff members are directly involved in MARC changes.

## PROCESSING LIMITATIONS

You're satisfied that the vendor or agency can read the records you send, and that the vendor's view of USMARC will be kept up to date. If you're paying for processing in ad-dition to tape maintenance, you need to know more about MARC handling. Reading USMARC is less complicated than processing USMARC. The vendor may be able to read all your records but may have some limits on processing. Chapter 11 shows some of the limits that may be present. Ask vendors about their limitations; every known system (in-cluding the major bibliographic services) has limitations, and vendors should be able and willing to specify what their own limitations are.

### Record Length and Complexity

How many access points can a single record generate? Archival and Manuscripts Con-trol records may contain more than 100 added entries; some sound recordings and other records may generate 50 or more entries. Can a system handle that many index points for a single record? Can it generate proper displays, with needed page breaks? Can it even store long records?

USMARC records are deliberately limited in complexity; subrecords and other multilevel structures have never been approved in USMARC, though they are used in UKMARC, INTERMARC, and other non-US MARC formats. Linking techniques as described in Chapter 8 do require special processing. Could your vendor handle them? Holdings information is the key to control of local collections. Can your vendor support OCLC or RLIN holdings data? When the USMARC Holdings format is approved, will your vendor support it? Would you ever actually attempt to enter serials holdings at the issue level and expect to have the holdings automatically compressed to the volume level?

### Other Limitations

A new vendor or agency, particularly a college computer center or city data processing department, may have problems with the Subfield delimiter and Field terminator, and with the extended characters. Any vendor that has successfully processed any MARC records will have resolved the delimiter and terminator problems, and most will have addressed the extended character situation.

Every known vendor, including the bibliographic services, has some presentation limits. The most common presentation limit involves extended characters. If a vendor translates extended characters in such a way that the product is meaningful, a limited character set may be acceptable and possibly even preferable. If a vendor simply ignores characters that cannot be printed, you will lose important information in many non-English records and a few English-language items as well.

You should understand the vendor's limits, and consider them in light of your needs, comparative pricing, and alternative sources. If you're doing a microfiche catalog, and 1% or 2% of your records have diacritics, look at the legibility and price of fiche with full diacritics before you insist that your vendor provide them. Fiche with diacritics are certainly available, but the benefits of diacritics may not outweigh the cost and diminished readability.

### Unrecognized and Unused Data

A vendor that is building a database from your records may not include everything that is in the records. Acquisitions information isn't relevant for a union list, and coded fields are rarely relevant for a batch product of any sort. You may also provide data that the vendor can't deal with, either because it is outside the vendor's scope or because your record supplier has added elements that the vendor doesn't know about yet. What does the vendor do with such data? Is it all stored and maintained, is it listed out as error reports, or is it just discarded? If you're satisfied with your current processing, you may not care; if you expect to add new functions later on, you'll want to be able to use the data. You should always remember: once data are lost, they are expensive or impossible to replace.

## Maintenance

Every vendor that accepts your MARC tapes is doing some form of record maintenance. Tape maintenance vendors do so directly; other processing agencies maintain records indirectly. You may be assuming more maintenance than a vendor expects to provide. If so, you may have problems when your library adds new functions or integrates old ones. "Maintenance" here means safeguarding records as received; records sent to a vendor in 1980 should be useful in 1986 when you bring up an online catalog. Vendors may take a more active role, eliminating duplicate records or even upgrading records through authority control, but maintenance of existing data is a fundamental requirement.

Will a vendor retain all the data you supply? More to the point, will the vendor retain all the data in the most current version of each record? When a vendor is creating a fiche catalog, the vendor may not be retaining data irrelevant to that catalog. You should never assume that a vendor is providing full data maintenance; any such requirement should be explicitly stated in writing. You need full retention if you're planning for the future. USMARC is a foundation for successful library automation; the integrated systems of the future will rely even more heavily on the versatility of USMARC.

If your full records are only on tape, as is usually the case, you should know how often the tapes are checked or rewritten. Tape is a useful but imperfect medium. Tape does age, both physically and electrically; old tapes that have never been refreshed are likely to be useless. The simple act of mounting a tape and winding it at high speed helps to maintain the tape's usefulness. Your archival tapes should probably be refreshed—checked or copied—at least twice a year; quarterly refreshing is even better.

Is the vendor building a database on disk? If so, how often is the disk backed up to tape? Has the vendor attempted to restore a disk from the tape backup? Magnetic disks are extremely reliable, but do fail; such failures can be catastrophic. Disks can be backed up in two ways: on duplicate disk, or on tape. A full set of duplicate disks can be maintained; this is the best, but most expensive, form of backup. Agencies that use this form are also likely to use tape backup. Tape backup copies all or portions of the database to magnetic tape on a regular basis, typically weekly. Daily transactions are also backed up, so that a faulty disk can be recreated from some combination of tapes. Backup methods need testing; there have been cases, not necessarily in library automation, where backups were done regularly, but files could not be recovered from the backups.

Security involves two other issues. Is the library's data protected against electronic intrusion and destructon? A surprising number of sociopaths have taken to breaking into computer systems; such intrusions can cause irreparable damage to existing files. A careful vendor will always have copies of your data in a form not accessible by telecommunications and may well have backup copies in remote storage, to protect against physical disasters.

A more sensitive security issue is business failure. What happens to your data if the vendor goes out of business? Do you have written safeguards to assure that your data, and the information necessary to process that data, will be available to you in case of bankruptcy or default? This last issue has nothing to do with USMARC as such, but is an extreme example of the need to be sure that your data are there when you need them.

## USING MARC

The measures noted above are designed to assure that your records are ready for use when your library is ready to use them. Whether you use a turnkey computer system, do your own programming, or use some mixture of the two, your future library automation plans should be based on USMARC.

USMARC provides a common reference, a standard, a vocabularly. The data storage format allows for fast and flexible processing, while the common content designators allow you to use cataloging done by others and modify the records to serve your own needs. USMARC isn't ideal for online storage, and full USMARC is overkill for many library operations. However, maintenance of full USMARC as a background activity preserves your options. Computers and storage are getting faster and less expensive, and users are becoming more sophisticated and more demanding. Where today's systems may not take advantage of USMARC's richness, tomorrow's systems are more likely to do so.

Even if you never actually see a tape reel of USMARC records, your library is likely to benefit from USMARC, now and in the future. Your awareness of the format and its implications help you to work with that future. In 1975, Henriette Avram expressed a number of hopes for the future; those hopes have been realized to a great extent, and should be realized more in the future. The full citation appears in Chapter 9, at the end of the brief history of early MARC; it all boils down to Mrs. Avram's final sentence, the real reason for USMARC:

Service to the user will be improved and that is really what MARC is all about.[1]

## NOTES AND REFERENCES

1. Henriette D. Avram. *MARC, Its History and Implications.* Washington, DC: Library of Congress; 1975: 31–32.

# Appendix A

# USMARC: Underlying Principles

On October 29, 1982, MARBI and the USMARC advisory group approved *The USMARC Formats: Underlying Principles.* While these principles change nothing in the formats, they establish a framework for considering change and explain some principles used in building USMARC. The document appears here in full, interspersed with annotations.

## UNDERLYING PRINCIPLES: PREFACE

The following statement of underlying principles for content designation in the USMARC formats was approved on October 29, 1982, by the American Library Association's RTSD/LITA/RASD Committee on the Representation in Machine-Readable Form of Bibliographic Information (MARBI), in consultation with representatives from the national libraries and bibliographic networks. This statement is intended to reflect those principles which account for the current state of the USMARC formats and to constitute a provisional set of working principles for further format development. The statement will be included as prefatory material in *MARC Formats for Bibliographic Data* and *Authorities: A MARC Format* and will be revised as necessary in the future.

The key statement in the Preface is "provisional set of working principles for further format development." This means that the *Underlying Principles* can serve as a filter for proposed changes. Those changes that do not follow the existing principles can be identified. If there is sufficient reason to violate the existing principles, the principles must be revised. For the first time, a written set of guidelines is available to use in considering format revision.

## SECTION 1. INTRODUCTION

1.1. The USMARC Formats are standards for the representation of bibliographic and authority information in machine-readable form.

1.2. A MARC record involves three elements: (1) the record *structure,* (2) the *content designation,* and (3) the data *content* of the record.

1.2.1. The structure of USMARC records is an implementation of the *American National Standard for Information Interchange on Magnetic Tape* (ANSI Z39.2-1979) and of *Documentation—Format for Bibliographic Information Interchange on Magnetic Tape* (ISO 2709-1981).

1.2.2. Content designation—the codes and conventions established explicitly to identify and further characterize the data elements within a record and to support the manipulaton of that data—is defined in the USMARC Formats.

1.2.3. The content of those data elements which comprise a traditional catalog record is defined by standards outside the formats—such as the *Anglo-American Cataloguing Rules* or the *National Library of Medicine Classification*. The content of other data elements—coded data (see Section 9. below)—is defined in the USMARC Formats.

1.3. A MARC format is a set of codes and content designators defined for encoding a particular type of machine-readable record.

1.3.1. At present, USMARC formats have been defined for two distinct types of records. *MARC Formats for Bibliographic Data* contains format specifications for encoding data elements needed to describe, retrieve, and control various types of bibliographic material. *Authorities: A MARC Format* contains format specifications for encoding data elements which identify or control the content and content designation of those portions of a bibliographic record which may be subject to authority control.

1.3.2. The *MARC Formats for Bibliographic Data* are a family of formats defined for the identification and description of different types of bibliographic material. USMARC Bibliographic formats have been defined for Books, Films, Machine-Readable Data Files, Manuscripts, Maps, Music and Serials.

1.3.3. The USMARC Formats have attempted to preserve consistency of content designation across formats where this is appropriate. As the formats proliferated and became more complex, however, definitions and usages have diverged. While complete consistency has not been achieved, a continuing effort is being made to promote consistent definition and usage across formats.

The introduction neatly separates content designation from content. USMARC deals with content definition, but only for coded elements and other elements outside the scope of traditional cataloging. A USMARC record contains the contents of a cataloging record, but USMARC itself does not define those contents.

The final paragraph attempts to strike a balance between theory and practice. This is always an uneasy balance in USMARC, and has grown more sensitive as use of USMARC has flourished. If a change to the formats will increase consistency but would require that OCLC change 100,000 records or that RLIN change 50,000 records, there are strong reasons to oppose the change. Those who work on the formats are frequently engaged in compromise between theoretical consistency and the value of existing records.

## SECTION 2. GENERAL CONSIDERATIONS

2.1. The USMARC Formats are communications formats, primarily designed to provide specifications for the exchange of records between systems. The communications formats do not mandate the internal formats to be used by individual systems, either for storage or display.

2.2. The USMARC Formats were designed to facilitate the exchange of information on magnetic tape. In addition, they have been widely adapted for use in a variety of exchange and processing environments.

These sections establish two important concepts: that USMARC does not mandate processing formats, and that USMARC is widely used for processing. The last sentence of the second paragraph is a key recognition of USMARC as a processing format, the first such recognition to appear in the published formats. Most online systems do not use USMARC structure, though they may use USMARC content designation. Many batch systems use all of USMARC, content designation and structure.

2.3. The USMARC Formats are designed for use within the United States. An attempt has been made to preserve compatibility with other national formats. Lack of international agreement on cataloging codes and practices has made complete compatibility impossible, however.

2.4. The USMARC Formats serve as a vehicle for bibliographic and authority data of all types, from all agencies. Historically and practically, the formats have always had a close relationship to the needs and the practices of the library community. In particular, the formats reflect the various cataloging codes applied by American libraries.

The first paragraph simply recognizes the impossibility of maintaining international compatibility within a national format. The second states, correctly, that the formats reflect library cataloging rules, but also explicitly says that the formats can serve to carry bibliographic data of all types, from all agencies. USMARC has been moving away from a strict mirroring of a single set of cataloging rules.

2.5. Historically, the USMARC Formats were developed to enable the Library of Congress to communicate its catalog records to other institutions. National agencies in the United States and Canada . . . are still given special emphasis in the formats, as sources of authoritative cataloging and as agencies responsible for certain data elements.

This paragraph says, in effect, that there is a legitimate historical basis for institutional bias (sometimes called "LC-centrism"). While institutional bias is generally disappearing from USMARC, the second sentence explicitly recognizes the continuing validity of special status for national agencies such as the Library of Congress and National Library of Medicine.

2.6. The institutions responsible for the content, content designation and transcription accuracy of data within a USMARC record are identified at the record level, in field 008, byte 39, and in field 040. This responsibility may be evaluated in terms of the following rule.

## The Responsible Parties Rule

2.6.1. Responsible Parties Rule.

(a) Unmodified records: The institution identified as the transcribing institution (field 040 ‡c) should be considered responsible for content designation and transcription accuracy for all data. Except for agency-assigned data (see Section 2.6.2.1 below), the institution identified as the cataloging institution (field 040 ‡a) should be considered responsible for content.

(b) Modified records: Institutions identified as transcribing or modifying institutions (field 040 ‡c,d) should be considered collectively responsible for content designation and transcription accuracy. Except for agency-assigned and authoritative-agency data (see Section 2.6.2 below), institutions identified as modifying or cataloging institutions (field 040 ‡a,d) should be considered collectively responsible for content.

2.6.2. Exceptions.

2.6.2.1. Certain data elements are defined in the USMARC formats as being exclusively assigned by particular agencies (for example, International Standard Serial Number, Library of Congress Card Number). The content of such *agency-assigned* elements is always the responsibility of the agency.

2.6.2.2. Certain data elements have been defined in the USMARC Formats in relation to one or more *authoritative agencies* which maintain the lists or rules upon which the data are based. Where it is possible for other agencies to create similar or identical values for these data elements, content designation is provided to distinguish between values actually assigned by the authoritative agency and values assigned by other agencies. In the former case, responsibility for content rests with the authoritative agency. In the latter case, the Responsible Parties Rule applies, and no further identification of source of data is provided. Authoritative-agency fields are:

050 Library of Congress Call Number
060 National Library of Medicine Call Number
082 Dewey Decimal Classification Number
    [DDC is maintained by the Library of Congress]

Section 2.6 is perhaps the most important new principle in the *Underlying Principles*. More than any other statement, the Responsible Parties Rule moved the formats from LC MARC to USMARC. It came after various proposals to show the source of each data element at the field level, or otherwise make it easier for a using library to tell who was responsible for a record's contents. MARBI was generally opposed to the idea of field-level source identification. The bibliographic services, which would have to support the record-keeping, were (in general) vehemently opposed. Some statement was required, which would identify those responsible for a record without overloading the record itself. Such a statement would be intended as a limit to source identification, with any exceptions specifically treated as such.[1]

The *Responsible Parties Rule* fills this need succinctly and thoroughly. It also indirectly addresses another need: opening the MARC formats for general use. Through 1982, and even into 1983, only a national agency could create a complete MARC record. Only a national agency could create a classification number, and only a national agency could assign subject headings (other than local headings). The two largest bibliographic services had users who skirted the latter rule; both were aware of the situation. Both services supported moves to open subject headings for general use; since both services rely on shared cataloging as a basis of operations, this is only natural.

2.7. In general, the USMARC Formats provide content designation only for data which is applicable to all copies of the bibliographic entity described.

2.7.1. Information which applies only to some copies (or even to a single copy) of a title may nevertheless be of interest beyond the institutions holding such copies. The USMARC Formats provide limited content designation for the encoding of such information and for indentifying the holding institutions (see, for example, subfield ‡5 in the 7XX fields).

2.7.2. Information which does not apply to all copies of a title, and is not of interest to other institutions, is coded in local fields (such as field 590).

2.8. Although a MARC record is usually autonomous, data elements have been provided which may be used to link related records. These linkages may be implicit, through identical access points in each record, or explicit, through a linking field. Linking fields (76X-78X) may contain either selected data elements which identify the related item or a control number which identifies the related record. An explicit code in the Leader identifies a record which is linked to another record through a control number.

Aspects of the Archival and Manuscripts Control Format make Section 2.7.1 somewhat questionable. The proposed Holdings format makes Section 2.7.1 even more questionable, and suggests that a different categorization of data elements is needed. Work on such a categorization has already begun; these sections of the *Underlying Principles* are likely to change.

## SECTION 3. STRUCTURAL FEATURES

3.1. The USMARC Formats are an implementation of the *American National Standard for Information Interchange on Magnetic Tape* (ANSI Z39.2-1979). They also incorporate other relevant ANSI standards, such as *Magnetic Tape Labels and File Structure for Information Interchange* (ANSI X3.27-1978).

3.2. All information in a MARC record is stored in character form. USMARC communication records are coded in Extended ASCII, as defined in Appendix III.B of *MARC Formats for Bibliographic Data.*

Only Extended ASCII characters are valid for communication of USMARC, but no such requirement exists for "MARC records" as a generic term. Character-form storage is a more fundamental requirement than is Extended ASCII. Most of the major processing systems using USMARC formats for processing use extended versions of IBM's EBCDIC (Extended Binary Coded Decimal Interchange Code); all, however, translate to Extended ASCII for communication.

3.3. The length of each variable field can be determined either from the "length of field" element in the directory entry or from the occurrence of the "field terminator" character [1E hex, 8-bit; 36 octal, 6-bit]. Likewise, the length of a record can be determined either from the "logical record length" element in the Leader or from the occurrence of the "record terminator" character [1D hex, 8-bit; 35 octal, 6-bit]. (In the past, the field terminator of the last field was omitted, and the record terminator identified the end of that field.) The location of each variable field is explicitly stated in the "starting character position" element in its directory entry.

## SECTION 4. CONTENT DESIGNATION

4.1. The goal of content designation is to identify and characterize the data elements which comprise a MARC record with sufficient precision to support manipulaton for a variety of functions.

4.2. For example, MARC content designation is designed to support such functions as:

(1) Display—the formatting of data for display on a CRT, for printing on 3 x 5 cards or in book catalogs, for production of COM catalogs, or for other visual presentation of the data.

(2) Information retrieval—the identification, categorization, and retrieval of any identifiable data element in a record.

4.3. Some fields serve multiple functions. For example, field 245 serves both as the bibliographic transcription of the title and statement of responsibility and as the access point for the title.

Early use of LC MARC went further in this direction; an indicator in the 1XX (main entry) field could specify that the main entry was also a subject—and, thus, should be traced and have a subject entry. This usage is now rare, though still recognized as valid.

4.4. The USMARC Formats provide for display constants (text which implicitly accompanies particular content designators). For example, subfield ‡x in field 490 (and in some other fields) implies the display constant "ISSN," and the combination of tag 780 and second indicator value "3" implies the display constant "Superseded in part by:". Such display constants are not carried in the data, but may be supplied for display by the processing system.

The provision and definition of display constants makes USMARC a relatively compact format in some cases. Quite a few fields have display constants, controlled in some cases by indicators. A specific processing system can define its own additional display constants or alternative display constants, but those defined in *MFBD* are most commonly used.

4.5. The USMARC Formats support the sorting of data only to a limited extent. In general, sorting must be accomplished through the application of external algorithms to the data.

Some fields have indicator values specifying a number of characters to be ignored in sorting (initial article length); title subfields do not have such values, however. Some bibliographic services and other processing systems have allowed use of special text to provide for better sorting. The most common method is the "triple backslash" technique. In this technique, text which prints differently than it sorts is handled by keying a "\" followed by the printing form, followed by a "\" followed by the sorting form, followed by a final "\". Thus, "Henry VIII" might be coded as "‡aHenry \VIII\EIGHTH\". Technically, this technique is improper in USMARC records. If a backslash is encountered in USMARC (other than in local fields), a fair presumption may exist that the technique is being used.

## SECTION 5. ORGANIZATION OF THE RECORD

5.1. A MARC record consists of three main sections: (1) the Leader, (2) the Directory, and (3) the Variable Fields.

5.2. The *Leader* consists of data elements which contain coded values and are identified by relative character position. Data elements in the Leader define parameters for processing the record. The Leader is fixed in length (24 characters) and occurs at the beginning of each MARC record.

5.3. The *Directory* contains the field identifier ("tag"), starting location and length of each field within the record. Directory entries for variable control fields appear first, in tag order. Entries for variable data fields follow, arranged in ascending order according to the first character of the tag. The order of fields in the record does not necessarily correspond to the order of directory entries. Duplicate tags are distinguished only by location of the respective fields within the record. The length of the directory entry is defined in the Entry Map elements in the Leader. In the USMARC Formats, the length of the directory entry is 12 characters. The Directory ends with a "field terminator" character.

5.4. The data content of a record is divided into *Variable Fields*. The USMARC Formats distinguish two types of variable fields: *Variable Control Fields* and *Variable Data Fields*. Control and data fields are distinguished only by structure (see Section 7.2 below). [The term "fixed fields" is occasionally used in MARC documentation, referring either to control fields generally or only to coded-data fields such as 007 or 008.]

## SECTION 6. VARIABLE FIELDS AND TAGS

6.1. The data in a MARC record is organized into fields, each identified by a three-character tag.

6.2. According to ANSI Z39.2-1979, the tag must consist of alphabetic or numeric basic characters (such as decimal integers 0–9 or lower-case characters a–z). To date, the USMARC Formats have used only numeric tags.

While USMARC has included only numeric tags, some local extensions to USMARC have used alphabetic tags. Designers of such extensions have made the reasonable assumption that USMARC will not use tags beginning with alphabetic characters.

6.3. The tag is stored in the directory entry for the field, not in the field itself.

6.4. Variable fields are grouped into blocks according to the first character of the tag, which identifies the function of the data within a traditional catalog record (such as main entry, added entry, subject entry). The type of information in the field (such as personal name, corporate name, title) is identified by the remainder of the tag.

6.4.1. For bibliographic records, the blocks are:

0XX = Variable control fields, identification and classification numbers, etc.
1XX = Main entry
2XX = Titles and title paragraph (title, edition, imprint)
3XX = Physical description
4XX = Series statements
5XX = Notes
6XX = Subject added entries
7XX = Added entries other than subject, series

8XX = Series added entries
9XX = Reserved for local implementation

Section 6.4.1 uses a notational convention common in discussion of USMARC; this convention is also followed elsewhere in this book. "0XX" means "all tags beginning with 0," that is, 001 through 099 (and 0a0 through 0zz). The notation may also appear as "0xx," with the same meaning. The modified notation "88x" means "all tags beginning with 88."

6.4.2. For authority records, the blocks are:
0XX = Variable control fields, identification and classification numbers, etc.
1XX = Heading
2XX = General see references
3XX = General see also references
4XX = See from tracings
5XX = See also from tracings
6XX = Treatment decisions, notes, cataloger-generated references
7XX = Not defined
8XX = Not defined
9XX = Reserved for local implementation

The blocks are not always quite as neat as they appear. For 7XX and 8XX, the "blocks" only cover up to 740 and 840, respectively. Higher 7XX and 8XX tags have been used for different purposes. 76X–78X have now been reserved for linking entries, and 88X is now reserved for links within a record. The proposed Holdings Format will use a group of tags from 851 through 866. Since USMARC has never used alphabetic tags, blocks aXX–zXX are not mentioned.

6.5. Certain blocks contain data which may be subject to authority control (1XX, 4XX, 6XX, 7XX, 8XX for bibliographic records; 1XX, 4XX, 5XX for authority records).
6.5.1. In these blocks, certain parallels of content designation are preserved. The following meanings are generally given to the final two characters of the tag:
X00 = Personal name
X10 = Corporate name
X11 = Conference name
X30 = Uniform title heading
X40 = Bibliographic title
X50 = Topical subject heading
X51 = Geographic name
Further content designation (indicators and subfield codes) for data elements subject to authority control are consistently defined across the bibliographic formats and in the authorities format. These guidelines apply only to the main range of fields in each block, not to secondary ranges such as the linking fields in 760–787 or the 87X fields. [Numerous exceptions to this principle presently exist in the formats.]
6.5.2. Within fields subject to authority control, data elements may exist which are not subject to authority control and which may vary from record to record containing the same heading (for example, subfield ‡e, Relator). Such data elements are not appropriate for inclusion in the 1XX field in the authorities format.
6.5.3. In the fields not subject to authority control, each tag is defined independently. Parallel meanings have been preserved whenever possible, however.

Section 6.5 was suggested by Walter Grutchfield of the New York Public Library at an open hearing on the *Underlying Principles*. It explicitly relates bibliographic and authority tags. Consistent definition of content designation makes it possible to carry out authority control by computer. USMARC shows more consistency in the fields mentioned above than in most other fields. Most tags in the 2XX, 3XX and 5XX ranges are defined as needed, since parallels are rarely available. Parallels at the subfield level are much more frequent.

6.6. Certain tags have been reserved for local implementation. Except as noted below, the USMARC Formats specify no structure or meaning for local fields. Communication of such fields between systems is governed by mutual agreements on the content and content designation of the fields communicated.

6.6.1. The 9XX block is reserved for local implementation.

6.6.2. In general, any tag containing the character "9" is reserved for local implementation within the block structure (see Section 6.4 above).

6.6.3. The historical development of the USMARC Formats has left the following exceptions to this general principle:

  009 Physical description fixed field for archival collections
  039 Level of bibliographic control and coding detail
  359 Rental price
  490 Series untraced or traced differently

Section 6.6 reserves areas for local implementation; this explicit inclusion (and another in Section 8.4.2.3) represent a recognition within USMARC of the need for local extensions.

Each of the exceptions in Section 6.6.3 represents a different historical situation. Field 009 typically contains copy-specific data, and was regarded as a "local" field when it was defined. Field 009 may well be made obsolete in the future; however, since it has already been defined, it is not really available for local implementation. Field 039 was added to the formats to support the National Level Bibliographic Record (NLBR) standards; it consists of five elements relating to level of effort used in cataloging and encoding a record. The field has not been well received (neither OCLC nor RLIN allowed users to create 039 fields as of mid-1983), and its form and function are being reconsidered on a national level. Field 359 is only defined for Films, and has never been used by the Library of Congress; it will become obsolete with implementation of the Visual Materials format.

Field 490 is the major exception to the "9s rule," and is a heavily used field. Definition of field 490 using a "9" took place before the "9s rule" was enunciated, at a time when "local data" was less important than it currently is.

The major bibliographic services do define "local" fields, and they also define their use. See Chapter 10 for examples of such definitions.

6.7. Theoretically, all fields (except 001 and 005) may be repeated. The nature of the data often precludes repetition, however. For example, a bibliographic record may contain only one title (field 245) and an authority record, only one entry (1XX fields). The repeatability/nonrepeatability of each field is defined in the USMARC Formats.

## SECTION 7. VARIABLE CONTROL FIELDS

7.1. 00X fields in the USMARC Formats are variable control fields.

7.2. Variable control fields consist of data and a field terminator. They do not contain either indicators or subfield codes (see Section 8.1 below).

7.3. Variable control fields contain either a single data element or a series of fixed-length data elements identified by relative character position.

Control fields are not always fixed-length fields. Field 001 is variable length, and different versions of field 007 vary in length. If a control field contains more than one element, all elements (except the last) must be fixed length: otherwise, identifying elements by relative character position wouldn't work.

## SECTION 8. VARIABLE DATA FIELDS

8.1. Three levels of content designation are provided for variable fields in ANSI Z39.2-1979:
(1) a three-character tag, stored in the directory entry;
(2) indicators stored at the beginning of each variable data field, the number of indicators being reflected in the Leader, byte 10; and
(3) subfield codes preceding each data element, the length of the code being reflected in the Leader, byte 11.
8.2. All fields except 00X are variable data fields.

This section does place one restriction on local extensions to USMARC: any field, local or national, that begins with characters other than "00" must contain two indicator positions and at least one subfield code.

### 8.3. Indicators

8.3.1. Indicators contain codes conveying information which interprets or supplements the data found in the field.
8.3.2. The USMARC Formats specify two indicator positions at the beginning of each variable data field.
8.3.3. Indicators are independently defined for each field. Parallel meanings are preserved whenever possible, however.
8.3.4. Indicator values are interpreted independently—that is, meaning is not ascribed to the two indicators taken together.
8.3.5. Indicators may be any lower-case alphabetic or numeric character or the blank. Numeric values are assigned first. A blank is used in an undefined indicator position, or to mean "no information supplied" in a defined indicator position.

This section explicitly chooses two as the number of indicator positions. It also adds 26 more values to the range of indicators possible in USMARC. No alphabetic indicators have ever been assigned in USMARC; Section 8.3.5 explicitly opens the way for such assignment, if needed in the future.

### 8.4. Subfield Codes

8.4.1. Subfield codes distinguish data elements within a field which do (or might) require separate manipulation.
8.4.2. Subfield codes in the USMARC Formats consist of two characters—a delimiter [1F hex, 8-bit; 37 octal, 6-bit] followed by a data element identifier. Identifiers defined in the USMARC communications formats may be any lower-case alphabetic or numeric character.
8.4.2.1. In general, numeric identifiers are defined for parametric data used to process the field, or coded data needed to interpret the field. (Note that not all numeric identifiers defined in the past have in fact identified parametric data.)
8.4.2.2. Alphabetic identifiers are defined for the separate elements which constitute the data content of the field.

8.4.2.3. The character "9" and the following graphic symbols are reserved for local definition as subfield identifiers:

9 ! " # $ % & ' ( ) * + , - . / : ; < = > ?

Most numeric subfields (but not all) can be suppressed in displaying or printing a field; some of them provide information useful in processing the field. Most alphabetic subfields (but not all) contain text which should be displayed as part of a field.

Adoption of the *Underlying Principles* recognized the possibility of adding local subfields to nationally defined fields, by explicitly reserving 22 symbols as locally defined subfield identifiers.

8.4.3. Subfield codes are defined independently for each field. Parallel meanings are preserved whenever possible, however.

8.4.4. Subfield codes are defined for purposes of identification, not arrangement. The order of subfields is specified by content standards, such as the cataloging rules. In some cases, such specifications may be incorporated in the format documentation.

8.4.5. Theoretically, all data elements may be repeated. The nature of the data often precludes repetition, however. The repeatability/nonrepeatability of each subfield code is defined in the USMARC Formats.

*MFBD* normally lists subfields in alphabetic order for convenience; there is no implication that subfields should be keyed in that order. A common misconception is that every variable data field begins with a ‡a subfield, which always appears first; this has never been true, is not implied by the formats, and is clearly wrong in certain cases. Field 040 (Cataloging source) frequently lacks subfield ‡a; subfield ‡p (Introductory phrase) in field 534 (Original version note) is always entered as the first subfield of the field, before subfield ‡a.

## SECTION 9. CODED DATA

9.1. In addition to content designation, the USMARC Formats include specifications for the content of certain data elements, particularly those which provide for the representation of coded values.

9.2. Coded values consist of fixed-length character strings. Individual elements within a coded-data field or subfield are identified by relative character position.

9.3. Although coded data occurs most frequently in the Leader, Directory, and Variable Control Fields, any field or subfield may be defined for coded-data elements.

9.4. Certain common values have been defined:

ᵇ = Undefined
n = Not applicable
u = Unknown
z = Other
| = Fill character [i.e. No information provided]

Historical exceptions do occur in the formats. In particular, the blank (ᵇ) has often been defined as "not applicable," or has been assigned a meaning.

Since discussion of the *Underlying Principles* began, changes in coded values have consistently worked toward more consistent use of these values. The values contain some small but important distinctions. The fill character "|" indicates that the cataloger has chosen not to provide information. The "n" means that the coded data is not applicable to the item, while the "u" means that the cataloger intended to supply a value but was unable to determine one. The blank indicates nothing: no information is given.

The special meaning of blank is crucial to the maintenance of the formats. When an indicator has not been defined, it is always blank; when it is later defined, existing records must still be valid. The blank is also more broadly used to mean "no information"—not "no information provided" or "information not applicable," but simply "no information."

## CHANGING PRINCIPLES

The *Underlying Principles* reflect 14 years of MARC format development. They reflect an evolving body of working principles, and make those principles available for broader use. New principles may be needed as the formats continue to evolve. Existing principles may require expansion or modification. There are two crucial principles that are not stated in the *Underlying Principles* but that play a major role in all USMARC change. Whatever changes there are in the *Underlying Principles,* these two will continue to be important.

### Preservation of Existing Data

While "the future is longer than the past," it is also based on that past. Literally tens of millions of USMARC bibliographic records are in use, representing an enormous investment of money and cataloging skills. Future changes in USMARC will assure that those records continue to be useful.

### Conservation of Maintenance Energy

"If it isn't broken, don't fix it." Those working on USMARC maintenance are interested in theoretical elegance, but not at the expense of proven workability. They also recognize the cost of keeping up with format changes (updating documentation and software); only changes that are justified by practical advantages should be approved.

## NOTES AND REFERENCES

1. David Weisbrod's study of LC MARC included wording for a proposed "Responsible Party Rule." This rule placed responsibility for a record on the last agency modifying that record. The rule was theoretically sound, but practically unworkable. For many records on bibliographic services, the "last agency" is the service itself, adding an NUC code as the result of computer edits applied against the record. Such edits rarely have anything to do with the content of the record, but the single-responsibility rule would suggest that the services were wholly responsible for such records.

# Appendix B

# Glossary

These definitions and discussions apply to this book, and may not always be universally applicable.

*AACR: Anglo-American Cataloguing Rules:* "AACR2" refers specifically to the second edition.

*ACRL:* Association of College and Research Libraries, a division of the American Library Association.

*ADABAS:* A commercial database management system which is fairly widely used in library automation. The Washington Library Network and University of California's MELVYL both use ADABAS.

*AFR:* Automatic Format Recognition; computer techniques to assign MARC tags and subfield codes to text strings automatically. AFR was thought to be an efficient method for retrospective conversion in the late 1960s and early 1970s. The technique, which can be fairly successful but can never produce comprehensive, fully designated records, is less popular in current thinking.

*ALA:* The American Library Association.

*AMC:* Archival and Manuscripts Control format.

*ANSI:* American National Standards Institute; the overall organization for voluntary standards in the United States, and the U.S. member of ISO, the International Organization for Standardization. ANSI standards are created by various standards committees. Of these, the National Information Standards Organization (Z39) is most directly involved with libraries.

*ARL:* The Association of Research Libraries.

*ASCII:* American Standard Code for Information Interchange. Computers store characters as combinations of bits (binary digits). ASCII assigns standard meanings to those combinations so that information can be interchanged. For instance, any computer that uses ASCII will treat the pattern "01000010" as the letter "B."

*Added Entry:* An entry, other than the main entry, by which an item is represented in a catalog.

*Agency-Assigned Elements:* Data elements that can only be assigned by a particular agency. The ISSN and LCCN are examples. Content of agency-assigned elements is always the responsibility of the agency, though transcription accuracy is the responsibility of the library that transcribes the information.

*Alternate Character Representation:* Field 880 in USMARC. This field can contain the contents of any other field in a record, but contains the data in some nonroman representation.

*Analytics:* Bibliographic records that describe part or parts of a larger item. An analytic record might describe an article in a journal, an illustration in a book, an individual piece of music on a sound recording. See also "Component Part."

*Archival and Manuscript Control Format:* A USMARC bibliographic format used in those cases where the processing of material is more significant than detailed bibliographic description, specifically for archival material. This format replaces the MARC Manuscripts format.

*Authoritative Agency:* Agencies that maintain lists or rules upon which a USMARC data element is based. As examples, the Library of Congress is the authoritative agency for fields 050 (Library of Congress Call Number) and 082 (Dewey Decimal Classification Number); the National Library of Medicine is the authoritative agency for field 060 (NLM call number).

*Authorities Format:* USMARC format for storage of information on headings, including established headings and cross references.

*Authority Control:* Maintenance of established headings, both within an authority file and within bibliographic files (including card catalogs). Authority control can be done manually or by a computer-based authority control system.

*Authority Record:* A record of an established heading or of a variant form with reference to an established heading.

*Automatic Format Recognition:* See "AFR."

*BALLOTS:* Bibliographic Automation of Large Library Operations using a Time-sharing System. A project begun at Stanford University in 1967, which eventually led to an online shared cataloging system. This system was adopted by the Research Libraries Group and transformed into RLIN.

*BPI:* Bits per inch. A measure of tape writing density. For nine-track tapes (most tapes used in USMARC communications), BPI is equal to characters per inch. Common values are 800 BPI, 1600 BPI and 6250 BPI.

*Base Address:* Bytes 12–16 of a MARC leader give the offset at which the first data character will be found. The first data character is always the first character of Field 001.

*Bibliographic Level:* Byte 7 of the USMARC leader, the second character in the Legend. This position is only used in USMARC bibliographic records. Common values are "m" (Monograph) and "s" (Serial). Four other values are used for analytics and collections: "a" (Component part, monographic), "b" (Component part, serial), "c" (Collection) and "d" (Subunit).

*Bibliographic Services:* A neutral term to describe OCLC, RLIN, UTLAS and WLN. "Bibliographic services" is the only single term that can fairly describe all four agencies.

*Bibliographic Utilities:* Common but misleading term for the four major bibliographic services (OCLC, RLIN, UTLAS and WLN). None of the four is a "utility" in the sense of gas, electric and telephone companies, and the term "utility" ignores the special characteristics of each service. This book uses "bibliographic services," which also oversimplifies the diverse natures of the four.

*Binary Data:* Technically, all machine-readable data is "binary data." The term is used to signify data that is stored in ways other than as strings of characters. The most common forms of binary data (or "pure binary data") are binary numbers (see "Binary Halfword") and bit strings, sometimes called "flags" or "switches." MARC explicitly disallows use of pure binary data within MARC records.

*Binary Digit:* The lowest level of computer data. Equivalent to Bit (which see).

*Binary Halfword:* For IBM computers and others with 32-bit words, a group of 16 Bits (which see) treated as a single number. The number can range from $-32,767$ to $+32,768$. Most computers and languages used in libraries store variable length data using a Binary Halfword for the length, thus limiting the maximum length of a record to 32,768 bytes or characters.

*Bit:* Short for "Binary digit," the basic unit of all computer data. A binary digit, or bit, has two possible values: on or off, normally interpreted as one or zero. All USMARC processing is done in terms of bytes or characters. In most cases, a byte (which see) is made up of eight bits.

*Books Format:* The oldest and most widely used USMARC bibliographic format, used for language material in print or microform which is not serially issued.

*Byte:* A group of binary digits which is treated as a single character in computer processing. "Byte" and

"Character" are generally synonymous, though a byte may not be printable, as it may contain a control code or an undefined character. In most cases, a byte is made up of eight bits.

*CANMARC:* Canadian MARC, maintained by the National Library of Canada and the Canadian Committee on MARC. Unlike other non-U.S. MARC formats, there is some ongoing effort to keep USMARC and CANMARC reasonably compatible. A liaison from NLC attends the meetings of the USMARC advisory group (which see).

*CIP:* Cataloging In Publication, a program of the Library of Congress which makes partial cataloging information available for items prior to publication. CIP records are distributed as MARC records; the data may also appear on the verso of title pages.

*CJK:* Chinese, Japanese and Korean: the brief name for the Research Libraries Group project to enable cataloging of such items in the original characters. Also used in "CJK terminal" or "CJK cluster," the terminal and group of terminals used to create, modify or access such records on RLIN.

*CLR:* Council for Library Resources, Inc.; a funding agency for a variety of projects in the library field.

*CONSER:* CONversion of SERials; a nationwide cooperative retrospective conversion project, based on OCLC and managed by OCLC for most of its life, building a large database of serials records.

*Card-centrism:* A charge leveled at MARC by those who feel that the catalog card is not an appropriate method for organizing or displaying bibliographic information. The concept of "main entry" is a favorite target of these critics, some of whom favor radically different approaches to organization of bibliographic information.

*Cataloging Code:* Any codified set of rules for descriptive or subject cataloging. The best known cataloging code is the Anglo-American Cataloguing Rules (AACR), but a number of special disciplines have other well-established cataloging codes.

*Cataloging Source:* Two elements in USMARC provide this information: field 008, position 39 (for a few coded values) and field 040, giving NUC codes for the cataloging agency, transcribing agency, and modifying agencies.

*Character Set:* A defined set of equivalences for graphic characters (on a screen or printer) and machine storage: the specification that the machine value "hexadecimal F2" is the graphic "2" (in EBCDIC), or that the graphic "2" is "hexadecimal 32" (in ASCII).

*Characters:* In MARC usage, those elements that can be portrayed as graphics (letters, numbers, special characters, punctuation, diacritics) and the four special characters currently used in MARC: the fill, subfield delimiter, field terminator, and record terminator. Excludes "pure binary" data.

*Chronology:* For holdings, the date information provided for individual issues, such as year, month, week.

*Coded Data:* Elements stored in coded rather than free-text form. Codes must be represented in some list; most such lists are contained within the *MARC Formats for Bibliographic Data*. Well-known examples of coded data include the Country of Publication, Language, and Descriptive Cataloging Form.

*Collection:* A group of material treated together for convenience in cataloging and control.

*Compatible:* As used in computing, "compatible" generally means "able to run on" or "can be used with" or "functions identically to," depending on the context. "MARC compatible" has a different range of meanings, generally ranging from "USMARC with additional fields" to "bears some resemblance to bibliographic data." See Chapter 11.

*Component Part:* Something which is physically part of a larger item, called the host item; that which is described by an analytic entry. A chapter is a component part of a book, because the chapter cannot be retrieved without retrieving the book. Thus, the description of the chapter must also include a description of the book of which it is a part. See also "Analytics."

*Content Designation:* "The codes and conventions established explicitly to identify and further characterize the data elements within a record and to support the manipulation of that data" (*Underlying Principles*, Section 1.2.2). Tags, indicators and subfield codes are the common forms of content designation defined in USMARC. ISBD punctuation is a form of content designation defined outside USMARC.

*Control Fields:* See "Variable Control Fields."

*Control Number:* Any distinctive number used by a system to identify a number. Most commonly, USMARC tag 001; can also apply to USMARC tag 035 or to local extensions.

*Copy-Specific Information:* Data that pertain only to a single copy of an item, as opposed to "bibliographic data," which normally pertain to all copies within an edition.

*Core Fields:* Fields commonly defined in all USMARC bibliographic formats, including all fields subject to authority control.

*DBMS:* DataBase Management System; any set of programs designed to build and maintain databases. The most popular commercial DBMS for bibliographic data is ADABAS. RLIN uses SPIRES as a DBMS; OCLC uses a proprietary DBMS.

*Data Element Identifier:* The character that follows a Subfield Delimiter and precedes the text of the subfield itself. The Data Element Identifier may be a lower-case alphabetic character, a digit, or any of 21 different punctuation symbols (see Chapter 3). The numeral "9" and the punctuation symbols are reserved for local extensions to national fields.

*Database:* Any organized system of data; specifically, for USMARC, a collection of USMARC records available through some set of indexes.

*Database Management System:* See "DBMS."

*Delimiter:* Special character used to set off elements within a MARC record. USMARC uses three different delimiters:

  Subfield Delimiter: hexadecimal "1F," preceding the Subfield Code;
  Field Terminator: hexadecimal "1E," at the end of each field (and directory);
  Record Terminator: hexadecimal "1D," at the end of the USMARC record.

*Descriptive Cataloging Form:* Position 18 of the USMARC leader. As currently defined, the Descriptive Cataloging Form can describe form of cataloging (AACR2), form of punctuation (ISBD or some variation), or neither.

*Directory:* A series of fixed-length entries, immediately following the MARC Leader, which define the contents of a record. See "Directory Entry" for the makeup of each 12-character portion of the directory.

*Directory Entry:* Twelve characters of the directory defining a single field. A directory entry has three parts, each of which is separately defined:

  Tag (bytes 0–2);
  Length of Field (bytes 3–6);
  Starting Character Position (bytes 7–11).

*Display Constant:* Text string that may precede a USMARC field or subfield when it is displayed or printed, but which is not entered or stored as part of the field or subfield. Display constants can be as short as "In," the display constant for field 773, or as long as "Superseded in part by:."

*EBCDIC:* Extended Binary Coded Decimal Interchange Code. IBM's standard character code, relating characters and controls to patterns of binary digits. EBCDIC serves the same function as ASCII (which see).

*Encoding Level:* A single character code carried as Byte 17 of a USMARC leader. The encoding level identifies the degree of completeness of the record. Blank means "full," and other codes identify other levels of completeness.

*Entry Map:* Bytes 20 through 23 of a MARC Leader define the directory entries. The four positions contain four single-digit numbers: Length of Field, Starting Character Position, Implementation-Defined Portion, and an Undefined Position. USMARC records always contain "4500" in bytes 20–23 of the leader.

*Enumeration:* Numbering, as in serial volume and issue numbering.

*Escape Sequence:* A sequence of three characters, beginning with the "Escape" control character (ASCII hexadecimal 27), that signals a change of character set. The second and third character indicate the character set being escaped to. Note: as of 1983, USMARC includes nonstandard two-character escape sequences to allow superscript and subscript numbers and three Greek letters.

*Extensions:* Additions to USMARC as defined in *MFBD*. Extensions can include subfields, fields, indicator values or even graphic representations for text.

*Field:* A string of characters as defined by a Directory Entry, identified by a Tag, beginning at the Starting Character Position and ending with a Field Terminator, with a total length defined by the Length of Field. The tag is not part of the field, but indicators and subfield codes (except for fields 001–009) and the field terminator are.

*Field Terminator:* The single character defined as ASCII 1/14 (hexadecimal "1E"). Appears at the end of the directory and at the end of each field in a USMARC record.

*Fill Character:* A special character (printed as a solid or broken vertical bar |) used in some coded position to indicate that no attempt has been made to provide any information. This is a subtly different meaning from blank, which indicates only that no information is provided.

*Films Format:* USMARC format used for motion pictures, video recordings, filmstrips, slides, and a number of other media. Changes approved in January 1984 will convert the Films Format into the Visual Materials Format.

*Fixed Fields:* Generally refers to fields 007 and 008, which contain fixed-length codes.

*Format:* In USMARC, a "format" is a defined set of fields and codes which is somehow distinguished from other formats. The USMARC Authorities format is clearly a format; as time goes on, it may be less clear whether there is a single USMARC bibliographic format or whether there are seven or more formats to describe bibliographic material. See "Format Integration."

*Format Integration:* Changes in USMARC working toward a single integrated bibliographic format, in which content designation is valid in any record for which it is appropriate.

*GPO:* Government Printing Office.

*Generating Agency:* The agency that actually writes a record to tape or through electronic transmission. Usually distinct from cataloging or transcribing agency, except that the largest cataloging agency, LC, is also one of the largest generating agencies. OCLC is a large generating agency but not a large cataloging agency. Generating agencies are responsible for USMARC structural maintenance.

*Graphic Materials:* Paintings, posters, prints, photographs, x-rays, and other nonprojected visual media.

*Hexadecimal:* A notation system widely used to annotate computer codes. Each digit can have 16 values, from 0 to 9 and from A to F. 15 decimal is F hexadecimal; 255 decimal is FF hexadecimal. A single byte or character can have 256 different values; hexadecimal notation allows all such values to be stated as two-digit strings, from 00 to FF.

*Holdings Format:* A proposed USMARC format to record holdings patterns and actual holdings for all forms of material (though most of the developmental effort concentrated on serials). The Holdings format is arranged so that Holdings fields can be carried along with a USMARC bibliographic record or as a separate record.

*Host Item:* An item that contains component parts (which see). If chapters within a book have been cataloged, the book becomes a host item to those chapters. See also "Analytics."

*ID:* Identification. In USMARC, Field 001.

*IFLA:* International Federation of Library Associations.

*ISBD:* International Standard Bibliographic Description. Best known in terms of ISBD punctuation, the distinctive punctuation pattern used in almost all USMARC cataloging since 1974.

*ISBN:* International Standard Book Number, carried in field 020. The field is also used for binding and price information, even where no ISBN exists. ISBNs are meaningful numbers, consisting of a publisher prefix followed by an item suffix.

*ISO:* International Organization for Standardization. The international body for voluntary standards, with representatives from various national standards organizations.

*ISSN:* International Standard Serial Number. Carried in field 022 and in subfield ‡x of 4XX and 76X–78X fields.

*ITAL: Information Technology and Libraries.* Official journal of the Library and Information Technology Association of ALA. Continues *Journal of Library Automation.*

*Identifier:* Equivalent to Subfield Code (which see). "Identifier" is the term used in ANSI Z39.2-1979, but "Subfield Code" is used throughout USMARC.

*Identifier Length:* A single-digit number stored as Byte 11 of MARC leaders. For USMARC records, the Identifier Length is always "2." "Identifier" is the ANSI version of "Subfield Code." An "Identifer Length" of 2 means that subfield codes in USMARC are always two characters (the delimiter and the data element identifier).

*Implementation-Defined:* Byte 22 of the MARC leader is a single digit number giving the length of a fourth portion of each directory entry, the "implementation-defined portion." USMARC carries "0" in Byte 22, since there is no implementation-defined portion in directory entries.

*Indicator:* Two indicators appear at the beginning of each USMARC variable data field. Indicators contain codes conveying information which interprets or supplements the data found in the field. Indicators are commonly used to show source of data, length of initial article, or appropriate display constant. Indicators can further define a field, or they can control generation of a note or added entry.

*Indicator Count:* A single digit carried as Byte 10 of any MARC leader, specifying the number of indicators carried in each variable-length field. For USMARC, the Indicator Count is always "2": each field begins with two indicators.

*Interchange Format:* An agreed-upon format for interchange of data. The ALA Interlibrary Loan Request form is a noncomputerized interchange format. MARC is a computerized interchange format.

*JOLA:* The *Journal of Library Automation.* Official journal of the Information Science and Automation Division of ALA, and of the Library and Information Technology Association until 1982, when it was continued by *Information Technology and Libraries.* Many significant articles on MARC appeared in *JOLA.*

*LC:* The Library of Congress.

*LC MARC:* Another name for MARC II. Also written as LC/MARC.

*LCCN:* Library of Congress Card Number. This element is stored in field 010 subfield ‡a, except on LC MARC Distribution Service tapes, where it is carried as the record number, field 001.

*LCSH:* Library of Congress Subject Headings.

*LITA:* Library and Information Technology Association, a division of the American Library Association. Formerly ISAD (Information Science and Automation Division). One of the divisions represented on MARBI.

*Leader:* The first 25 characters of a USMARC record. The Leader contains elements that allow a program to process the remainder of the record.

*Legend:* Bytes 6 through 9 of the USMARC leader. Byte 6 is the Type of Record, byte 7 is the Bibliographic Level. Bytes 8 and 9 have not been defined as of 1983. The Legend says which USMARC format a record belongs to, and must be used to interpret Field 008 correctly.

*Length of Field:* Four digits (carried as characters) in each USMARC directory entry, immediately following the tag, giving the length of the field (including the field terminator).

*Linked Record Code:* Position 19 of the USMARC leader. Nearly always blank. An "r" in this position means that a Linking Entry Field in the record contains the record number for another record, but has no descriptive information on the related item. The other record is, therefore, required in order to process this record completely.

*Linking Entry:* Any field with a tag between 760 and 788. Linking entries establish some relationship between the record containing them and some other bibliographic entity or record. Examples of linking entry fields include 780, Preceding Item, and 773, Host Item.

*Logical Record Length:* The length of a logical record (that is, a self-contained MARC record). The "logical record" distinction arises because MARC records are communicated in a manner which separates "physical records" (what the computer treats as a record) from "logical records" (what the program treats as a record).

*MARBI:* ALA RTSD/LITA/RASD Committee on the Representation in Machine-Readable Form of Bibliographic Information. A committee that reviews proposed changes to USMARC, in cooperation with LC and liaisons from other national libraries, the four major bibliographic services, and other interested parties. MARBI advises LC, but does not actually determine the content of USMARC.

*MARC:* MAchine-Readable Cataloging. The term was coined in 1966, at the time of MARC I and the MARC Pilot Project. MARC is a general term covering a variety of formats in different countries. USMARC, formerly LC MARC or MARC II, is frequently referred to as MARC—a broader term that also covers UKMARC, CANMARC, SUPERMARC, InterMARC, and a number of other MARC formats.

*MARC I:* The initial MAchine-Readable Cataloging format, promulgated by the Library of Congress for the MARC Pilot Project (1966–1968).

*MARC II:* The overall record structure designed by the Library of Congress in 1968. The term also applies to all of the MARC formats, including the six bibliographic formats implemented prior to 1984 and the Authorities Format. MARC II was succeeded by USMARC in 1983.

*MARC-Compatible:* Formats and systems that can accept any pure USMARC record and, as needed, regenerate the same USMARC record without loss of content, content designation or structure.

*MFBD:* The *MARC Formats for Bibliographic Data,* published by the Library of Congress as a looseleaf publication with quarterly updates. The single reference for content designation in USMARC bibliographic formats.

*MRDF:* Machine-Readable Data Files Format. A new USMARC format to describe items that are machine-readable. First developed for data files such as census tapes, the format is being extended to cover micro-computer software.

*MUDG:* MARC Users Discussion Group, a group within ISAD and LITA which met to discuss and hear about various MARC issues. The group merged with the Library Automation Discussion Group in the late 1970s to form the Library and Information Technology Discussion Group.

*Machine-Readable Data Files:* See "MRDF."

*Manuscripts Format:* A USMARC format that was not widely adopted or used; replaced in 1984 by the Archival and Manuscripts Control Format.

*Maps Format:* A USMARC format to accommodate cartographic materials, including maps, atlases and globes.

*Music Format:* The USMARC format that is used to describe sound recordings, both musical and nonmusical, and printed music.

*NAL:* National Agricultural Library.

*NISTF:* National Information Systems Task Force, a task force headed by David Bearman and representing the interests of the Society of American Archivists (SAA) in developing the USMARC Archival and Manuscripts Control Format. (The group also had other functions.)

*NLBR:* National Level Bibliographic Record. A series of documents establishing standards for bibliographic records.

*NLC:* National Library of Canada.

*NLM:* National Library of Medicine.

*NOTIS:* Northwestern Online Technical Information System, the library automation system developed by Northwestern University.

*NSDP:* National Serials Data Program, the control agency for ISSNs and key titles in the United States.

*NUC:* National Union Catalog; also used to refer to NUC Codes.

*NUC Code:* Code identifying a library in the National Union Catalog and, later, in MARC records. The NUC code is used in field 040 subfields and in a number of other places as a distinct, nationally known identifying string. NUCs are geographically based, and vary in length from two to eight characters. Upper and lower case letters have different meanings within an NUC code.

*Networks:* There are dozens or hundreds of library networks in the United States, some of them computer-based, others not. "Network" is sometimes used to refer to the four major bibliographic services (OCLC, RLIN, UTLAS and WLN). While each of these does maintain an online network, the term is too broad: SOLINET, PALINET and multicounty borrowing networks are also networks.

*OCLC:* Online Computer Library Center. The largest bibliographic service in the United States. A complex of computers, people and data providing shared cataloging for several thousand libraries. Formerly OCLC, Inc., and before that Ohio College Library Center.

*OCLC MARC:* USMARC with OCLC extensions, as defined and generated by OCLC.

*Offset:* Relative position from the beginning. The first position is always offset 0. The second character in a text string is at offset 1.

*RASD:* Reference and Adult Services Division of ALA, one of the three divisions represented on MARBI.

*RBMS:* The Rare Books and Manuscripts Section of ALA's Association of College and Research Libraries. The RBMS Standards Committee was an interested party in the development of the USMARC Archival and Manuscripts Control Format.

*RLG:* The Research Libraries Group, Inc. A corporation owned by a number of research institutions and libraries, working in a number of fields to forward common aims of its members. Operates the Research Libraries Information Network (RLIN), a large online shared cataloging system.

*RLIN:* The Research Libraries Information Network. The computer support for RLG, and a large bibliographic service, with more than 12 million bibliographic records and more than 600 terminals.

*RTSD:* Resources and Technical Services Division, one of three ALA divisions represented on MARBI.

*Record Length:* See "Logical Record Length."

*Record Number:* USMARC field 001; also known as Record ID or Control Number.

*Record Status:* Position 5 of the USMARC leader, a single character code. The commonly used values are "n" (New record), "c" (Changed record), and "d" (Deleted record).

*Record Terminator:* The single character ASCII 1/13 (hexadecimal '1D'). Every MARC record, and every USMARC record, has a Record Terminator as a final character.

*Repeatability:* While all USMARC fields are theoretically repeatable, fields and subfields are specifically defined in the format documentation as being repeatable or nonrepeatable.

*SAA:* Society of American Archivists.

*Scores:* Printed or manuscript music notation, recorded in the USMARC Music Format.

*Self-defining:* Data that carry their own identification. USMARC is self-defining to the extent that fields are labeled in the directory. For those who find "245" meaningful, USMARC records are self-defining. For others, USMARC is dependent on an external dictionary, the *MARC Formats for Bibliographic Data.*

*Sequence Control Number:* Subfield ‡6 in the proposed USMARC Holdings format, containing a number that can be used to sort fields 853–855 into proper order and to sort fields 863–865 and relate them to appropriate 853–855 fields.

*Serials Format:* A USMARC format to describe printed or microform language material issued in successive parts bearing numerical or chronological designations and intended to be continued indefinitely.

*Starting Character Position:* Five digits (carried as characters) in each directory entry, following the Length of Field. The Starting Character Position is the offset of the first character of a field, relative to the first character in the first field. Thus, the Starting Character Position for field 001 is always "00000." The actual position of a field is the Starting Character Position plus Base Address.

*Subfield:* Portion of a USMARC field, identified by a leading Subfield Code and terminated by either a Subfield Delimiter or a Field Terminator.

*Subfield Delimiter:* A single character, stored as ASCII 1/15 (more commonly, hexadecimal "1F"). Always followed by a Data Element Identifier (which see) and the contents of the subfield. The subfield delimiter is displayed as a double dagger (‡), slashed equal sign (≠) or dollar sign ($).

*Superset:* A format is a superset of the another format if all elements of the second the are included in the first, but not the reverse. OCLC MARC and RLIN MARC are both supersets of USMARC, but neither is a superset of the other.

*Tag:* Each variable field in a USMARC record is identified by a three-character tag, stored in the directory. Tags are the level of content designation used to define independent elements of a record.

*Turnkey System:* Properly, an automation system that includes hardware, software, training and documentation: all you do is turn the key and use it.

*Type of Record:* Byte 6 of a USMARC leader, the first character of the Legend. This code distinguishes physical formats and special record types. The character "a" is "Language material, printed or microform"; "j" is "Sound recordings, musical"; "z" is "Authority."

*UKMARC:* The MARC format used in the United Kingdom.

*USMARC:* Current name for the machine-readable cataloging format used in the United States. Formerly known as LC MARC, LC/MARC, MARC II or just MARC.

*USMARC advisory group:* A group that meets to advise LC on development and maintenance of the USMARC formats. The group includes MARBI (which see), liaisons from the major bibliographic services, liaisons from national libraries within the United States and Canada, and other interested parties. The USMARC advisory group normally meets quarterly.

*UTLAS:* University of Toronto Library Automation Systems; the largest bibliographic service in Canada, with a large online network and extensive batch services.

*Utilities:* An inaccurate but common term for OCLC, RLIN, UTLAS and WLN. This book uses the term "bibliographic services" (which see).

*Variable Control Fields:* USMARC tags 001–009, and potentially 00a–00z. Control fields do not have indicators or tags, and can be composed of one or more data elements. Such fields are not necessarily fixed-length, but any elements other than the last one in a field must be fixed-length, since elements are identified by their position in the field. Most common examples: 001, 005, 008.

*Vernacular Data:* Bibliographic data carried in the language of the publication, where that language is not the language of the cataloging agency. More specifically, such data in languages that do not use the roman alphabet.

*Visual Materials Format:* New name for the USMARC Films Format, since it is expanded to include graphics and other materials.

*WLN:* The Washington Library Network. WLN is both a bibliographic service (serving the Pacific Northwest) and a set of computer programs in use in Australia, at the University of Illinois (Urbana-Champaign), at SOLINET, and elsewhere.

# Appendix C

# Bibliography and Reading List

The following list is neither exhaustive nor specifically chosen for merit. A comprehensive bibliography on USMARC and its uses would run to thousands of items. A number of the articles and monographs listed have bibliographies that can lead to other sources; where appropriate, these are noted. Items are listed in alphabetical order. Also note that some of these items are not available in published form, but are included because they were used in preparing this book.

Allison, Anne Marie; Allan, Ann G., eds. *OCLC, A National Library Network*. Short Hills, NJ: Enslow; 1979. 248 p. Extensive bibliography.

*Anglo-American Cataloguing Rules*. 2nd ed. Chicago: American Library Association; 1978. 620 p.

American National Standards Institute. *American National Standard Format for Bibliographic Information Interchange on Magnetic Tape*. New York: ANSI; 1979. (ANSI Z39.2-1979.)

Aronofsky, Julius S.; Korfhage, Robert R. "Telecommunication in Library Networks: A Five-Year Projection." *Journal of Library Automation*. 10(1): 5-27; 1977 March.

Atherton, Pauline; Miller, Karen B. "LC/MARC on MOLDS; An Experiment in Computer-Based, Interactive Bibliographic Storage, Search, Retrieval and Processing." *Journal of Library Automation*. 3(2): 142-165; 1970 June.

Atherton, Pauline; Tessier, Judith. "Teaching with MARC Tapes." *Journal of Library Automation*. 3(1): 24-35; 1970 March.

Attig, John C. "The Concept of a MARC Format." *Information Technology and Libraries*. 2(1): 7-17; 1983 March.

Attig, John C. *Integration of USMARC Bibliographic Formats*. 1983 August. 9 p. (MARBI discussion paper no. 7.) [Unpublished.]

Attig, John C. "The USMARC Formats—Underlying Principles." *Information Technology and Libraries*. 1(2): 169-174; 1982 June. The next-to-final version of the *Underlying Principles*.

*Audiovisual Media Format*. Columbus: OCLC; 1980. 264 p.

Auld, Larry. "Authority Control: An Eighty-Year Review." *Library Resources & Technical Services*. 26(4): 319-330; 1982 October/December.

Avram, Henriette D.; Droz, Julius R. "MARC II and COBOL." *Journal of Library Automation.* 1(4): 261-272; 1968 December.

Avram, Henriette D.; Freitag, Ruth S.; Guiles, Kay D. *A Proposed Format for a Standardized Machine-Readable Catalog Record: A Preliminary Draft.* Washington, DC: Library of Congress; 1965. [Out of print; not consulted for this work.]

Avram, Henriette D.; Knapp, John F.; Rather, Lucia J. *The MARC II Format: A Communications Format for Bibliographic Data.* Washington, DC: Library of Congress; 1968. 167 p.

Avram, Henriette D. "The Library of Congress View on Its Relation to the ALA MARC Advisory Committee." *Journal of Library Automation.* 7(2): 119-125; 1974 June. Proposal which led to MARBI's role in USMARC.

Avram, Henriette D. *MARC, Its History and Implications.* Washington, DC: Library of Congress; 1975. 49 p. Includes bibliography, pages 37-49.

Avram, Henriette D. *The MARC Pilot Project: Final Report on a Project Sponsored by the Council on Library Resources, Inc.* Washington, DC: Library of Congress; 1968. 183 p. Includes reports from participants.

Avram, Henriette D. [and others]. "MARC Program Research and Development: A Progress Report." *Journal of Library Automation* 2(4): 242-265; 1969 December.

Avram, Henriette D.; Markuson, Barbara Evans. "Library Automation and Project MARC." *The Brasenose Conference on the Automation of Libraries.* London: Mansell; 1967: 97-127. Early report. Includes bibliography.

Avram, Henriette D.; Maruyama, Lenore S. "The RECON Pilot Project: A Progress Report, October 1970-May 1971." *Journal of Library Automation.* 4(3): 159-169; 1971 September.

Avram, Henriette D. "The RECON Pilot Project: A Progress Report." *Journal of Library Automation.* 3(2): 102-114; 1970 June.

Avram, Henriette D. [and others]. "The RECON Pilot Project: A Progress Report, November 1969-April 1970." *Journal of Library Automation.* 3(3): 230-251; 1970 September.

Avram, Henriette D.; Maruyama, Lenore S. "The RECON Pilot Project: A Progress Report, April-September 1970." *Journal of Library Automation.* 4(1): 38-51; 1971 March.

Avram, Henriette D. *RECON Pilot Project.* Washington, DC: Library of Congress; 1972. 49 p.

Avram, Henriette D. [and others]. "Status of Processing Services Automation in the Library of Congress." *Information Technology and Libraries.* 2(2): 135-141; 1983 June.

Avram, Henriette D. "Toward a Nationwide Library Network." *Journal of Library Automation.* 11(4): 285-298; 1978 December.

Balfour, Frederick M. "Conversion of Bibliographic Information to Machine Readable Form Using On-line Computer Terminals." *Journal of Library Automation.* 1(4): 217-226; 1968 December.

Betz, Elizabeth W. *Graphic Materials: Rules for Describing Original Items and Historical Collections.* Washington, DC: Library of Congress; 1982. 155 p.

*Bibliographic Input Standards.* 2d ed. Columbus: OCLC; 1982. 158 p.

Bierman, Kenneth John; Blue, Betty Jean. "A MARC Based SDI Service." *Journal of Library Automation.* 3(4): 304-319; 1970 December.

Bierman, Kenneth John; Blue, Betty Jean. "Processing of MARC Tapes for Cooperative Use." *Journal of Library Automation.* 3(1): 36-64; 1970 March.

*Books Field Guide.* Stanford: RLG; 1982 September 1. 367 p.

*Books Format.* Columbus: OCLC; 1980. 320 p.

Bowden, Virginia M.; Miller, Ruby B. "MARCIVE: A Cooperative Automated Library System." *Journal of Library Automation.* 7(3): 183-200; 1974 September. An early MARC-based multilibrary project, still succeeding.

Brown, Georgia L. "AACR2: OCLC's Implementation and Database Conversion." *Journal of Library Automation*. 14(3): 161-173; 1981 September.

Buckland, Lawrence F. *The Recording of Library of Congress Bibliographical Data in Machine Form; A Report Prepared for the Council on Library Resources, Inc.* Washington, DC: Council on Library Resources, Inc.; 1965. 54 p. [Not consulted for this work.]

Buhr, Lorne R. "Selective Dissemination of MARC: A User Evaluation." *Journal of Library Automation*. 6(4): 237-256; 1973 December.

Butler, Brett. "Automatic Format Recognition of MARC Bibliographic Elements: A Review and Projection." *Journal of Library Automation*. 7(1): 27-42; 1974 March.

Butler, Brett. "State of the Nation in Networking." *Journal of Library Automation*. 8(3): 200-220; 1975 September.

Carrington, David K.; Mangan, Elizabeth U. *Data Preparation Manual for the Conversion of Map Cataloging Records to Machine-Readable Form*. Washington, DC: Library of Congress; 1971. 317 p.

*Cartographic Materials: A Manual of Interpretation for AACR2*. Chicago: American Library Association; 1982. x, 258 p.

*Cataloging: User Manual*. Columbus: OCLC; 1979 February. 280 p.

Christoffersson, John G. "Automation at the University of Georgia Libraries." *Journal of Library Automation*. 12(1): 22-38; 1979 March.

"A Composite Effort to Build an On-line National Serials Data Base." *Journal of Library Automation*. 7(1): 60-64; 1974 March. Early work eventually leading to CONSER.

*Conversion of Retrospective Catalog Records to Machine-Readable Form*. Washington, DC: Library of Congress; 1969. 230 p. An early cost and feasibility study.

Crawford, Walt. "Building a Serials Key Word Index." *Journal of Library Automation*. 9(1): 34-47; 1976 March.

Crawford, Walt. "EBCDIC Bibliographic Character Sets—Sources and Uses: A Brief Report." *Journal of Library Automation*. 12(4): 380-383; 1979 December.

Crawford, Walt. "Library Standards for Data Structures and Element Identification: U.S. MARC in Theory and Practice." *Library Trends*. 23(4): 265-281; 1982 Fall.

Crawford, Walt. "The RLIN Reports System: A Tool for MARC Selection and Listing." *Information Technology and Libraries*. 3(1): 3-14; 1984 March.

Curran, Ann T. "Library Networks: Cataloging and Bibliographic Aspects." *Proceedings of the 1969 Clinic on Library Applications of Data Processing*. Urbana: U. of Illinois; 1970: 31-41. Includes bibliography.

Davison, Wayne E. "The WLN/RLG/LC Linked Systems Project." *Information Technology and Libraries*. 2(1): 34-46; 1983 March. Includes bibliography.

Dodd, Sue A. "Building an On-line Bibliographic/MARC Resource Data Base for Machine-Readable Data Files." *Journal of Library Automation*. 12(1): 6-21; 1979 March.

Dodd, Sue A. *Cataloging Machine-Readable Data Files: An Interpretive Manual*. Chicago: American Library Association, 1982. xix, 247 p.

Epstein, A.H.; Veaner, Allen B. "A User's View of BALLOTS." *Proceedings of the 1972 Clinic on Library Applications of Data Processing*. Urbana: U. of Illinois; 1972: 109-137.

Epstein, Hank. "MITINET/Retro: Retrospective Conversion on an Apple." *Information Technology and Libraries*. 2(2): 166-173; 1983 June.

*Films Field Guide*. Stanford: RLG; 1982 September 1. 396 p.

*Format for Standardized MARC Bibliographic Records. LHF3*. Toronto: UTLAS; 1981 March 23. 98 p.

Furlong, Elizabeth J. "Index Access to On-line Records: An Operational View." *Journal of Library Automation*. 11(3): 223-238; 1978 September. A description of NOTIS at Northwestern.

Gapen, D. Kaye. "MARC Format Simplification." *Journal of Library Automation.* 14(4): 286-292; 1981 December. Brief version of a 22-page report prepared for the Association of Research Libraries.

Gibson, Liz. "BIBCON—A General Purpose Software System for MARC-based Book Catalog Production." Journal of Library Automation. 6(4): 237-256; 1973 December.

Gillespie, Veronica M. *MARC Conversion Manual—Books.* Washington, DC: Library of Congress; 1981. 455 p. Draft. [Unpublished.]

Goossens, Paula. "Techniques for Special Processing of Data within Bibliographic Text." *Journal of Library Information.* 7(3): 168-182; 1974 September.

Grosch, Audrey N. "The Minnesota Union List of Serials." *Journal of Library Automation.* 6(3): 167-181; 1973 September.

Hagler, Ronald. *The Bibliographic Record and Information Technology.* Chicago: American Library Association; 1982. 346 p. Includes detailed description of CANMARC.

Hajnal, Peter I. [and others]. "MARC and CODOC: A Case Study in Dual Format Use in a University Library." *Journal of Library Automation.* 10(4): 358-373; 1977 December.

Hannan, Chris. "The Australian Bibliographic Network—An Introduction." *Information Technology and Libraries.* 1(3): 222-230; 1982 September.

Hensen, Steven L. *Archives, Personal Papers, and Manuscripts: A Cataloging Manual for Archival Repositories, Historical Societies, and Manuscript Libraries.* Washington, DC: Library of Congress; 1983. 51 p.

Hickey, Thomas B. *Research Report on Field, Subfield, and Indicator Statistics in OCLC Bibliographic Records.* Dublin, OH: OCLC; 1981 March 23. 146 p. Tables of figures based on a 1% sample of the OCLC database.

Hickey, Thomas B.; Rypka, David J. "Automation Detection of Duplicate Monographic Records." *Journal of Library Automation.* 12(2): 125-142; 1979 June. Detecting duplicates within OCLC.

Hirshon, Arnold. "Considerations in the Creation of a Holdings Record Structure for an Online Catalog." *Library Resources & Technical Services.* 28(1): 25-40; 1984 January/March.

Holley, Robert F.; Flecker, Dale. "Processing OCLC MARC Subscription Tapes at Yale University." *Journal of Library Automation.* 12(1): 88-91; 1979 March.

Horner, William C. "Processing OCLC MARC Subscription Tapes at North Carolina State University." *Journal of Library Automation.* 12(1): 91-94; 1979 March.

Hudson, Judith. "Revisions to Contributed Cataloging in a Cooperative Cataloging Database." *Journal of Library Automation.* 14(2): 116-120; 1981 June.

Hyman, Richard J. *From Cutter to MARC: Access to the Unit Record.* Flushing: Queens College Press; 1977. 40 p. Extensive bibliography.

"Inclusion of Nonroman Character Sets." *Journal of Library Automation.* 14(3): 210-215; 1981 September.

"In-Depth: University of California MELVYL." *Information Technology and Libraries.* 1(4): 350-380; 1982 December, and 2(1): 58-115; 1983 March. Eight pieces describing a large, sophisticated MARC-based online catalog.

International Organization for Standardization. *Documentation—Format for Bibliographic Information Interchange on Magnetic Tape.* 1973. 4 p. [ISO 2709-1973(E).] [Not consulted for this work.]

[ISAD Institute on a National Bibliographic Network. Proceedings.] *Journal of Library Automation.* 10(2): 101-180; 1977 June. Nine papers covering a variety of viewpoints on the topic.

Jacobs, Mary Ellen [and others]. *Online Resource Sharing II—A Comparison of: OCLC, Incorporated, Research Libraries Information Network, and Washington Library Network.* CLASS; 1979 January. 99 p.

Johnson, Carolyn A. "Retrospective Conversion of Three Library Collections." *Information Technology and Libraries.* 1(2): 133-139; 1982 June.

Jones, Barbara; Kastner, Arno. "Duplicate Records in the Bibliographic Utilities: A Historical Review of the Printing versus Edition Problem." *Library Resources & Technical Services.* 27(2): 211-220; 1983 April/June.

Kelly, Betsy [and others]. "Bibliographic Access and Control System." *Information Technology and Libraries.* 1(2): 125-132; 1982 June.

Kennedy, John P. "File Size and the Cost of Processing MARC Records." *Journal of Library Automation.* 4(1): 1-12; 1971 March.

Kennedy, John P. "A Local MARC Project: The Georgia Tech Library." *Proceedings of the 1978 Clinic on Library Applications of Data Processing.* Urbana: U. of Illinois; 1969: 199-215.

Kessler, Brett; Shaw, Debora. "SOLOS: A Student-oriented Information Retrieval System Using MARC Records." *Information Technology and Libraries.* 2(3): 272-279; 1983 September.

Kilgour, Frederick G. "Initial System Design for the Ohio College Library Center: A Case History." *Proceedings of the 1968 Clinic on Library Applications of Data Processing.* Urbana: Univ. of Illinois; 1969: 79-88.

Kilgour, Frederick G. [and others]. "The Shared Cataloging System of the Ohio College Library Center." *Journal of Library Automation.* 5(3): 157-183; 1972 September. Major introduction to OCLC online.

Kim, David U. "OCLC-MARC Tapes and Collection Management." *Information Technology and Libraries.* 1(1): 22-27; 1982 March.

King, Gilbert W. [and others]. *Automation and the Library of Congress: A Survey Sponsored by the Council on Library Resources, Inc.* Washington, DC: Library of Congress; 1963. 88 p. [Out of print; not consulted for this work.]

Landgraf, Alan L. [and others]. "Corporate Author Entry Records Retrieved by Use of Derived Truncated Search Keys." *Journal of Library Automation.* 6(3): 156-161; 1973 September.

Landgraf, Alan L.; Kilgour, Frederick G. "Catalog Records Retrieved by Personal Author Using Derived Search Keys." *Journal of Library Automation.* 6(2): 103-108; 1973 June.

"The LC Network Technical Architecture Group." *Journal of Library Automation.* 10(3): 276-283; 1977 September.

Legard, Lawrence K.; Bourne, Charles P. "An Improved Title Word Search Key for Large Catalog Files." *Journal of Library Automation.* 9(4): 318-327; 1976 December.

Leung, Shirley W. "MARC CIP Records and MARC LC Records: An Evaluative Study of Their Discrepancies." *Cataloging and Classification Quarterly.* 4(2): 27-39; 1983 Winter.

Levine, Jamie J.; Logan, Timothy. *On-line Resource Sharing: A Comparison of BALLOTS and OCLC.* CLASS; 1977 June. 121 p.

*Library Automation: The State of the Art II.* Chicago: ALA; 1975. 191 p. See especially pages 56-86 and the bibliography, 156-191.

Library of Congress. Automated Systems Office. *MARC Formats for Bibliographic Data.* Washington, DC: Library of Congress, 1980. Looseleaf, with quarterly updates.

Library of Congress. Automation Planning and Liaison Office. *Authorities: A MARC Format.* Washington, DC: Library of Congress; 1981. [160] p. Updated in 1983 June.

Library of Congress. Information Systems Office. *Maps: A MARC Format; Specifications for Magnetic Tapes Containing Catalog Records for Maps.* Washington, DC: Library of Congress; 1970. 45 p. [Out of print.]

Library of Congress. Information Systems Office. *MARC Manuals Used by the Library of Congress.* Chicago: American Library Association; 1969. 355 p.

Library of Congress. MARC Development Office. *Authorities: A MARC Format.* Preliminary edition. Washington, DC: Library of Congress; 1976. [Out of print.]

Library of Congress. MARC Development Office. *Books: A MARC Format; Specifications for Magnetic Tapes Containing Catalog Records for Books.* 5th ed. Washington, DC: Library of Congress; 1972. 106 p. [Out of print.]

Library of Congress. MARC Development Office. *Films: A MARC Format; Specifications for Magnetic Tapes Containing Records for Motion Pictures, Filmstrips, and Other Pictorial Media Intended for Projection.* Washington, DC: Library of Congress; 1970. 65 p. [Out of print.]

Library of Congress. MARC Development Office. *Manuscripts: A MARC Format; Specifications for Magnetic Tapes Containing Catalog Records for Single Manuscripts or Manuscript Collections.* Washington, DC: Library of Congress; 1973. 47 p. [Out of print.]

Library of Congress. MARC Development Office. *MARC User Survey, 1972.* Washington, DC: Library of Congress; 1972. 58 p.

Library of Congress. MARC Development Office. *Music: A MARC Format; Specifications for Magnetic Tapes Containing Catalog Records for Music Scores and Musical and Non-Musical Sound Recordings.* Draft. Washington, DC: Library of Congress; 1973 [Out of print.]

Library of Congress. MARC Development Office. *Serials: A MARC Format; Specifications for Magnetic Tapes Containing Catalog Records for Serials.* Washington, DC: Library of Congress; 1974. 104 p. [Out of print.]

Library of Congress. MARC Standards Office. *USMARC Archival and Manuscripts Control Content Designators (January 1983).* Unpaged. [Unpublished.]

Library of Congress. Processing Services. *National Level Authority Record.* Preliminary edition. Washington, DC: Library of Congress; 1982 March. 181 p.

Library of Congress. Processing Services. *National Level Bibliographic Record—Books.* Washington, DC: Library of Congress; 1980 May. 220 p.

Library of Congress. Processing Services. *National Level Bibliographic Record—Films.* Washington, DC: Library of Congress; 1981 February. 243 p.

Library of Congress. Processing Services. *National Level Bibliographic Record—Maps.* Washington, DC: Library of Congress; 1981 August. 253 p.

Library of Congress. Processing Services. *National Level Bibliographic Record—Music.* Washington, DC: Library of Congress; 1981 June. 299 p.

Library of Congress. Processing Services. *National Level Bibliographic Record—Serials.* Washington, DC: Library of Congress; 1981 September. 341 p.

Long, Philip L.; Kilgour, Frederick G. "Name-Title Entry Retrieval from a MARC File." *Journal of Library Automation* 4(4): 211-212; 1971 December.

Long, Philip L.; Kilgour, Frederick G. "A Truncated Search Key Title Index." *Journal of Library Automation.* 5(1): 17-20; 1972 March.

*Machine-Readable Data Files: A MARC Format.* Final draft. Washington, DC: Library of Congress; 1981 June. 156 p. (MARBI proposal 80-4.) [Unpublished.]

MacLaury, Keith D. "Automatic Merging of Monographic Data Bases—Use of Fixed-Length Keys Derived from Title Strings. *Journal of Library Automation.* 12(2): 143-155; 1979 June.

Malinconico, S. Michael; Rizzolo, James A. "The New York Public Library Automated Book Catalog Subsystem." *Journal of Library Automation.* 6(1): 3-36; 1973 March.

Malinconico, S. Michael [and others]. "Vernacular Scripts in the NYPL Automated Bibliographic Control System." *Journal of Library Automation.* 10(3): 205-225; 1977 September.

*Manuscripts Format.* Columbus: OCLC; 1980. 236 p.

*Maps Field Guide.* Stanford: RLG; 1982 September 1. 358 p.

*Maps Format.* Columbus: OCLC; 1980. 254 p.

*MARC Format for Holdings and Locations.* 1983 September 14. Unpaged, ab. 150 p. (MARBI proposal 82-20.) [Unpublished.]

*MARC Serials Editing Guide.* Second CONSER ed. Washington, DC: Library of Congress; 1981. 510 p. Bimonthly updates.

Martin, Susan K. *Library Networks, 1976-77.* White Plains: Knowledge Industry Publications, Inc.; 1976. 131 p. Bibliography.

Martin, Susan K. *Library Networks, 1978-79.* White Plains: Knowledge Industry Publications, Inc.; 1978. 144 p. Bibliography.

Martin, Susan K. *Library Networks, 1981-82.* White Plains: Knowledge Industry Publications, Inc.; 1981. 160 p. Bibliography.

Maruskin, Albert F. *OCLC: Its Governance, Function, Financing and Technology.* New York: Dekker; 1980. 145 p.

Matson, Susan. "Desiderata for a National Series Authority File." *Library Resources & Technical Services.* 26(4): 331-334; 1982 October/December.

Mauerhoff, Georg R.; Smith, Richard G. "A MARC II-based Program for Retrieval and Dissemination." *Journal of Library Automation.* 4(3): 141-158; 1971 September.

McCallum, Sally H.; Godwin, James L. "Statistics on Headings in the MARC File." *Journal of Library Automation.* 14(3): 194-201; 1981 September.

McCallum, Sally H. "MARC Record-linking Technique." *Information Technology and Libraries.* 1(3): 281-291; 1982 September.

Meyer, Richard W.; Knapp, John F. "COM Catalog Based on OCLC Records." *Journal of Library Automation.* 8(4): 312-321; 1975 December.

*Music Online Input Manual.* Washington, DC: Library of Congress; 1982 May 3. Unpaged, ab. 200 p. [Unpublished.]

Nasatir, Marilyn. "Machine-readable Data Files and Networks." *Information Technology and Libraries.* 2(2): 159-164; 1983 June.

*OCLC: A Bibliography.* Columbus: OCLC; 1979 May. 16 p.

*OCLC-MARC Subscription Service Documentation.* Columbus: OCLC; 1978. 20 p.

Olson, Nancy B. *Cataloging of Audiovisual Materials.* Mankato: Minnesota Scholarly Press; 1981. 154 p. See especially pages 95-153.

Palmer, Foster M. "A Librarian's View of Data Processing." *Proceedings of the 1969 Clinic on Library Applications of Data Processing.* Urbana: U. of Illinois; 1970: 1-13.

Pringle, William R. "Computing the Effective Length of a MARC Tag." *Journal of Library Automation.* 12(4): 387-390; 1979 December.

*Proceedings of the 1970 Clinic on Library Applications of Data Processing: MARC Uses and Users.* Urbana: U. of Illinois; 1971. 113 p. Several sets of early references.

Project BALLOTS and the Stanford University Libraries. "Stanford University's BALLOTS System." *Journal of Library Automation.* 8(1): 31-50; 1975 March. BALLOTS was the precursor of RLIN.

*Proposal 80-5.1: MARC Subrecord Technique.* Washington, DC: Library of Congress; 1980 December 31. [Unpublished.]

Rather, John C.; Pennington, Jerry G. "The MARC Sort Program." *Journal of Library Automation.* 2(3): 125-138; 1969 September.

*Recordings Field Guide.* Stanford: RLG; 1982 September 1. 404 p.

Reed, Mary Jane Pobst. "Cost Figures: Washington Library Network." *Information Roundup . . . Proceedings of the 4th ASIS Mid-Year Meeting.* Washington, DC: ASIS; 1975: 62-66.

Reed, Mary Jane Pobst. "The Washington Library Network's Computerized Bibliographic System." *Journal of Library Automation.* 8(3): 174-199; 1975 September.

Reynolds, Dennis. "Entry of Local Data on OCLC: The Options and Their Impact on the Processing of Archival Tapes." *Information Technology and Libraries.* 1(1): 5-14; 1982 March.

*RLG CJK Input Manual.* [Stanford]: RLG; 1983 June. 264 p. Describes the RLIN vernacular Chinese-Japanese-Korean system and its use of Field 886 and Subfield ‡6 for links.

*The Role of the Library of Congress in the Evolving National Network.* Washington, DC: Library of Congress; 1978. 141 p. Includes notes on networks.

Ruecking, Frederick H., Jr. "Bibliographic Retrieval from Bibliographic Input; the Hypothesis and Construction of a Test." *Journal of Library Automation.* 1(4): 227-238; 1968 December. MARC I experiments at Rice University.

Ryans, Cynthia C. "A Study of Errors Found in Non-MARC Cataloging in a Machine-assisted System." *Journal of Library Automation.* 11(2): 125-132; 1978 June. An early discussion of errors in contributed cataloging—with an interesting use of "non-MARC," meaning "non-LC."

Salmon, Stephen R. *Library Automation Systems.* New York: Dekker; 1975. 291 p. See especially pages 73-146 and bibliography.

Sawyer, Jeanne. "An Archive Tape Processing System for the Triangle Research Libraries Network." *Library Resources & Technical Services.* 26(4): 362-369; 1982 October/December.

*Scores Field Guide.* [Stanford]: RLG; 1982 September 1. 380 p.

*Scores Format.* Columbus: OCLC; 1980. 280 p.

*Serials Field Guide.* Stanford: RLG; 1982 September 1. 458 p.

*Serials Format.* Columbus: OCLC; 1980. 374 p.

"Sharing Machine-Readable Bibliographic Data: A Progress Report on a Series of Meetings Sponsored by the Council on Library Resources." *Journal of Library Automation.* 7(1): 57-60; 1974 March.

Siebert, Donald. *The MARC Music Format: From Inception to Publication.* Philadelphia: Music Library Association; 1982. 42 p. (MLA Technical report no. 13.)

Silberstein, Stephen M. "Computerized Serial Processing System at the University of California, Berkeley." *Journal of Library Automation.* 8(4): 299-311; 1975 December.

*Sound Recordings Format.* Columbus: OCLC: 1980. 292 p.

Spalding, Helen H. "A Computer-Produced Serials Book Catalog with Automatically Generated Indexes." *Library Resources & Technical Services.* 24(4): 352-360; 1980 Fall.

Torkington, Roy B. "MARC and Its Application to Library Automation." *Advances in Librarianship* 4: 2-23; 1979.

Uluakar, Tamer [and others]. "Design Principles for a Comprehensive Library System." *Journal of Library Automation.* 14(2): 78-89; 1981 June.

*The University of Chicago Library Data Mangement System.* Chicago: U. of Chicago Library; 1976 March. 62 p.

University of Oregon Library. "A Comparison of OCLC, RLG/RLIN, and WLN." *Journal of Library Automation.* 14(3): 215-230; 1981 September.

"The USMARC Formats: Underlying Principles." *LC Information Bulletin.* 1983 May 9.

*UTLAS MARC Coding Manual for Monographs.* Toronto: UTLAS; 1982. Unpaged; ab. 500 p.

Veaner, Allen B. "BALLOTS—The View from Technical Services." *Library Resources & Technical Services.* 21(2): 127-146; 1977 Spring.

*Visual Arts Format.* 1983 May 23. Unpaged; ab. 150 p. (MARBI Proposal 82-21.)

Wajenberg, Arnold S. "MARC Coding of DDC for Subject Retrieval." *Information Technology and Libraries.* 2(3): 246-251; 1983 September.

Wanninger, Patricia Dwyer. "Is the OCLC Database Too Large? A Study of the Effect of Duplicate Records in the OCLC System." *Library Resources & Technical Services*. 26(4): 353-361; 1982 October/December. Also responses in v. 27.

Weisbrod, David. "NUC Reporting and MARC Redistribution: Their Functional Confluence and Its Implication for a Redefinition of the MARC Format." *Journal of Library Automation*. 10(3): 226-239; 1977 September.

[Weisbrod, David]. *Principles of MARC Format Content Designation*. Washington, DC: Library of Congress; 1981 May 1. 66 p. (MARBI Proposal 81-4.) [Unpublished.]

Williams, Martha E.; MacLaury, Keith D. "Automatic Merging of Monographic Data Bases—Identification of Duplicate Records in Multiple Files: The IUCS Scheme." *Journal of Library Automation*. 12(2): 156-168; 1979 June.

Williams, Martha E.; Shefner, Gordon J. "Data Element Statistics for the MARC II Data Base." *Journal of Library Automation*. 9(2): 89-100; 1976 June.

Williams, Martha E. [and others]. "Summary Statistics for Five Years of the MARC Data Base." *Journal of Library Automation*. 12(4): 314-337; 1979 December.

[Woods, Elaine W.] *Discussion Paper Number 5*. Numerous versions, 1981-1982, differing pagination. [Unpublished.]

# Index

# About the Author

Walt Crawford has been manager of the Product Batch Group in the Computer Systems and Services Division of the Research Libraries Group (RLG) since 1980. He began at RLG in 1979 as a programmer/analyst. Previously, he was a programmer/analyst in the Library Systems Office of the University of California, Berkeley, from 1972 to 1979. His experience in library automation began in 1968 when he designed and implemented a circulation system (based on punched cards) for the Circulation Department of UC Berkeley's Doe Library.

Mr. Crawford has served as a liaison from RLG to the USMARC advisory group since early 1981, and has been developing MARC-based products and services since 1972. He has been active in the American Library Association since 1975, and a member of the Technical Standards for Library Automation (TESLA) committee of ALA's Library and Information Technology Association (LITA) from 1978 to 1982 (chair 1980-1981). Mr. Crawford founded LITA's Programmer/Analysts Discussion Group in 1982, serving as chair in 1982 and 1983.

Mr. Crawford has published articles on MARC, library automation, technical standards and microcomputers in several professional journals. He is currently beginning work on a new book, *Technical Standards: a Non-Technical Introduction,* to be published by Knowledge Industry Publications, Inc.